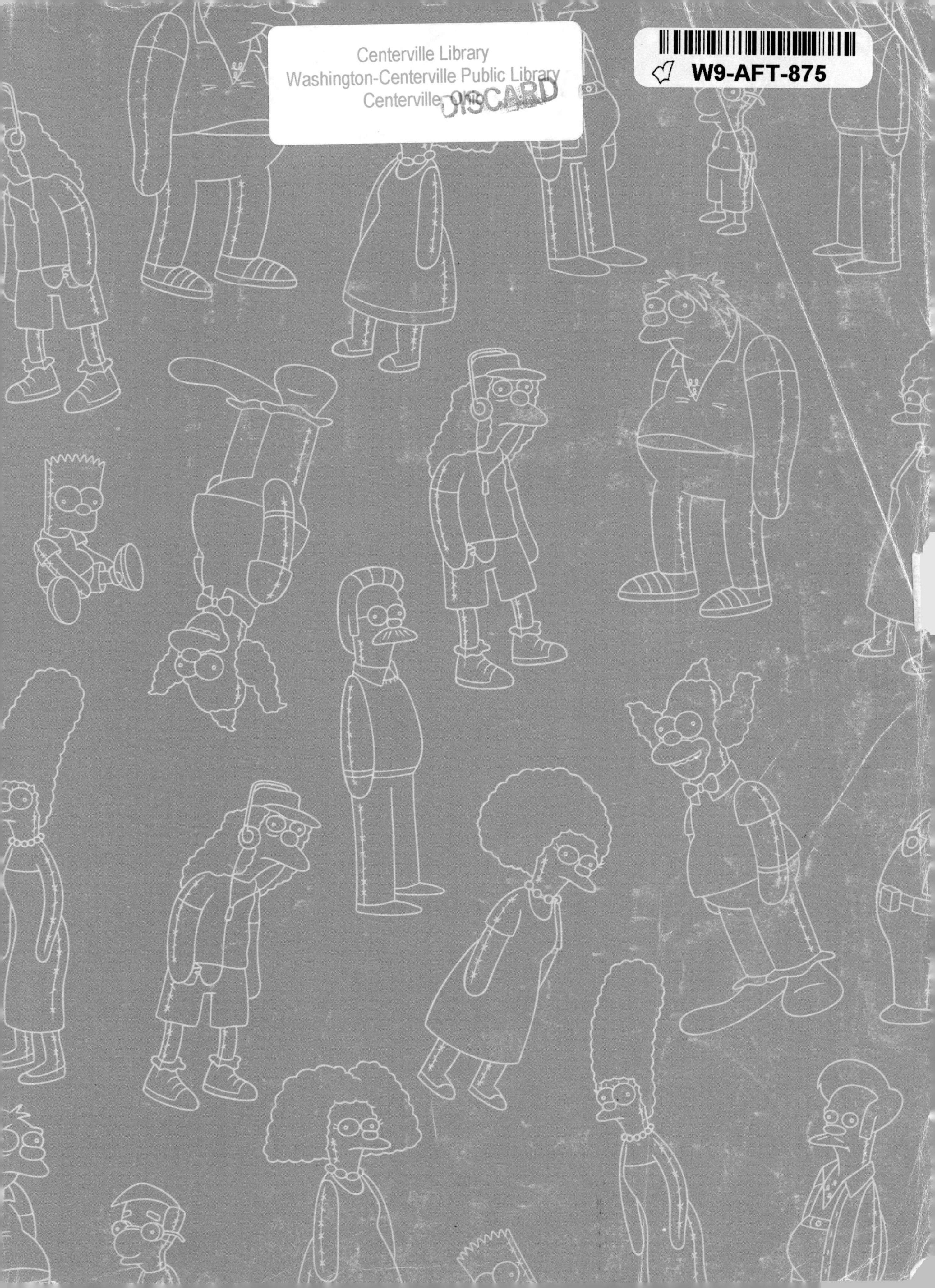

THE SIMPSONS™

TREEHOUSE OF HORROR

HOODOO VOODOO BROUHAHA

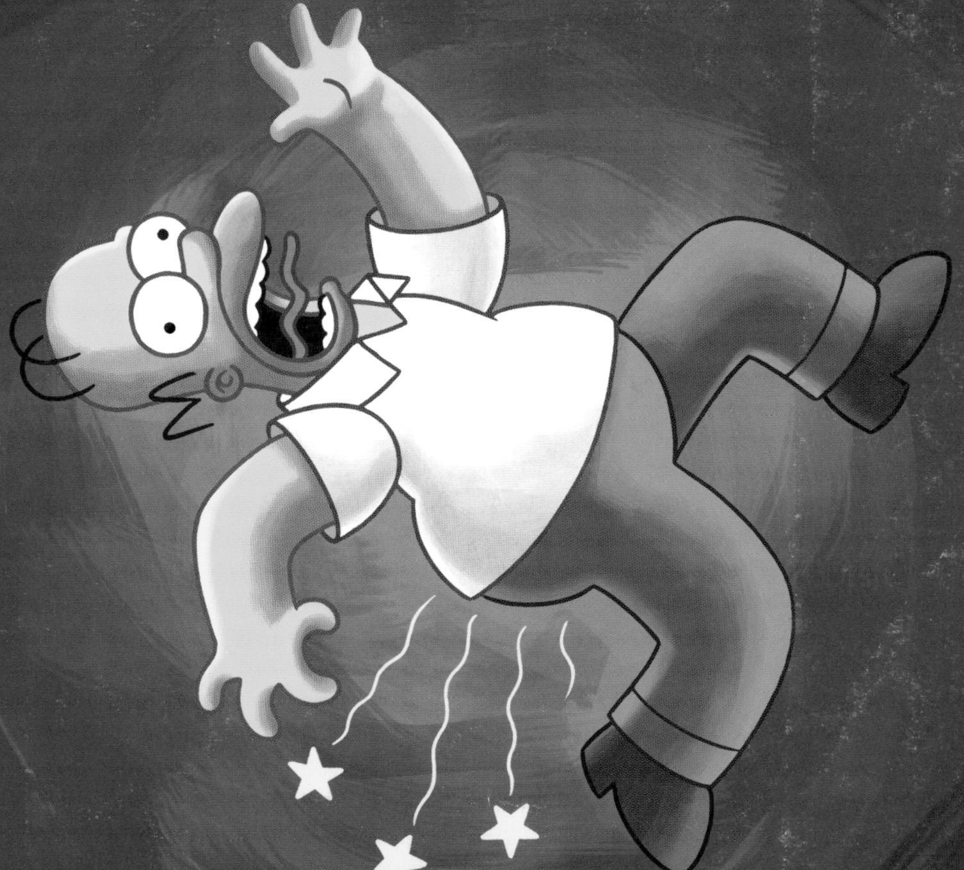

HARPER

NEW YORK • LONDON • TORONTO • SYDNEY

THE SIMPSONS™ TREEHOUSE OF HORROR HOODOO VOODOO BROUHAHA

Printed in the United States of America.

HarperCollins books may be purchased for educational, business, or sales
promotional use. For information please write:
Special Markets Department,
HarperCollins Publishers,
10 East 53rd Street, New York, NY 10022.

FIRST EDITION

ISBN-10: 0-06-114872-5
ISBN-13: 978-0-06-114872-9

06 07 08 09 10 11 QWM 10 9 8 7 6 5 4 3 2 1

Publisher: Matt Groening
Creative Director: Bill Morrison
Managing Editor: Terry Delegeane
Director of Operations: Robert Zaugh
Art Director: Nathan Kane
Art Director Special Projects: Serban Cristescu
Production Manager: Christopher Ungar
Production/Design: Karen Bates, Art Villanueva
Production Assistance: Chia-Hsien Jason Ho, Nathan Hamill, Mike Rote
Administration: Sherri Smith
Legal Guardian: Susan A. Grode

Book Concepts and Design: Serban Cristescu

Contributing Artists:
Hilary Barta, Karen Bates, Dan Brereton, Serban Cristescu, Luis Escobar, Chia-Hsien Jason Ho,
Nathan Kane, Istvan Majoros, Gary Spencer Millidge, Bill Morrison, Ted Naifeh, Kevin M. Newman,
Joey Nilges, Rick Reese, Mike Rote, Scott Shaw!, Robert Stanley, Dave Stewart, Ty Templeton, Jill Thompson, Art Villanueva

Contributing Writers:
Neil Alsip, Hilary Barta, Ian Boothby, Paul Dini, Evan Dorkin, Gary Spencer Millidge,
Scott Shaw!, Gail Simone, Stephen Sullivan, Ty Templeton

HarperCollins Editors: Hope Innelli, Casey Kait

Special Thanks to:
Pete Benson, N. Vyolet Diaz, Deanna MacLellan, Mili Smythe, and Ursula Wendel

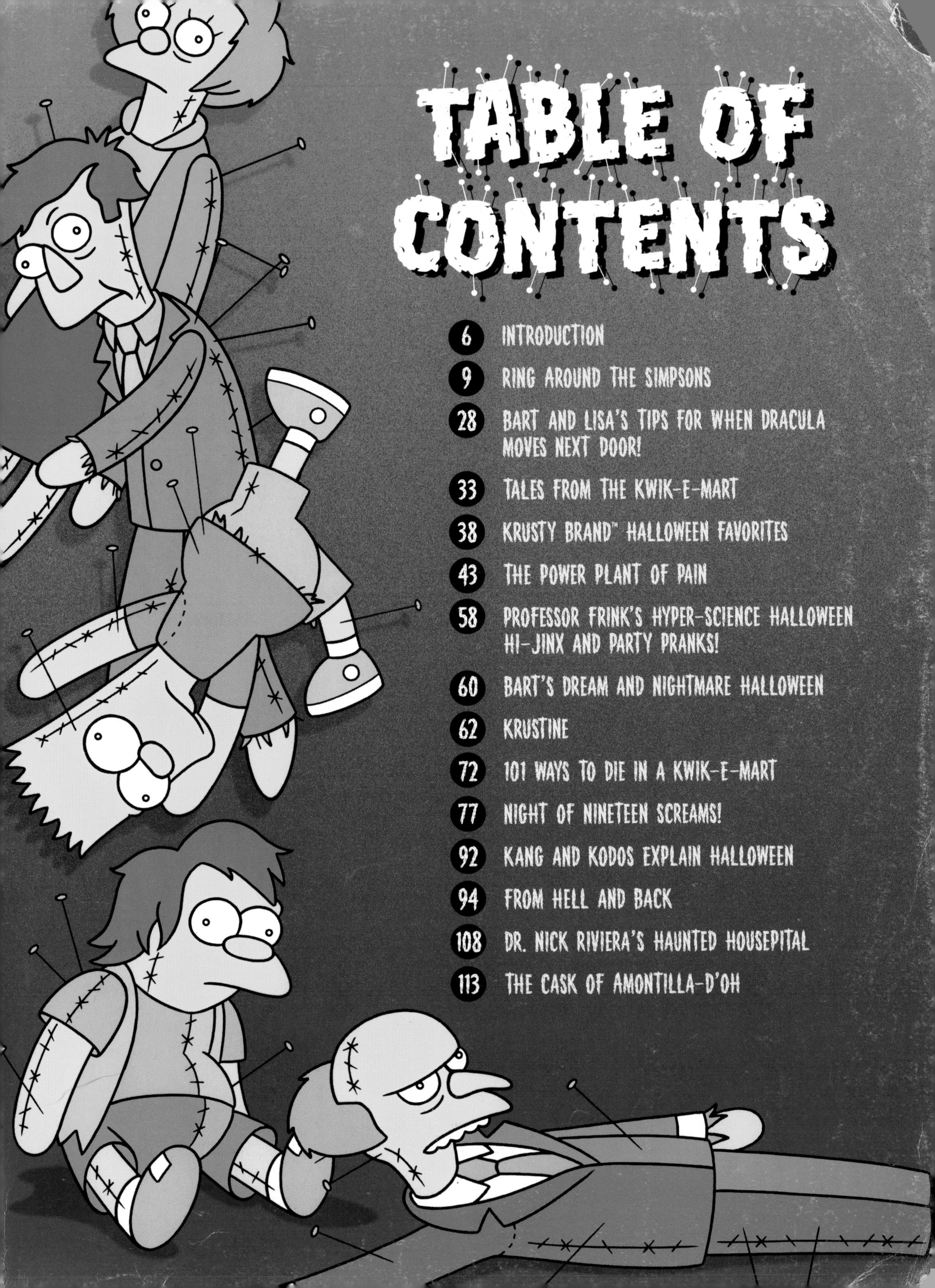

TABLE OF CONTENTS

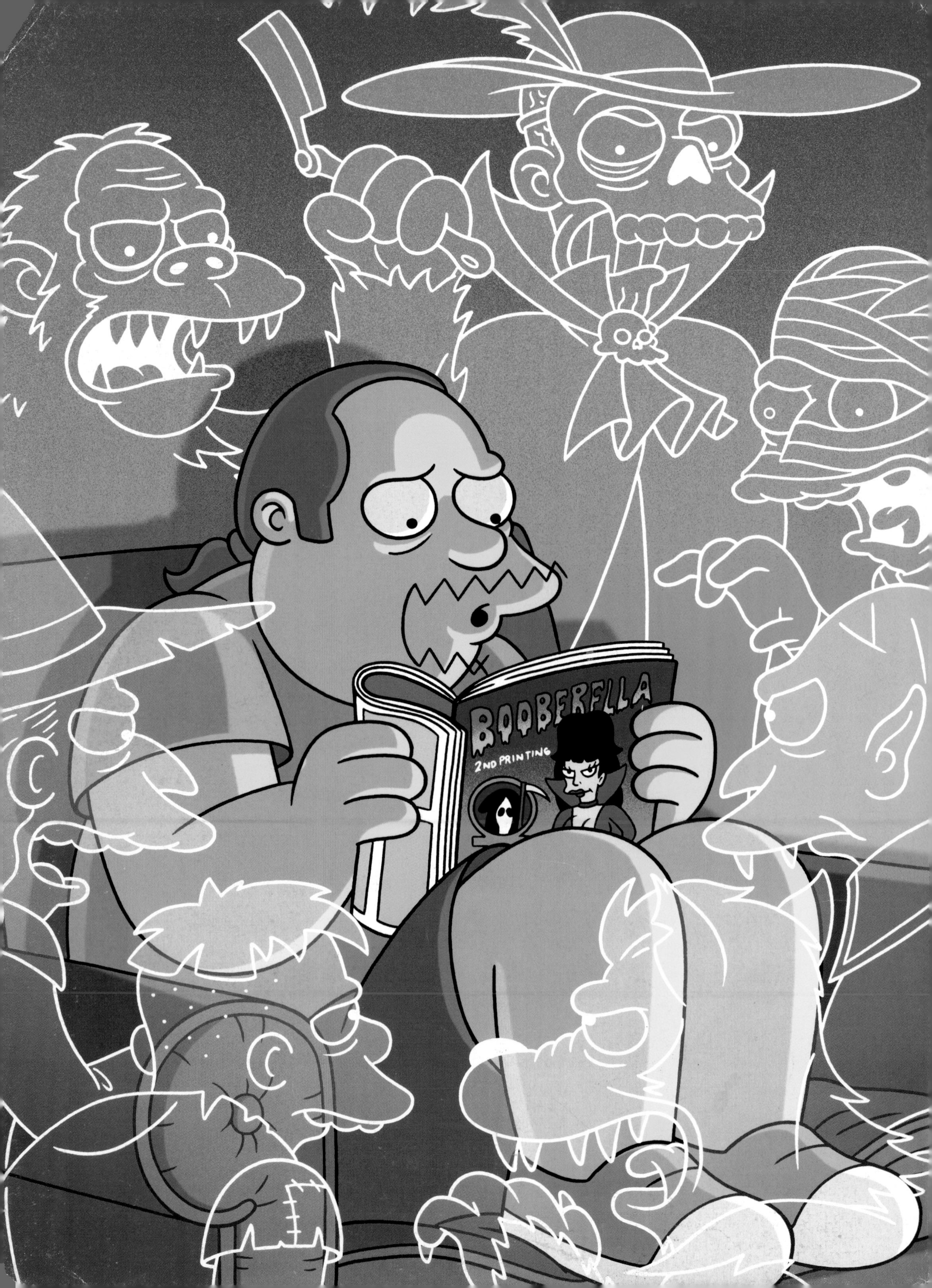
BOOBERELLA
2ND PRINTING

Greetings, fright fans. Welcome to The Simpsons Treehouse of Horror Hoodoo Voodoo Brouhaha, a collection of terrifying tales and tidbits featuring stories and art by the "scream de la scream" of modern-day comic book masters.

As the proprietor of The Android's Dungeon & Baseball Card Shop and lifelong comic book aficionado, I have spent untold hours delighting to fearsome four-color fables of werewolves, ghouls, vampires, mummies, and monsters of all sorts. From "All-Psycho " to "Zombies on Parade" I have relished every salacious page, every grisly panel. And yet, horror comics have never really frightened me. I find the line between horror and humor to be tenuous at best, and a good, garish terror tale always makes me laugh. So, you must be wondering what it is that does frighten me. I have prepared a short list:

- A slobbering child in the vicinity of a near mint-condition Golden Age comic book
- Having to wear long pants
- The precarious developmental state of the Ant Man feature film
- Furries
- What may lurk beneath my beard
- The possibility that I have squandered my life on adolescent power fantasies, lurid and juvenile portrayals of women, and the ceaseless pursuit of rare action figures
- The thought of living my life without adolescent power fantasies, lurid and juvenile portrayals of women, and the ceaseless pursuit of rare action figures
- Being outbid on eBay
- Getting cellophane tape stuck on a rare comic book while removing it from its mylar bag
- Inflated prices in the new, updated, comic book price guides (when I'm buying, not selling)
- Having to answer "Sports & Leisure" questions while playing Trivial Pursuit
- Restraining orders
- Burritos gaining a sentient consciousness and taking revenge on those who have eaten oh-so-many of them (This phobia is due to a burrito-induced nightmare I had in 1987)

But what scares me the most? Poorly executed comic books. Every piece of awful graphic literature I've read cannot be unread. The hours spent cannot be added back to my lifespan. And since much of what I read is awful, said mediocrity has eaten up approximately 17.4 years of my allotted time on Earth. Sooner or later, the days I have left to live will be in deficit to the amount of time I have spent reading paper drive classics like "David Niven Adventures" or "Radioactive Man Vs. The New York Times Crossword Puzzle." This realization chills me to the bone.

Thankfully, there exist comics that rise above the rubbish. They amuse, they thrill, they terrify, and, yes, they even inspire. And this tome of hilarious horror tales you hold in your sweaty hands may well be one of those. In fact, it may be the best comics collection ever!

I don't know. I haven't had time to read it yet.

Comic Book Guy
Springfield, USA

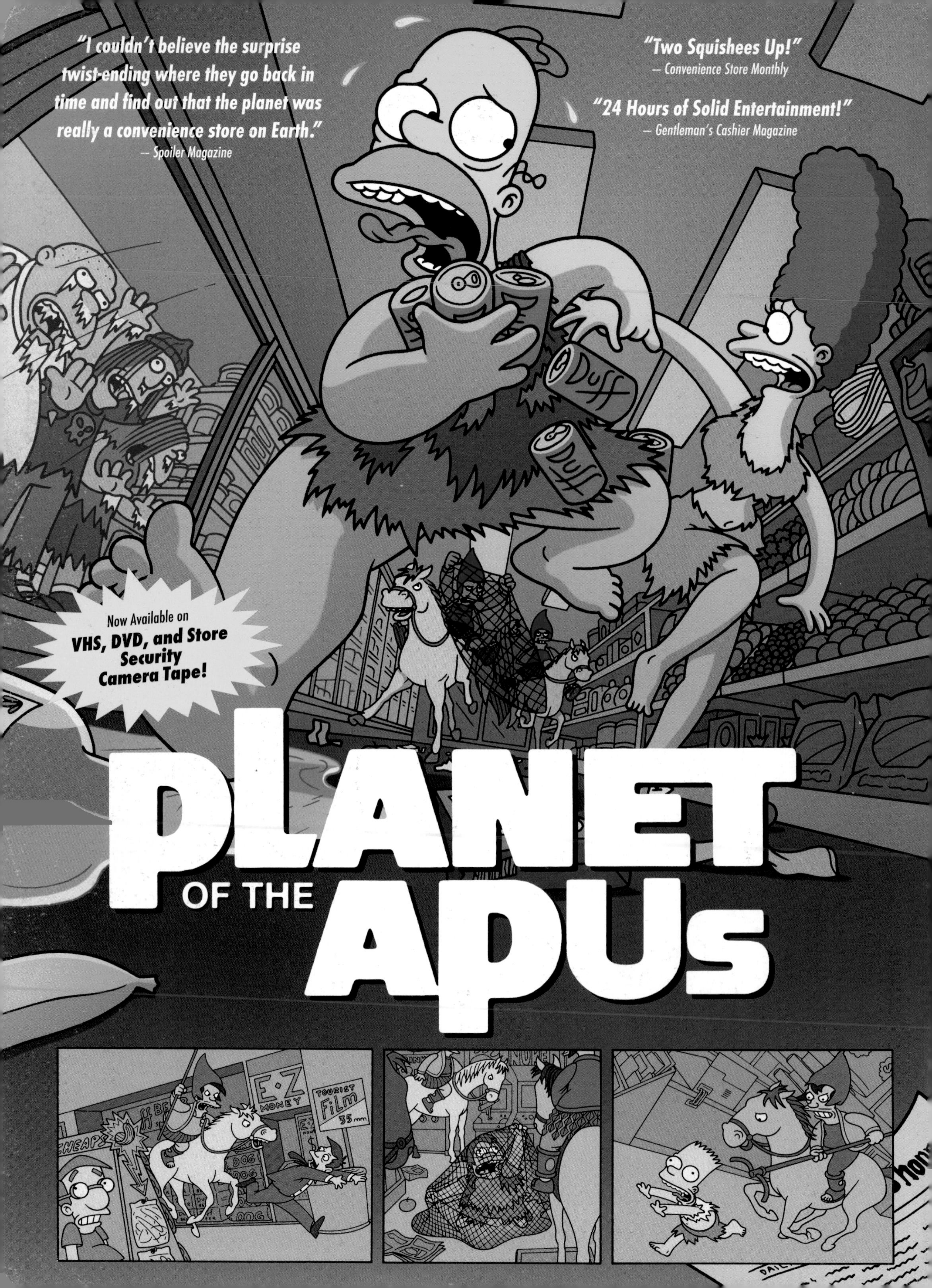
"I couldn't believe the surprise twist-ending where they go back in time and find out that the planet was really a convenience store on Earth."
— Spoiler Magazine
"Two Squishees Up!"
— Convenience Store Monthly
"24 Hours of Solid Entertainment!"
— Gentleman's Cashier Magazine
Duff
Duff
Now Available on
VHS, DVD, and Store Security Camera Tape!
PLANET
OF THE
APUs
E-Z MONEY
TOURIST Film 35mm
CHEAP
DOG
DOG
DOG

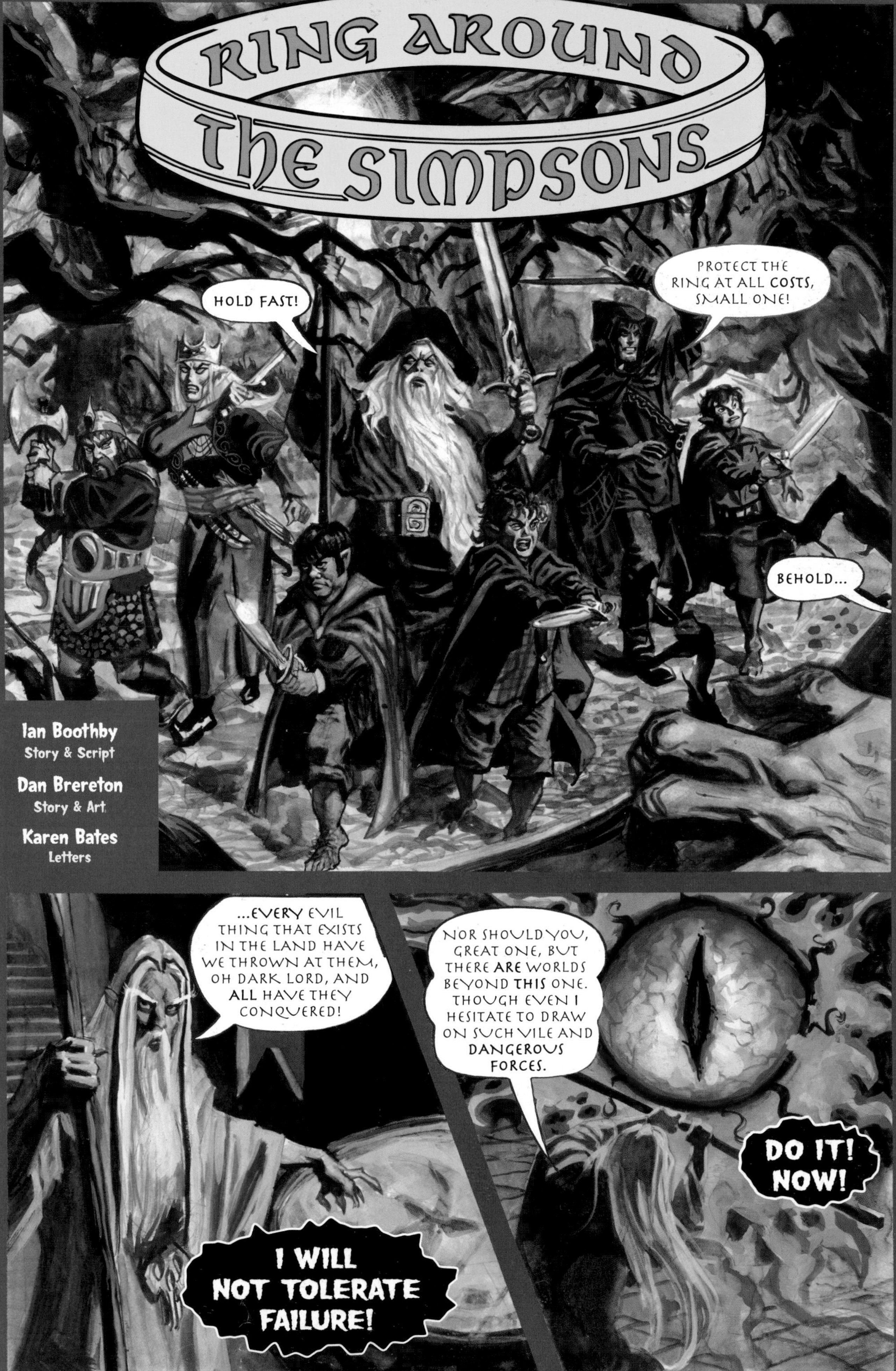
RING AROUND THE SIMPSONS
HOLD FAST!
PROTECT THE RING AT ALL COSTS, SMALL ONE!
BEHOLD...
Ian Boothby
Story & Script
Dan Brereton
Story & Art
Karen Bates
Letters
...EVERY EVIL THING THAT EXISTS IN THE LAND HAVE WE THROWN AT THEM, OH DARK LORD, AND ALL HAVE THEY CONQUERED!
I WILL NOT TOLERATE FAILURE!
NOR SHOULD YOU, GREAT ONE, BUT THERE ARE WORLDS BEYOND THIS ONE. THOUGH EVEN I HESITATE TO DRAW ON SUCH VILE AND DANGEROUS FORCES.
DO IT! NOW!

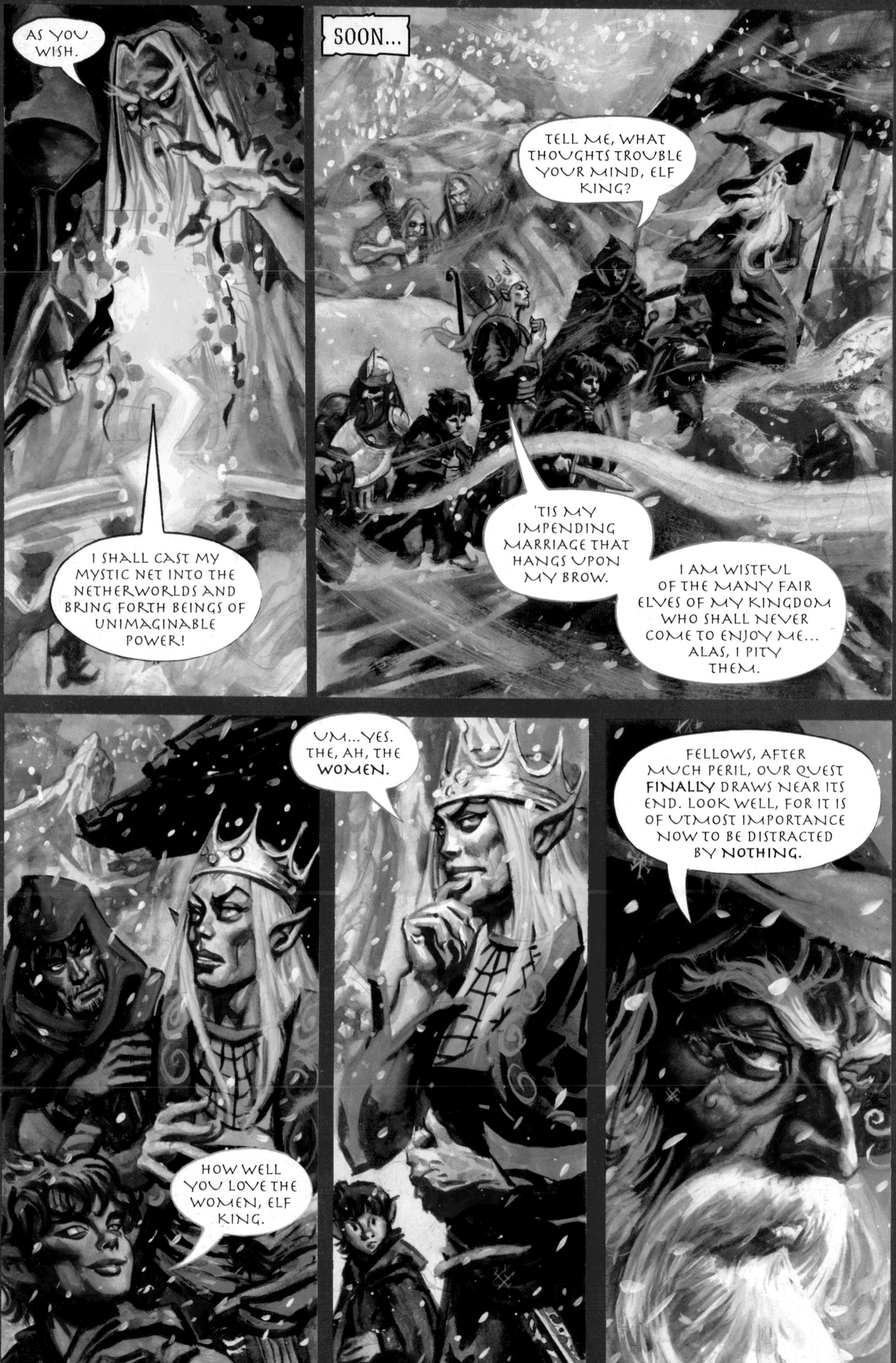
AS YOU WISH.
I SHALL CAST MY MYSTIC NET INTO THE NETHERWORLDS AND BRING FORTH BEINGS OF UNIMAGINABLE POWER!
SOON...
TELL ME, WHAT THOUGHTS TROUBLE YOUR MIND, ELF KING?
'TIS MY IMPENDING MARRIAGE THAT HANGS UPON MY BROW.
I AM WISTFUL OF THE MANY FAIR ELVES OF MY KINGDOM WHO SHALL NEVER COME TO ENJOY ME... ALAS, I PITY THEM.
HOW WELL YOU LOVE THE WOMEN, ELF KING.
UM...YES. THE, AH, THE **WOMEN.**
FELLOWS, AFTER MUCH PERIL, OUR QUEST **FINALLY** DRAWS NEAR ITS END. LOOK WELL, FOR IT IS OF UTMOST IMPORTANCE NOW TO BE DISTRACTED BY **NOTHING.**

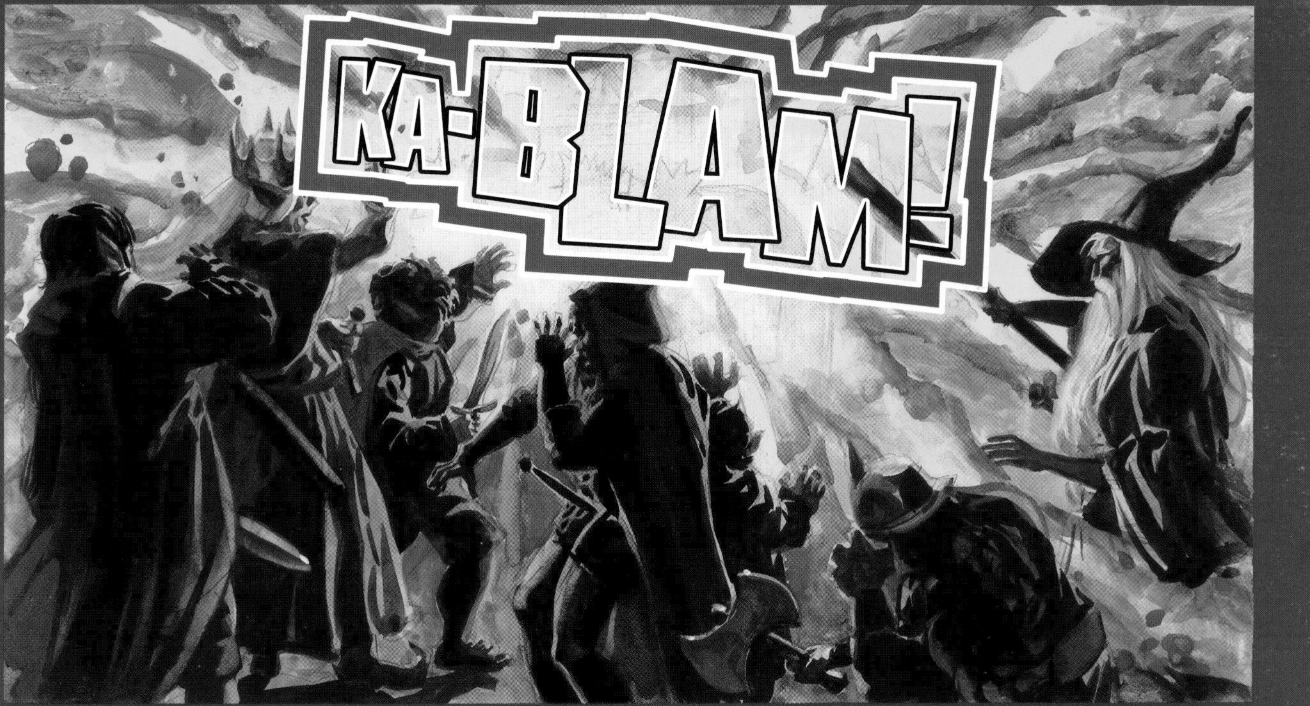
KA-BLAM!

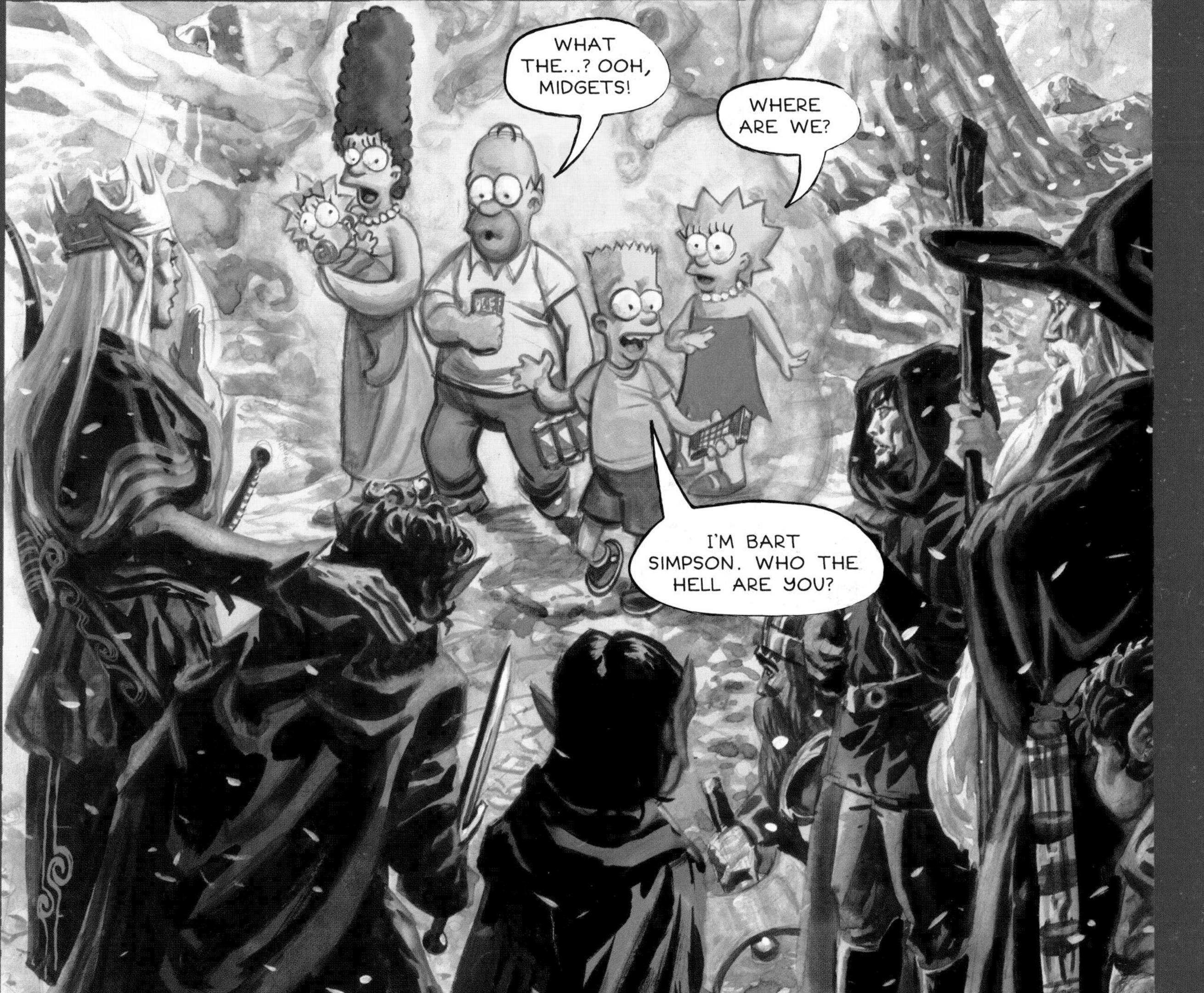
WHAT THE...? OOH, MIDGETS!
WHERE ARE WE?
I'M BART SIMPSON. WHO THE HELL ARE YOU?

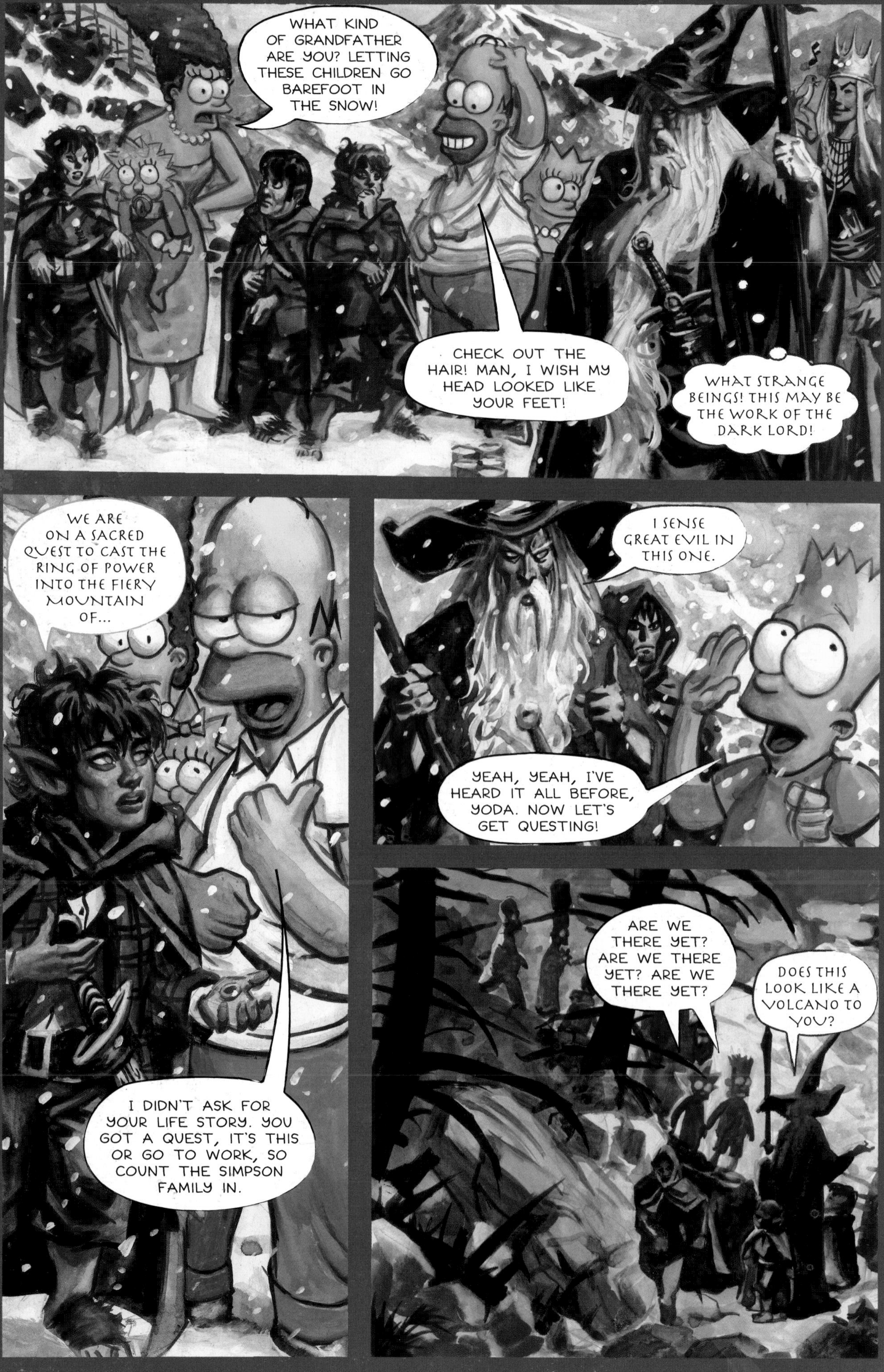
WHAT KIND OF GRANDFATHER ARE YOU? LETTING THESE CHILDREN GO BAREFOOT IN THE SNOW!
CHECK OUT THE HAIR! MAN, I WISH MY HEAD LOOKED LIKE YOUR FEET!
WHAT STRANGE BEINGS! THIS MAY BE THE WORK OF THE DARK LORD!
WE ARE ON A SACRED QUEST TO CAST THE RING OF POWER INTO THE FIERY MOUNTAIN OF...
I DIDN'T ASK FOR YOUR LIFE STORY. YOU GOT A QUEST, IT'S THIS OR GO TO WORK, SO COUNT THE SIMPSON FAMILY IN.
I SENSE GREAT EVIL IN THIS ONE.
YEAH, YEAH, I'VE HEARD IT ALL BEFORE, YODA. NOW LET'S GET QUESTING!
ARE WE THERE YET? ARE WE THERE YET? ARE WE THERE YET?
DOES THIS LOOK LIKE A VOLCANO TO YOU?

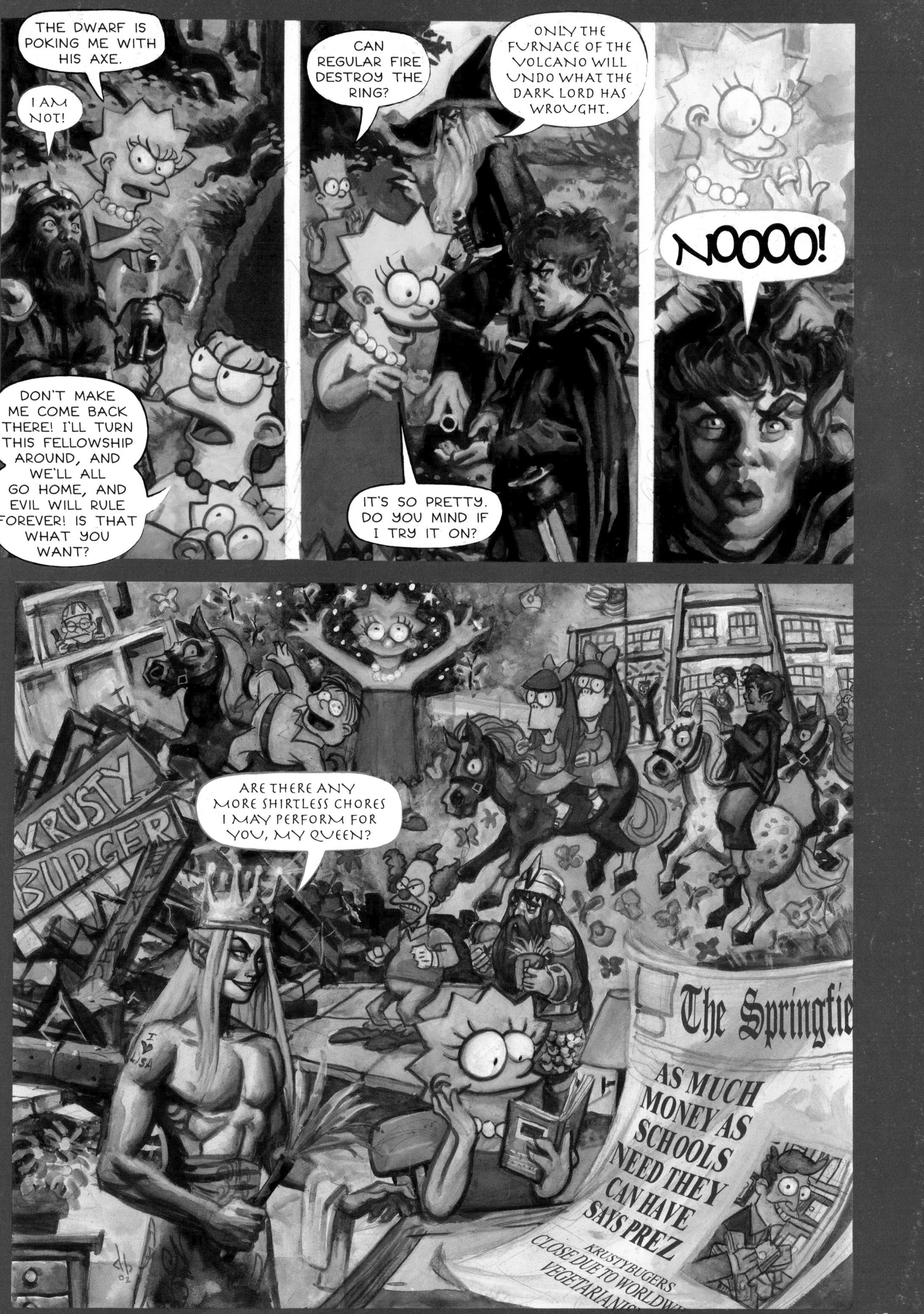
THE DWARF IS POKING ME WITH HIS AXE.
I AM NOT!
DON'T MAKE ME COME BACK THERE! I'LL TURN THIS FELLOWSHIP AROUND, AND WE'LL ALL GO HOME, AND EVIL WILL RULE FOREVER! IS THAT WHAT YOU WANT?
CAN REGULAR FIRE DESTROY THE RING?
ONLY THE FURNACE OF THE VOLCANO WILL UNDO WHAT THE DARK LORD HAS WROUGHT.
IT'S SO PRETTY. DO YOU MIND IF I TRY IT ON?
NOOOO!
KRUSTY BURGER
ARE THERE ANY MORE SHIRTLESS CHORES I MAY PERFORM FOR YOU, MY QUEEN?
I ♥ LISA
The Springfie
AS MUCH MONEY AS SCHOOLS NEED THEY CAN HAVE SAYS PREZ
KRUSTYBUGERS

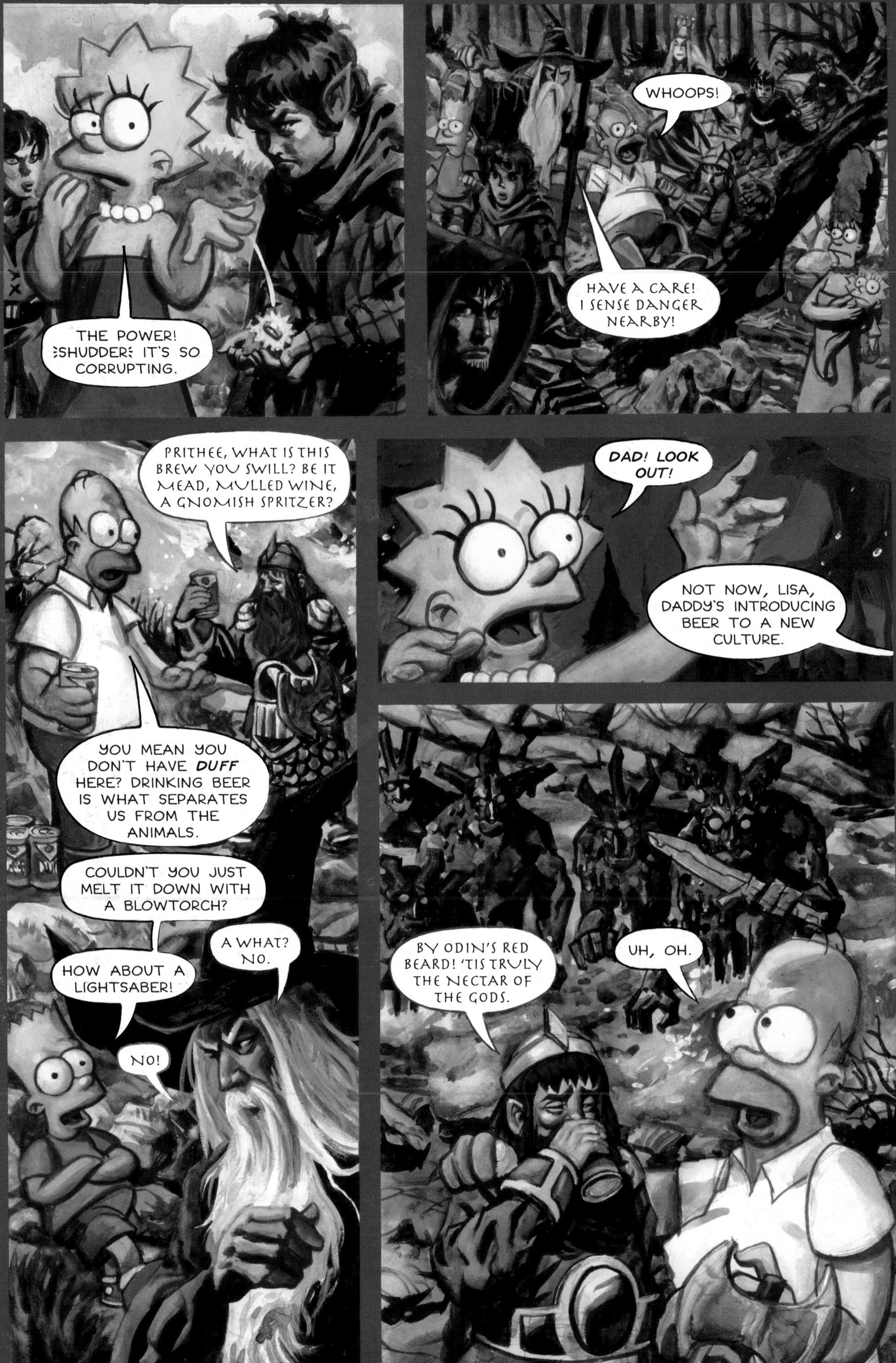

THE POWER! :SHUDDER: IT'S SO CORRUPTING.
WHOOPS!
HAVE A CARE! I SENSE DANGER NEARBY!
PRITHEE, WHAT IS THIS BREW YOU SWILL? BE IT MEAD, MULLED WINE, A GNOMISH SPRITZER?
YOU MEAN YOU DON'T HAVE DUFF HERE? DRINKING BEER IS WHAT SEPARATES US FROM THE ANIMALS.
COULDN'T YOU JUST MELT IT DOWN WITH A BLOWTORCH?
A WHAT? NO.
HOW ABOUT A LIGHTSABER!
NO!
DAD! LOOK OUT!
NOT NOW, LISA, DADDY'S INTRODUCING BEER TO A NEW CULTURE.
BY ODIN'S RED BEARD! 'TIS TRULY THE NECTAR OF THE GODS.
UH, OH.

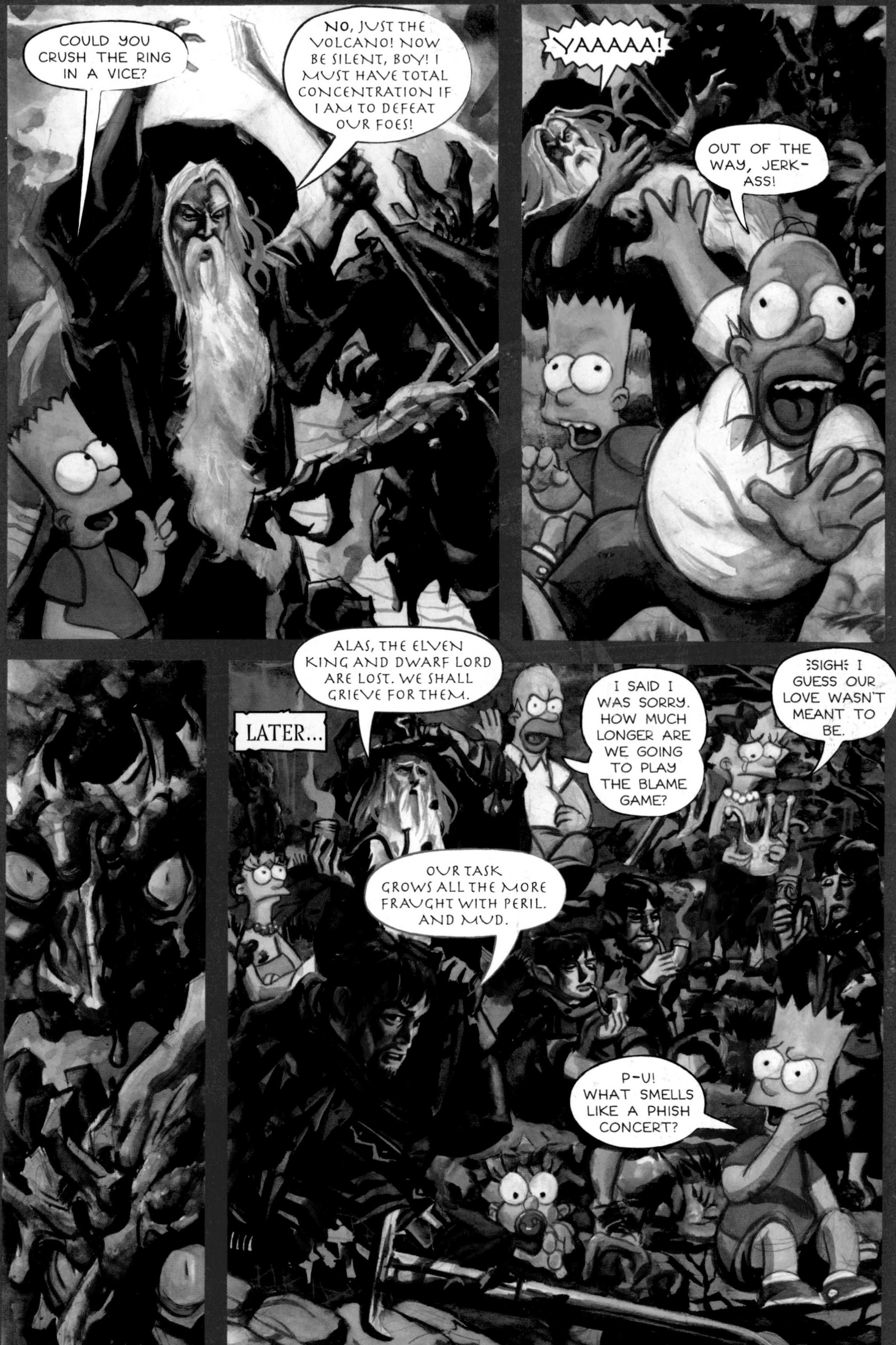

COULD YOU CRUSH THE RING IN A VICE?
NO, JUST THE VOLCANO! NOW BE SILENT, BOY! I MUST HAVE TOTAL CONCENTRATION IF I AM TO DEFEAT OUR FOES!
YAAAAA!
OUT OF THE WAY, JERK-ASS!
LATER...
ALAS, THE ELVEN KING AND DWARF LORD ARE LOST. WE SHALL GRIEVE FOR THEM.
I SAID I WAS SORRY. HOW MUCH LONGER ARE WE GOING TO PLAY THE BLAME GAME?
SIGH I GUESS OUR LOVE WASN'T MEANT TO BE.
OUR TASK GROWS ALL THE MORE FRAUGHT WITH PERIL. AND MUD.
P-U! WHAT SMELLS LIKE A PHISH CONCERT?

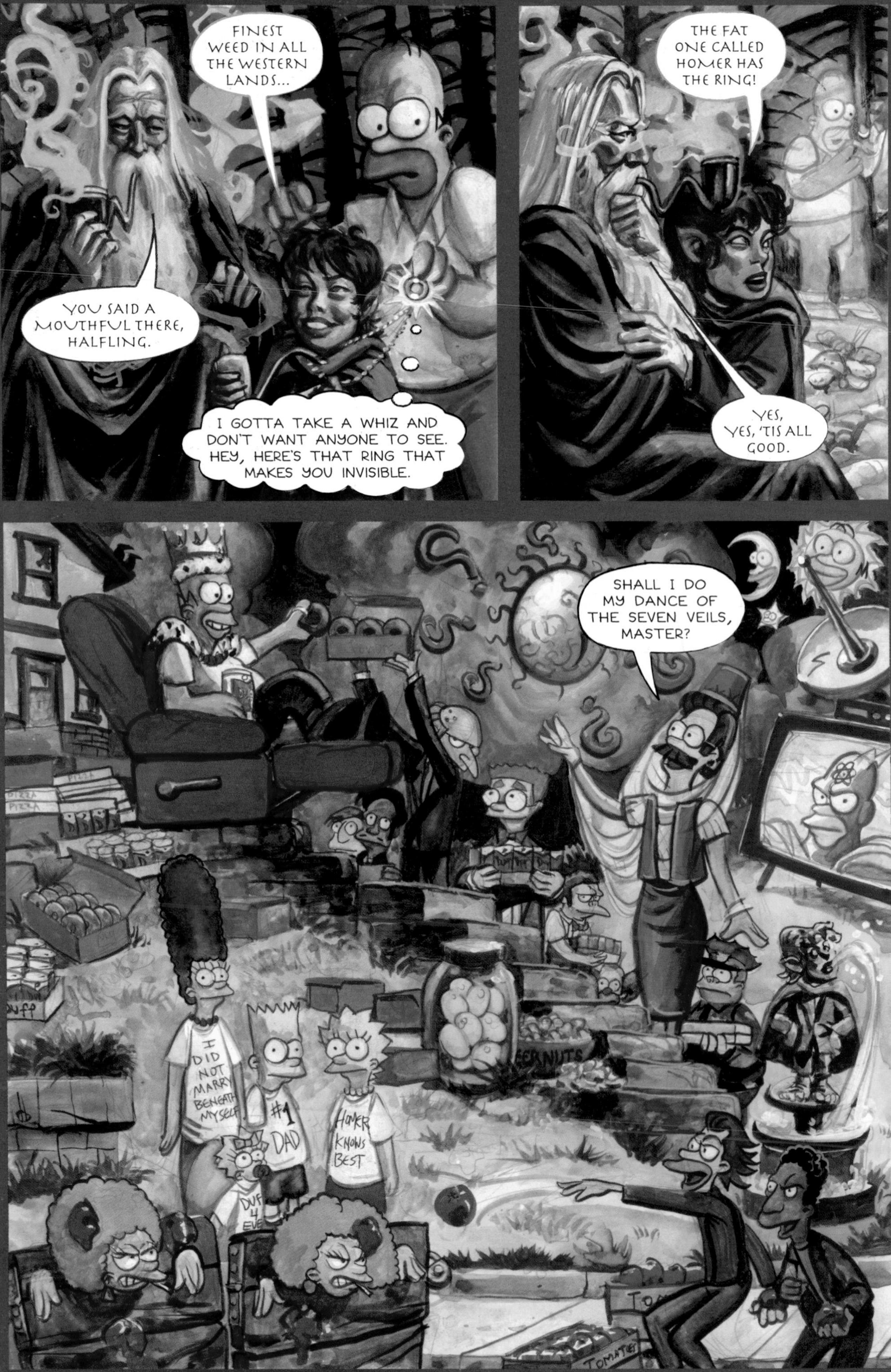
FINEST WEED IN ALL THE WESTERN LANDS...
YOU SAID A MOUTHFUL THERE, HALFLING.
I GOTTA TAKE A WHIZ AND DON'T WANT ANYONE TO SEE. HEY, HERE'S THAT RING THAT MAKES YOU INVISIBLE.
THE FAT ONE CALLED HOMER HAS THE RING!
YES, YES, 'TIS ALL GOOD.
SHALL I DO MY DANCE OF THE SEVEN VEILS, MASTER?
I DID NOT MARRY BENEATH MYSELF
#1 DAD
HOMER KNOWS BEST

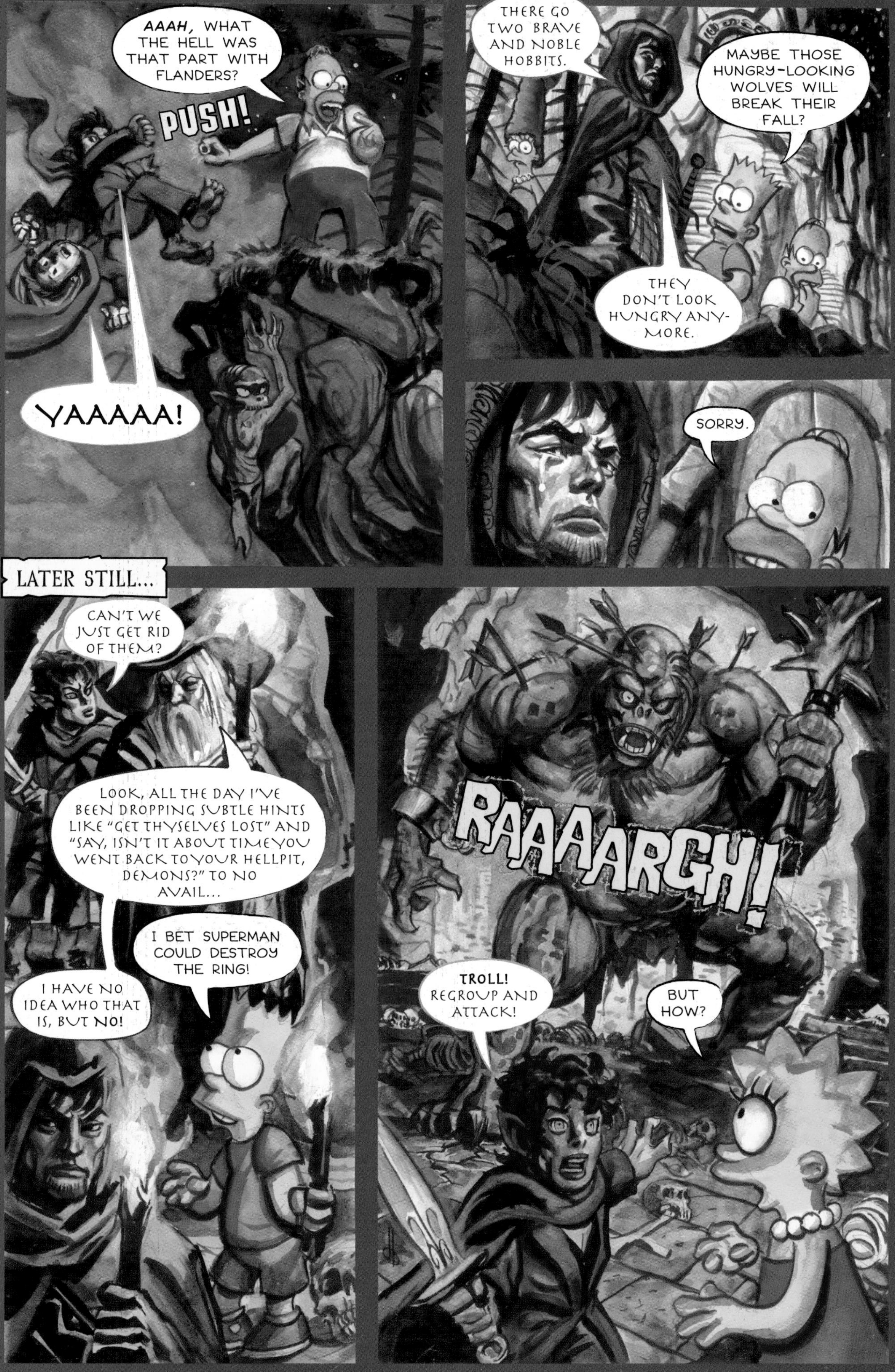
AAAH, WHAT THE HELL WAS THAT PART WITH FLANDERS?
PUSH!
YAAAAA!
THERE GO TWO BRAVE AND NOBLE HOBBITS.
MAYBE THOSE HUNGRY-LOOKING WOLVES WILL BREAK THEIR FALL?
THEY DON'T LOOK HUNGRY ANY-MORE.
SORRY.
LATER STILL...
CAN'T WE JUST GET RID OF THEM?
LOOK, ALL THE DAY I'VE BEEN DROPPING SUBTLE HINTS LIKE "GET THYSELVES LOST" AND "SAY, ISN'T IT ABOUT TIME YOU WENT BACK TO YOUR HELLPIT, DEMONS?" TO NO AVAIL...
I BET SUPERMAN COULD DESTROY THE RING!
I HAVE NO IDEA WHO THAT IS, BUT NO!
RAAAARGH!
TROLL! REGROUP AND ATTACK!
BUT HOW?

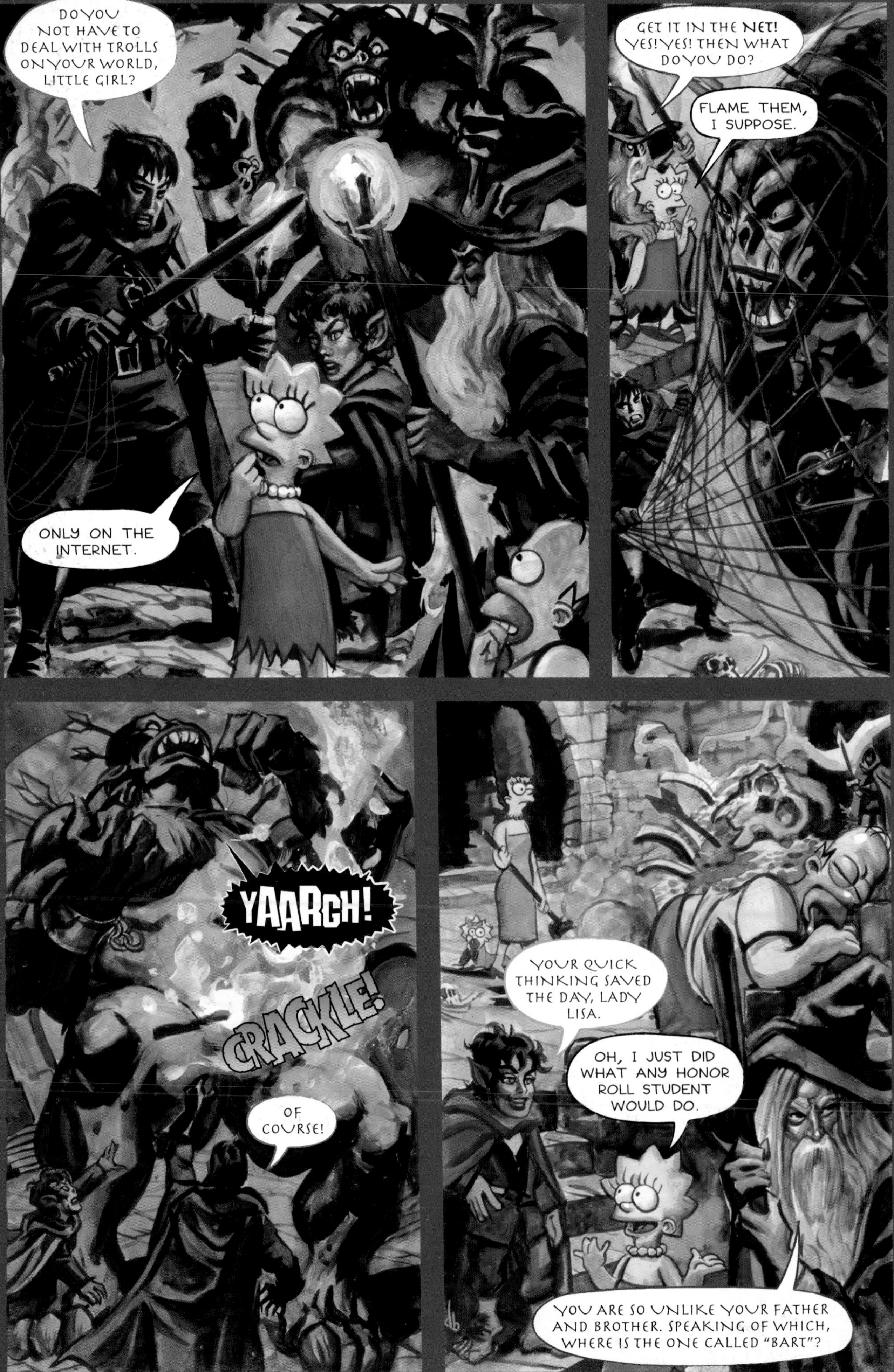
DO YOU NOT HAVE TO DEAL WITH TROLLS ON YOUR WORLD, LITTLE GIRL?
ONLY ON THE INTERNET.
GET IT IN THE NET! YES! YES! THEN WHAT DO YOU DO?
FLAME THEM, I SUPPOSE.
YAARGH!
CRACKLE!
OF COURSE!
YOUR QUICK THINKING SAVED THE DAY, LADY LISA.
OH, I JUST DID WHAT ANY HONOR ROLL STUDENT WOULD DO.
YOU ARE SO UNLIKE YOUR FATHER AND BROTHER. SPEAKING OF WHICH, WHERE IS THE ONE CALLED "BART"?

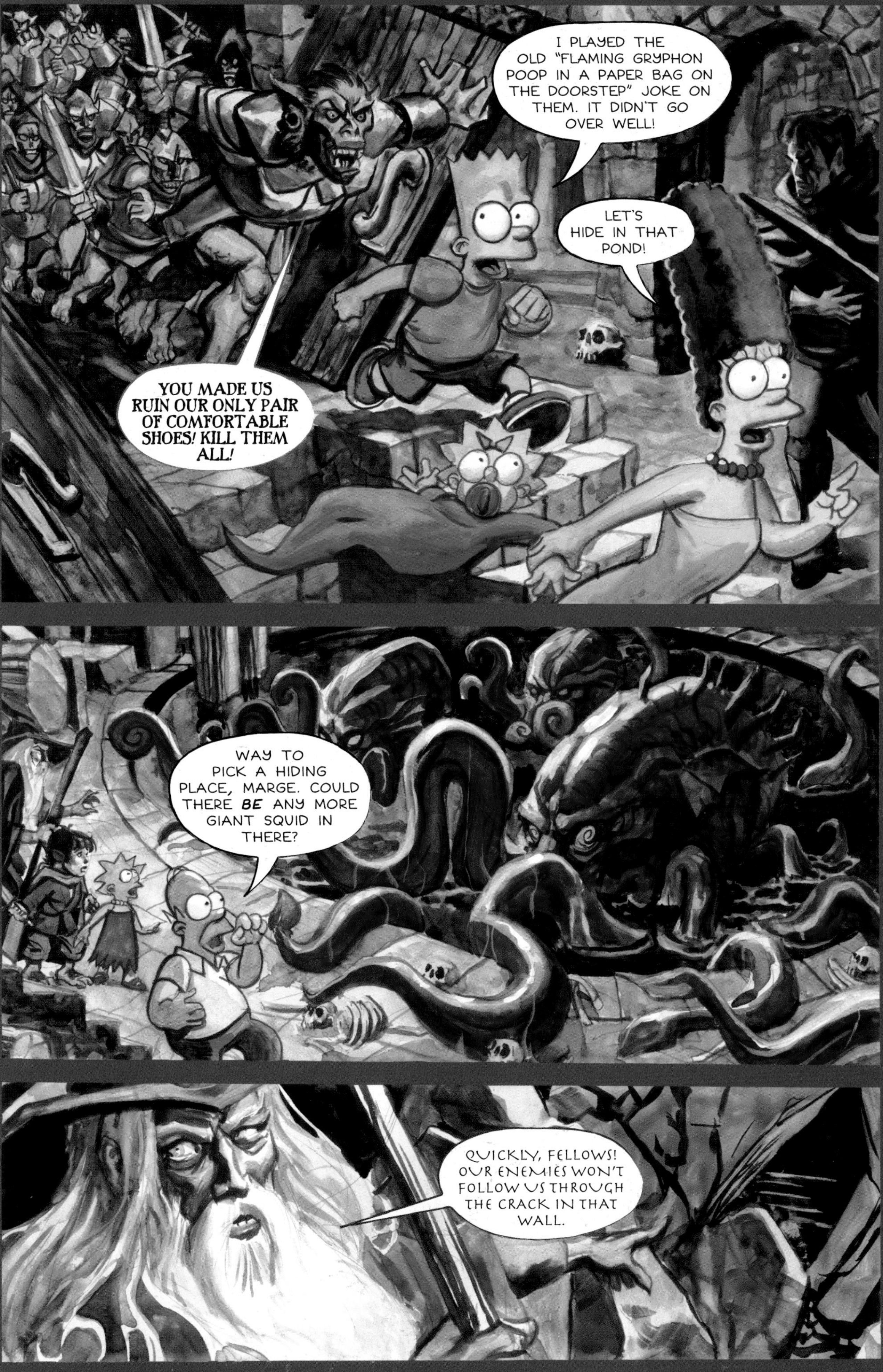
I PLAYED THE OLD "FLAMING GRYPHON POOP IN A PAPER BAG ON THE DOORSTEP" JOKE ON THEM. IT DIDN'T GO OVER WELL!
YOU MADE US RUIN OUR ONLY PAIR OF COMFORTABLE SHOES! KILL THEM ALL!
LET'S HIDE IN THAT POND!
WAY TO PICK A HIDING PLACE, MARGE. COULD THERE *BE* ANY MORE GIANT SQUID IN THERE?
QUICKLY, FELLOWS! OUR ENEMIES WON'T FOLLOW US THROUGH THE CRACK IN THAT WALL.

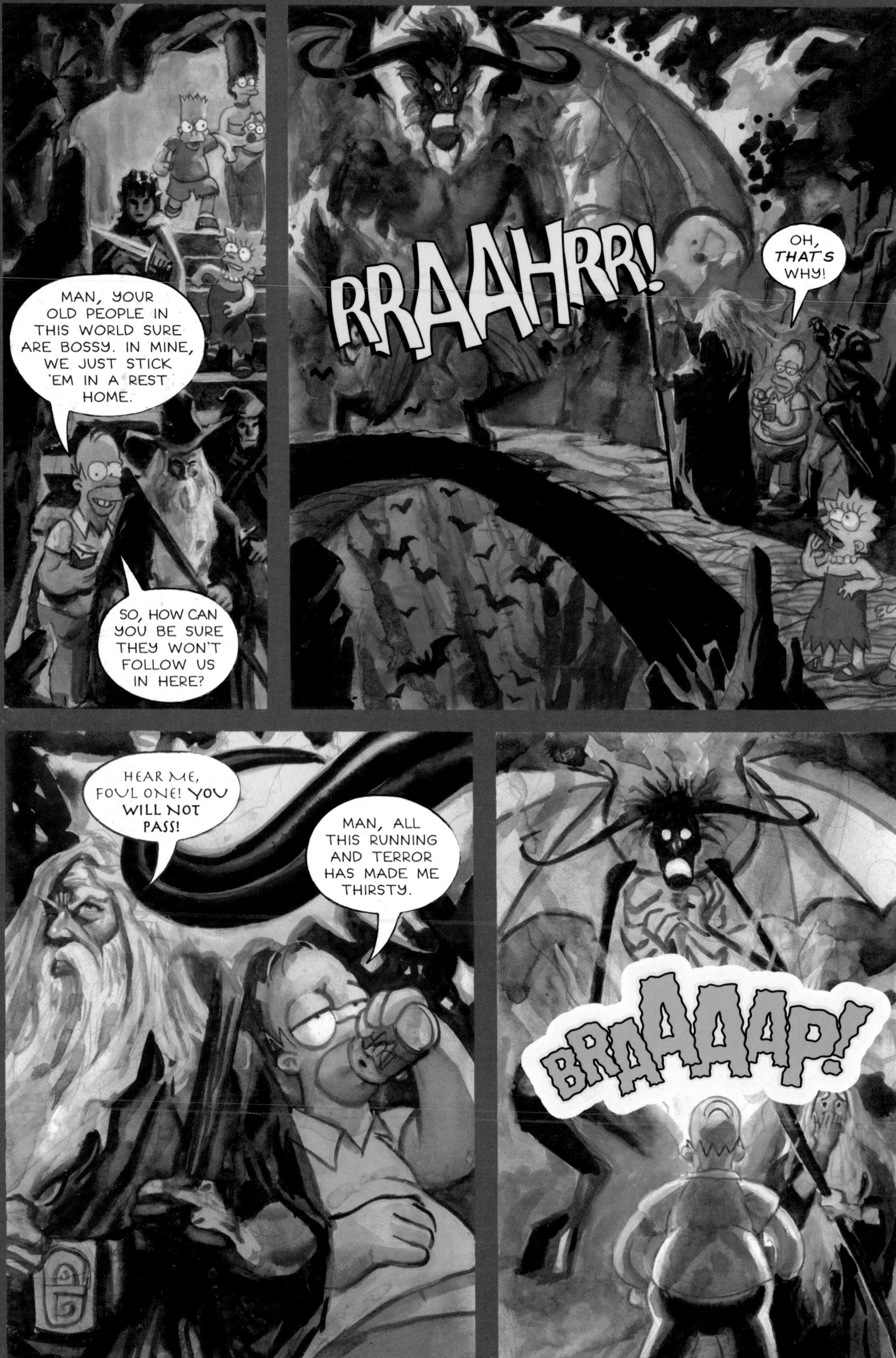
MAN, YOUR OLD PEOPLE IN THIS WORLD SURE ARE BOSSY. IN MINE, WE JUST STICK 'EM IN A REST HOME.
SO, HOW CAN YOU BE SURE THEY WON'T FOLLOW US IN HERE?
BRAAHRR!
OH, THAT'S WHY!
HEAR ME, FOUL ONE! YOU WILL NOT PASS!
MAN, ALL THIS RUNNING AND TERROR HAS MADE ME THIRSTY.
BRAAAAP!

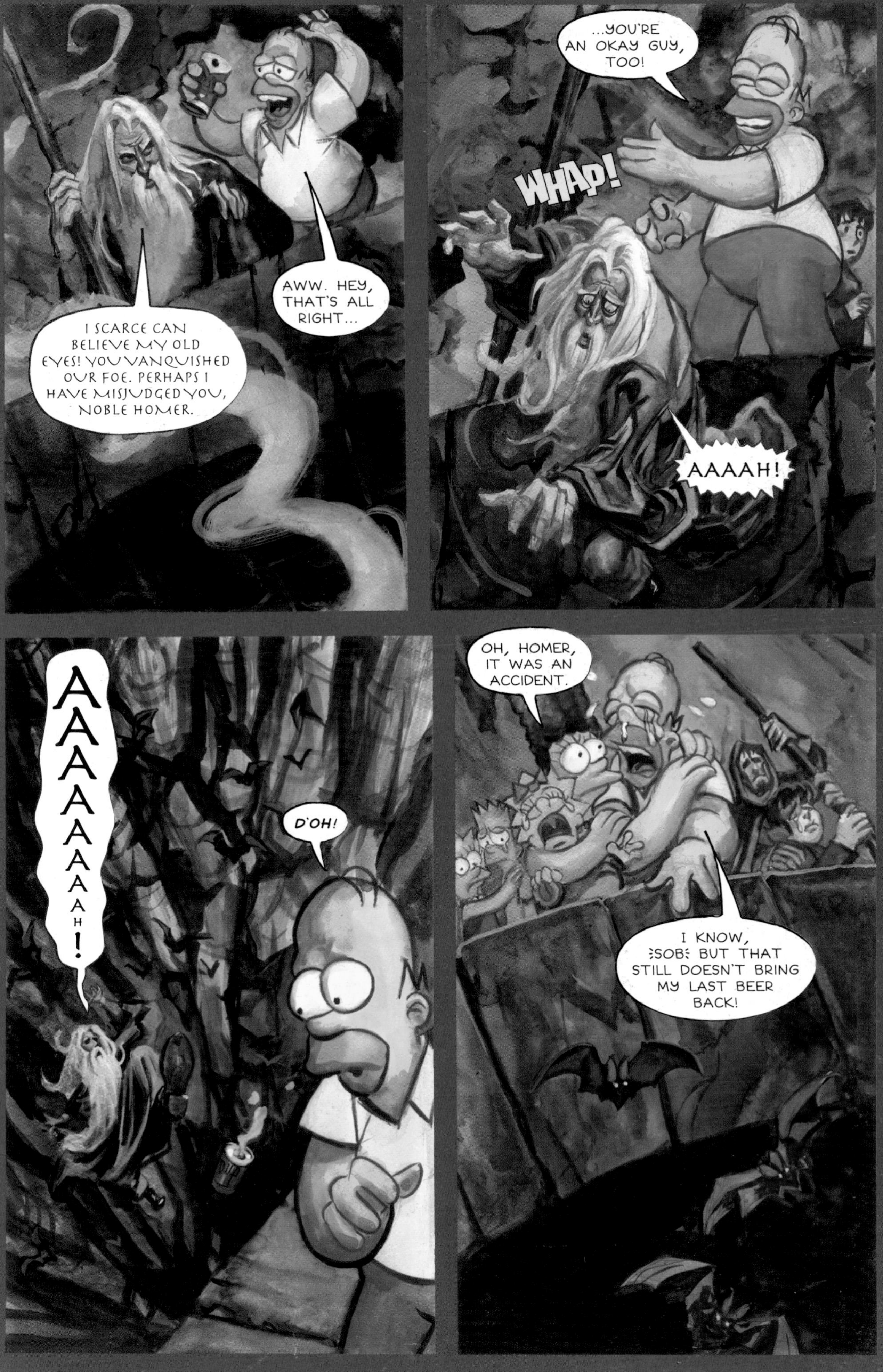
I SCARCE CAN BELIEVE MY OLD EYES! YOU VANQUISHED OUR FOE. PERHAPS I HAVE MISJUDGED YOU, NOBLE HOMER.
AWW. HEY, THAT'S ALL RIGHT...
...YOU'RE AN OKAY GUY, TOO!
WHAP!
AAAAH!
AAAAAAAAH!
D'OH!
OH, HOMER, IT WAS AN ACCIDENT.
I KNOW, ≤SOB≥ BUT THAT STILL DOESN'T BRING MY LAST BEER BACK!

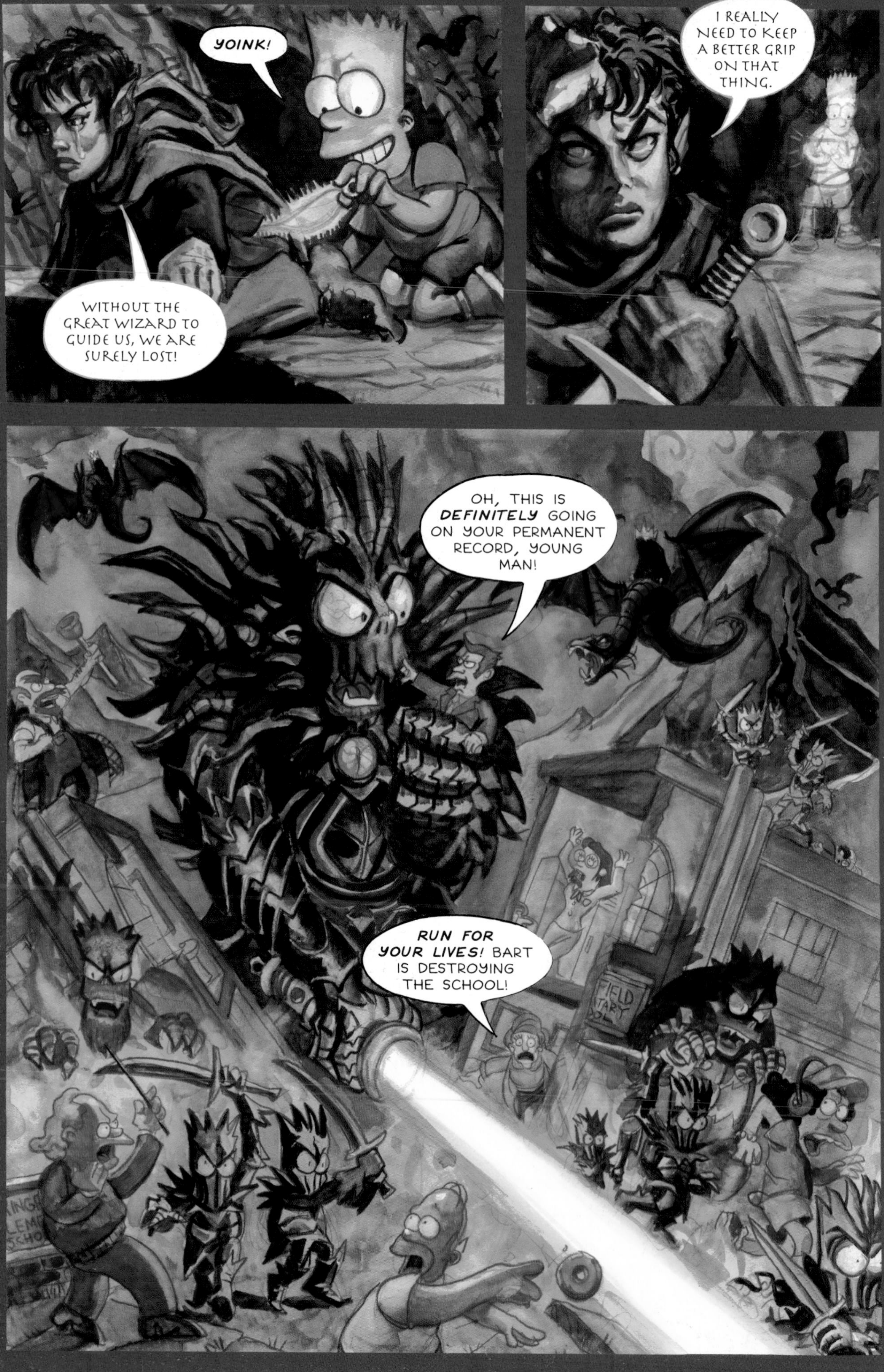
YOINK!
WITHOUT THE GREAT WIZARD TO GUIDE US, WE ARE SURELY LOST!
I REALLY NEED TO KEEP A BETTER GRIP ON THAT THING.
OH, THIS IS DEFINITELY GOING ON YOUR PERMANENT RECORD, YOUNG MAN!
RUN FOR YOUR LIVES! BART IS DESTROYING THE SCHOOL!

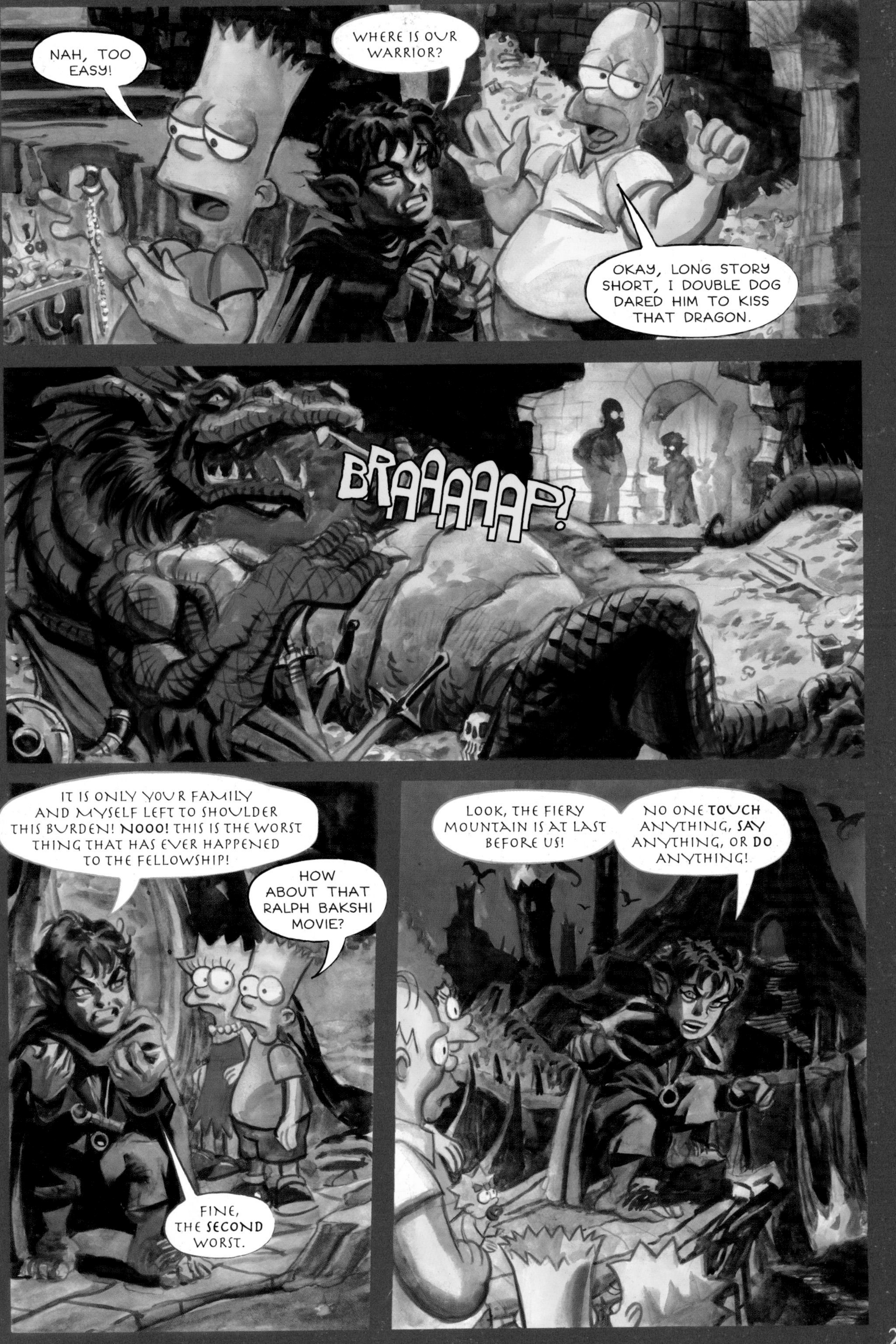

NAH, TOO EASY!
WHERE IS OUR WARRIOR?
OKAY, LONG STORY SHORT, I DOUBLE DOG DARED HIM TO KISS THAT DRAGON.
BRAAAAAAP!
IT IS ONLY YOUR FAMILY AND MYSELF LEFT TO SHOULDER THIS BURDEN! NOOO! THIS IS THE WORST THING THAT HAS EVER HAPPENED TO THE FELLOWSHIP!
HOW ABOUT THAT RALPH BAKSHI MOVIE?
FINE, THE SECOND WORST.
LOOK, THE FIERY MOUNTAIN IS AT LAST BEFORE US!
NO ONE TOUCH ANYTHING, SAY ANYTHING, OR DO ANYTHING!

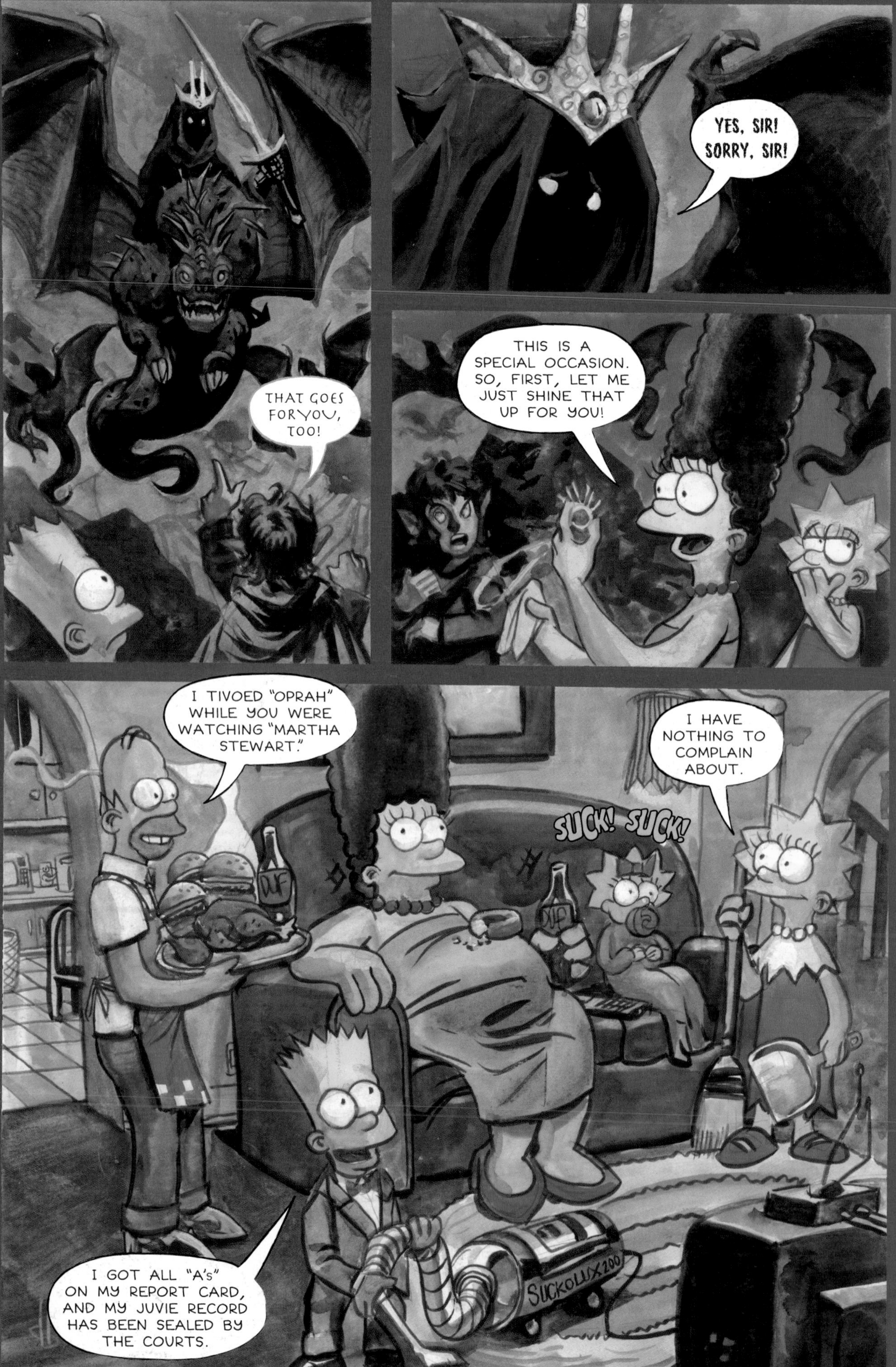
YES, SIR!
SORRY, SIR!
THAT GOES FOR YOU, TOO!
THIS IS A SPECIAL OCCASION. SO, FIRST, LET ME JUST SHINE THAT UP FOR YOU!
I TIVOED "OPRAH" WHILE YOU WERE WATCHING "MARTHA STEWART."
I HAVE NOTHING TO COMPLAIN ABOUT.
SUCK! SUCK!
I GOT ALL "A's" ON MY REPORT CARD, AND MY JUVIE RECORD HAS BEEN SEALED BY THE COURTS.
SUCKOLUX 200

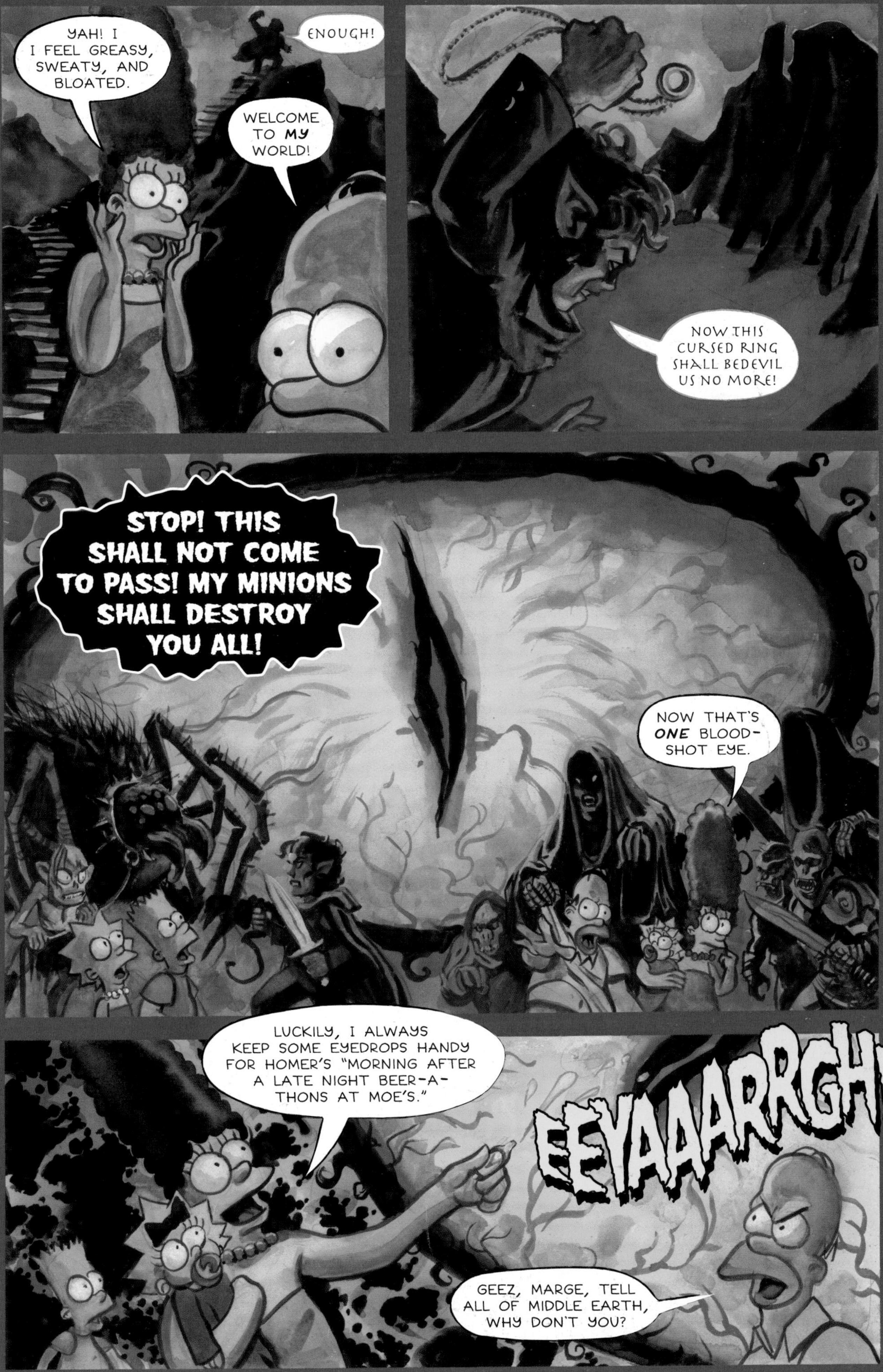
YAH! I
I FEEL GREASY,
SWEATY, AND
BLOATED.
ENOUGH!
WELCOME TO **MY** WORLD!
NOW THIS CURSED RING SHALL BEDEVIL US NO MORE!
STOP! THIS SHALL NOT COME TO PASS! MY MINIONS SHALL DESTROY YOU ALL!
NOW THAT'S **ONE** BLOOD-SHOT EYE.
LUCKILY, I ALWAYS KEEP SOME EYEDROPS HANDY FOR HOMER'S "MORNING AFTER A LATE NIGHT BEER-A-THONS AT MOE'S."
EEYAAARRGH!
GEEZ, MARGE, TELL ALL OF MIDDLE EARTH, WHY DON'T YOU?

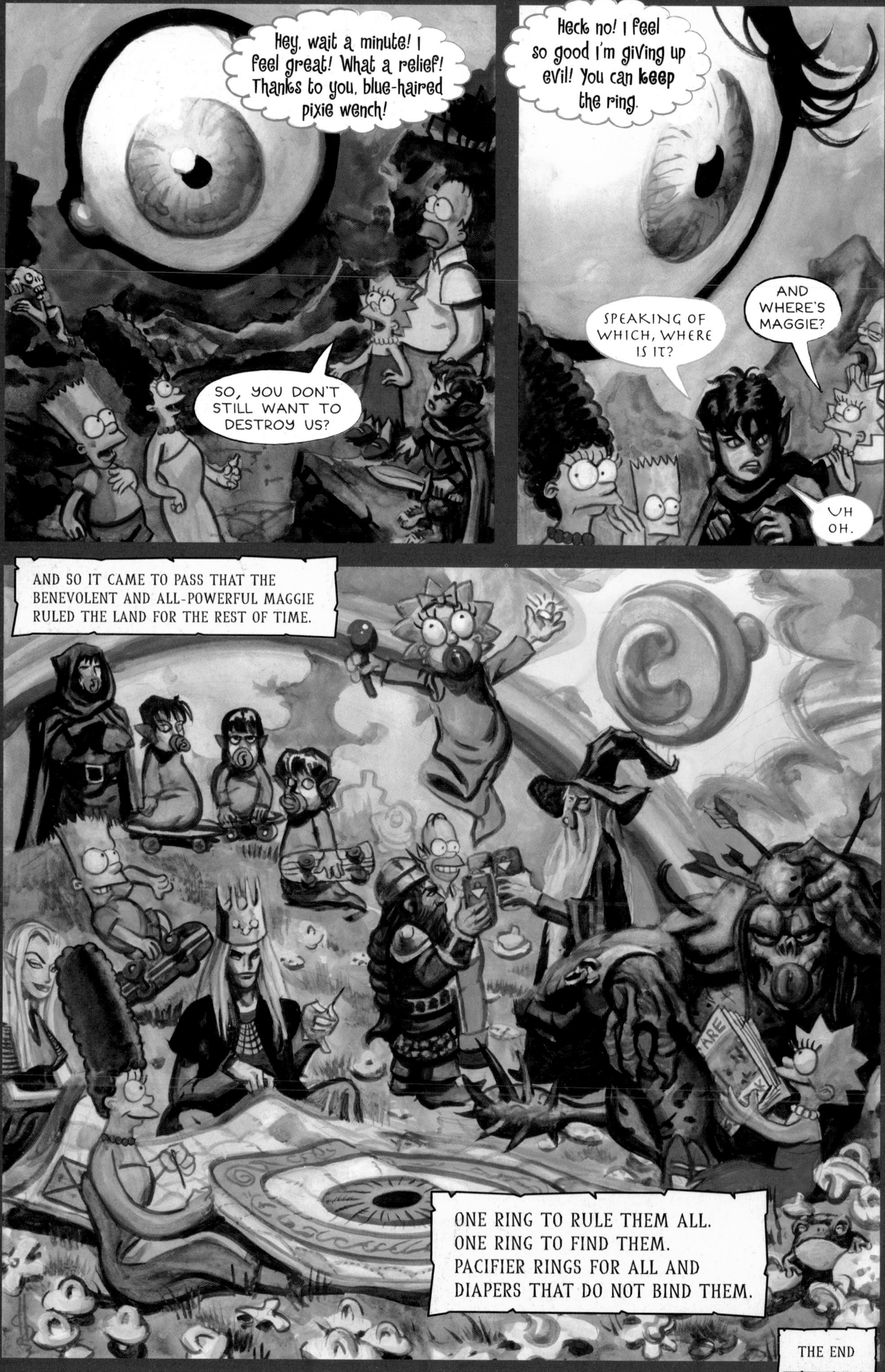
Hey, wait a minute! I feel great! What a relief! Thanks to you, blue-haired pixie wench!
SO, YOU DON'T STILL WANT TO DESTROY US?
Heck no! I feel so good I'm giving up evil! You can keep the ring.
SPEAKING OF WHICH, WHERE IS IT?
AND WHERE'S MAGGIE?
UH OH.
AND SO IT CAME TO PASS THAT THE BENEVOLENT AND ALL-POWERFUL MAGGIE RULED THE LAND FOR THE REST OF TIME.
ONE RING TO RULE THEM ALL.
ONE RING TO FIND THEM.
PACIFIER RINGS FOR ALL AND
DIAPERS THAT DO NOT BIND THEM.
THE END

COMIC BOOK GUY'S
Best Costumes Ever - Part 1

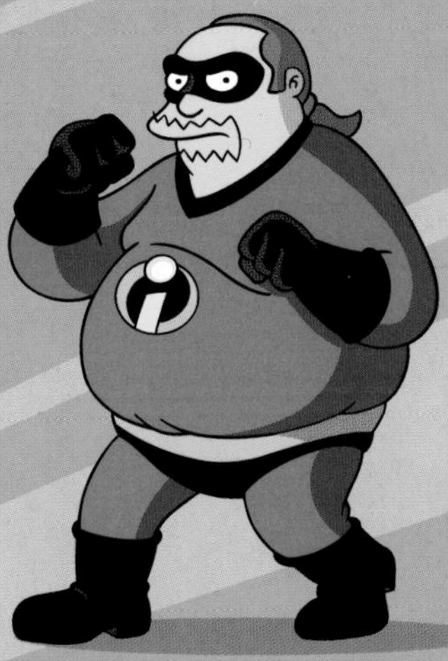

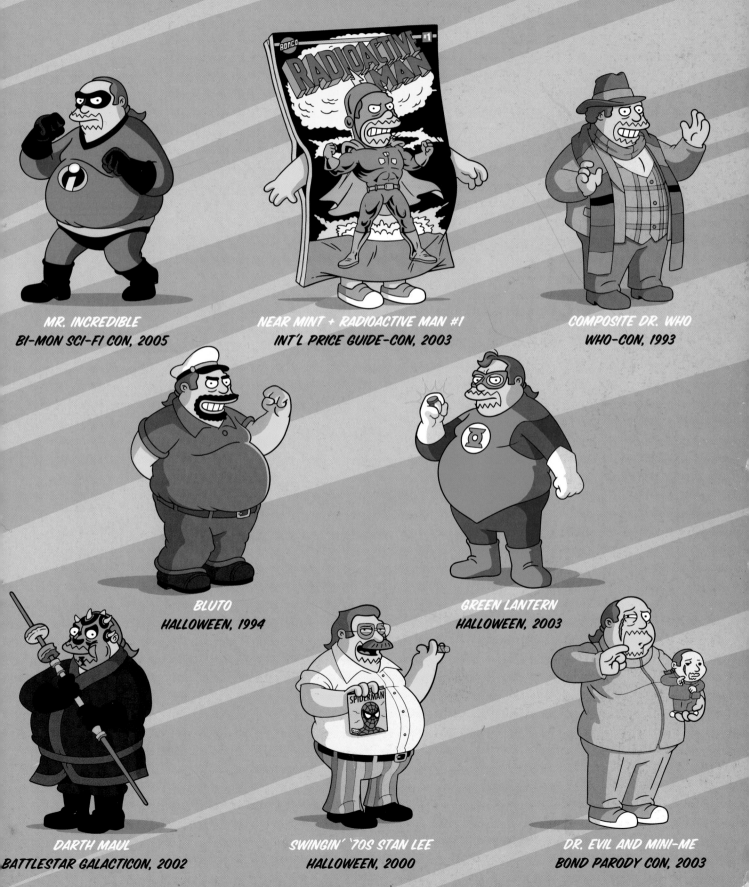

MR. INCREDIBLE
BI-MON SCI-FI CON, 2005

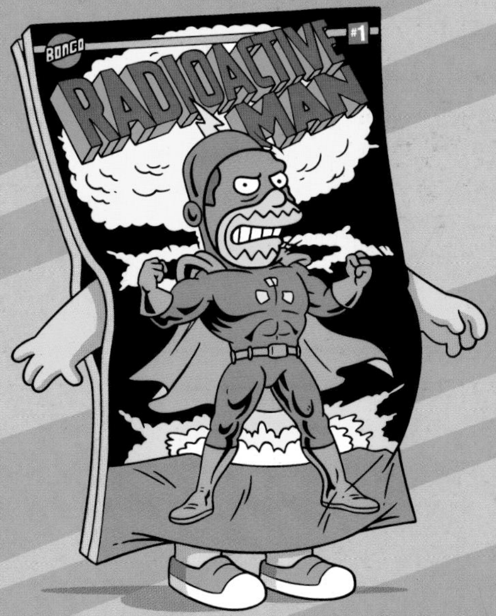
BONGO
RADIOACTIVE MAN
#1

NEAR MINT + RADIOACTIVE MAN #1
INT'L PRICE GUIDE-CON, 2003

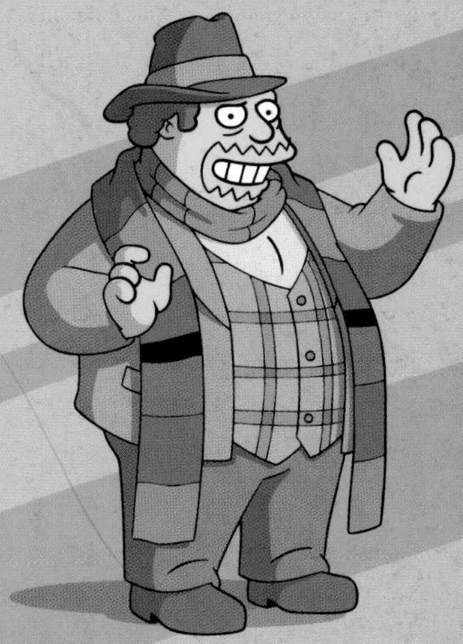

COMPOSITE DR. WHO
WHO-CON, 1993

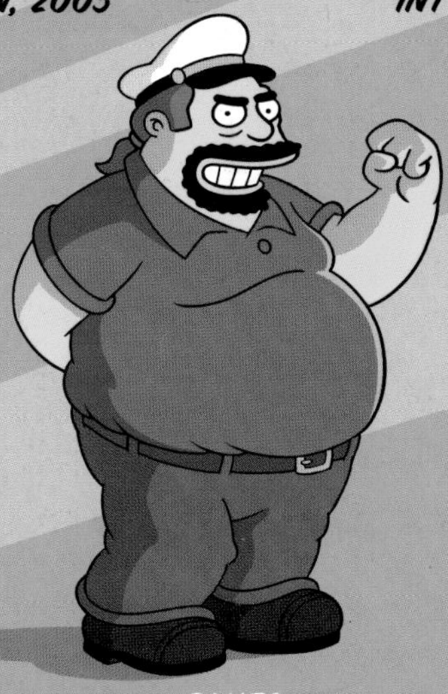

BLUTO
HALLOWEEN, 1994

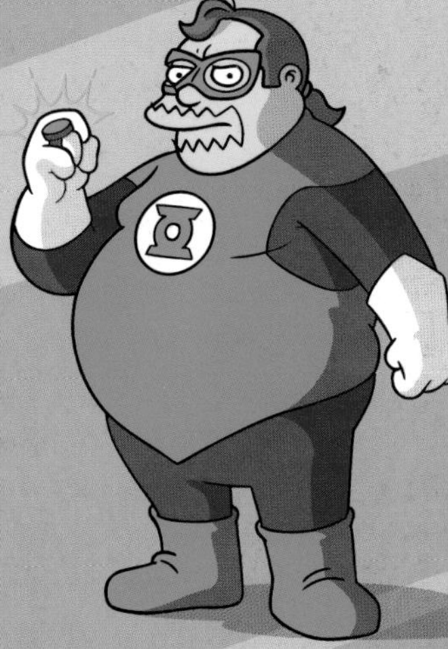

GREEN LANTERN
HALLOWEEN, 2003

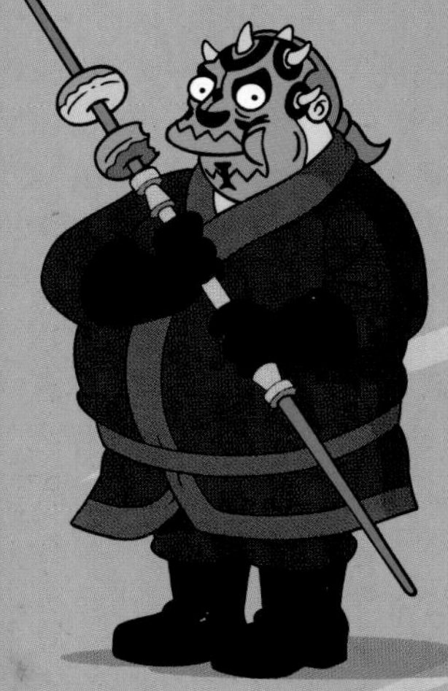

DARTH MAUL
BATTLESTAR GALACTICON, 2002

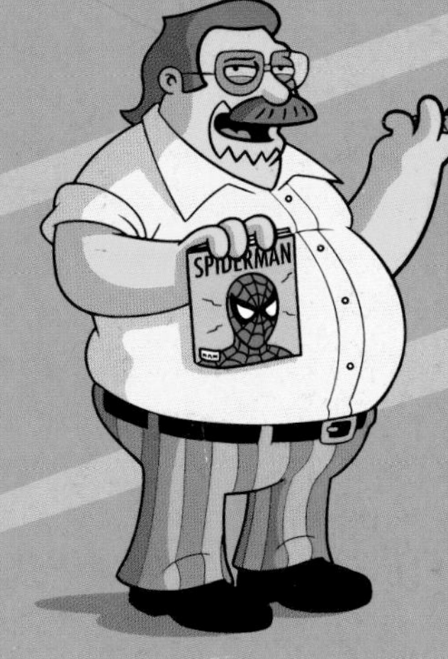
SPIDERMAN

SWINGIN' '70S STAN LEE
HALLOWEEN, 2000

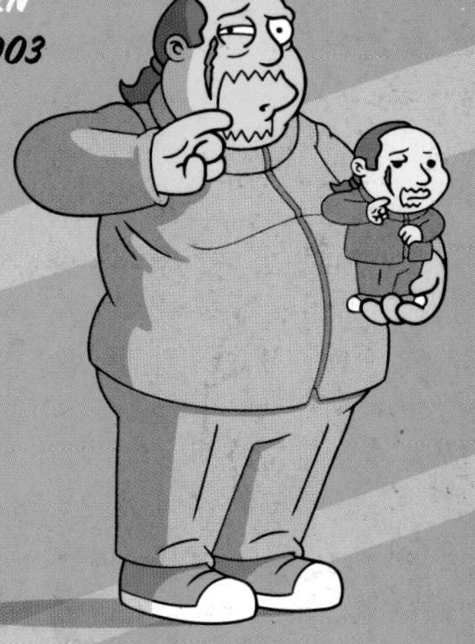

DR. EVIL AND MINI-ME
BOND PARODY CON, 2003

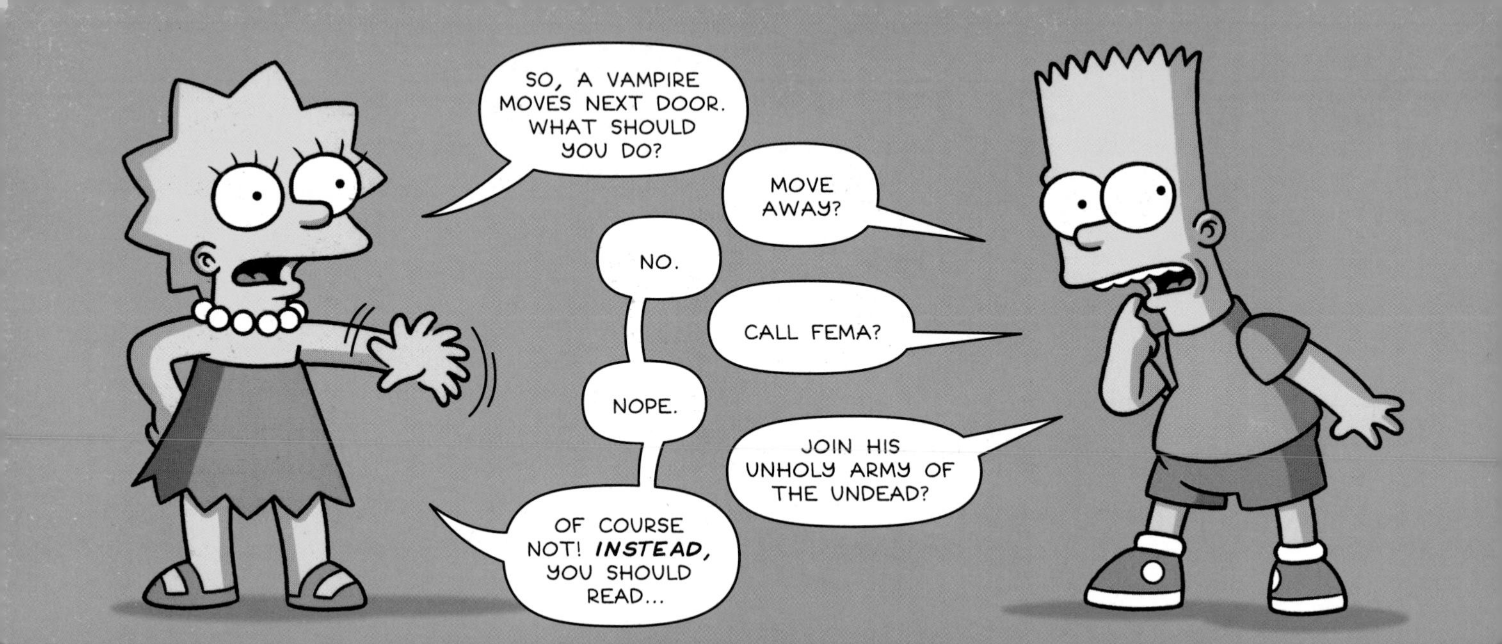
SO, A VAMPIRE MOVES NEXT DOOR. WHAT SHOULD YOU DO?
MOVE AWAY?
NO.
CALL FEMA?
NOPE.
JOIN HIS UNHOLY ARMY OF THE UNDEAD?
OF COURSE NOT! *INSTEAD,* YOU SHOULD READ...

BART AND LISA'S TIPS FOR WHEN DRACULA MOVES NEXT DOOR!

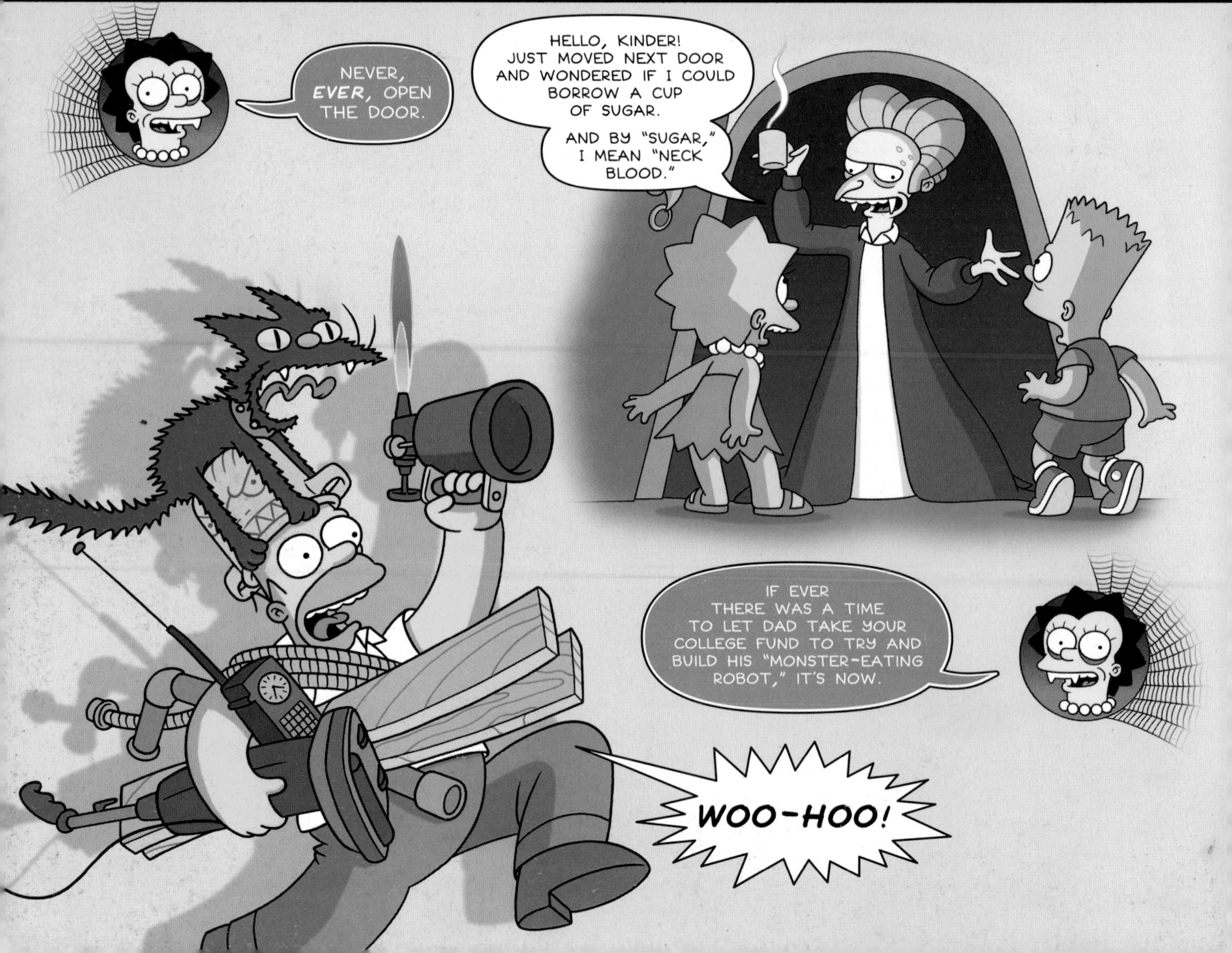
NEVER, *EVER,* OPEN THE DOOR.
HELLO, KINDER! JUST MOVED NEXT DOOR AND WONDERED IF I COULD BORROW A CUP OF SUGAR.
AND BY "SUGAR," I MEAN "NECK BLOOD."
IF EVER THERE WAS A TIME TO LET DAD TAKE YOUR COLLEGE FUND TO TRY AND BUILD HIS "MONSTER-EATING ROBOT," IT'S NOW.
WOO-HOO!

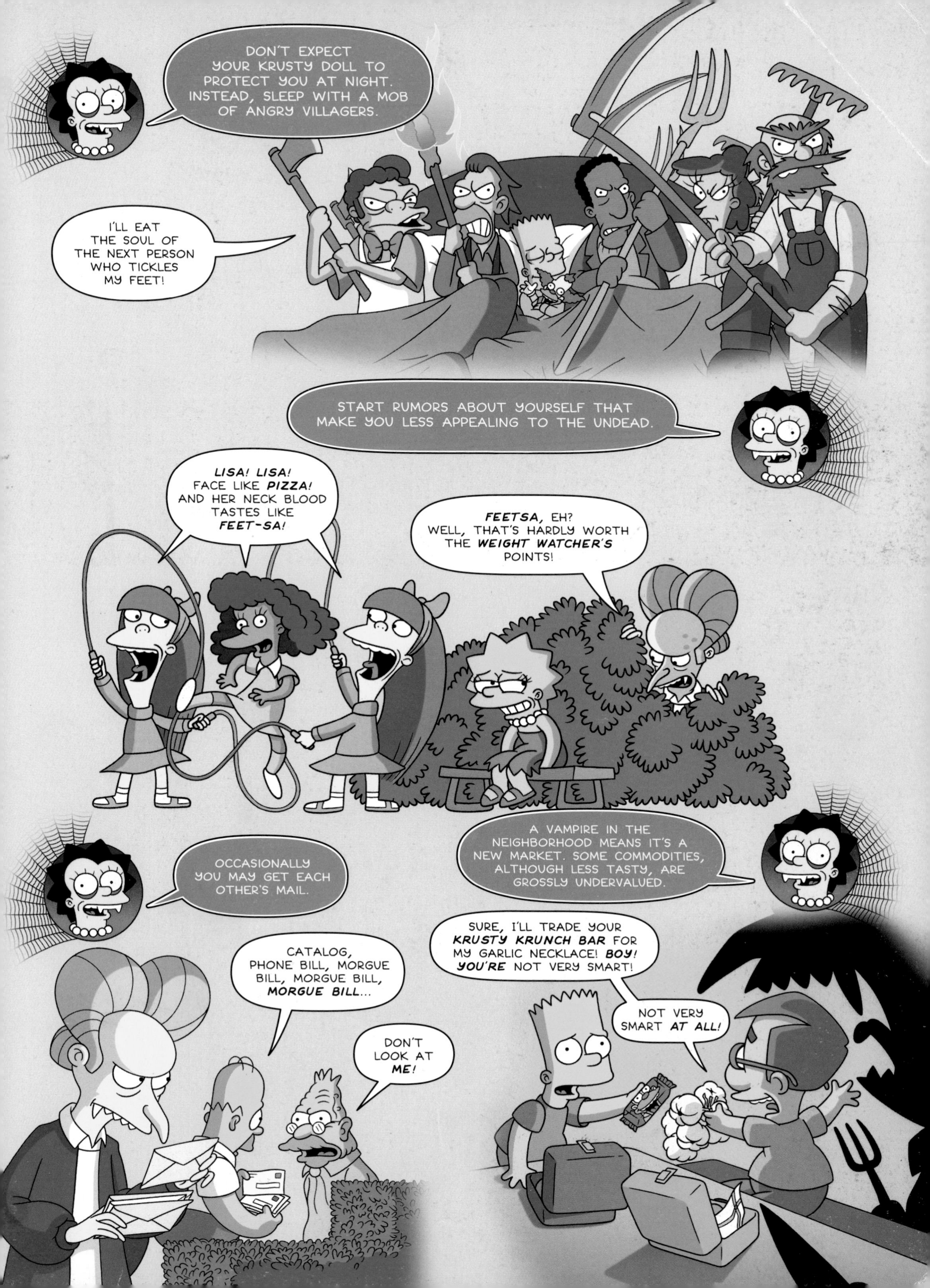

DON'T EXPECT YOUR KRUSTY DOLL TO PROTECT YOU AT NIGHT. INSTEAD, SLEEP WITH A MOB OF ANGRY VILLAGERS.
I'LL EAT THE SOUL OF THE NEXT PERSON WHO TICKLES MY FEET!
START RUMORS ABOUT YOURSELF THAT MAKE YOU LESS APPEALING TO THE UNDEAD.
LISA! LISA! FACE LIKE PIZZA! AND HER NECK BLOOD TASTES LIKE FEET-SA!
FEETSA, EH? WELL, THAT'S HARDLY WORTH THE WEIGHT WATCHER'S POINTS!
OCCASIONALLY YOU MAY GET EACH OTHER'S MAIL.
A VAMPIRE IN THE NEIGHBORHOOD MEANS IT'S A NEW MARKET. SOME COMMODITIES, ALTHOUGH LESS TASTY, ARE GROSSLY UNDERVALUED.
CATALOG, PHONE BILL, MORGUE BILL, MORGUE BILL, MORGUE BILL...
DON'T LOOK AT ME!
SURE, I'LL TRADE YOUR KRUSTY KRUNCH BAR FOR MY GARLIC NECKLACE! BOY! YOU'RE NOT VERY SMART!
NOT VERY SMART AT ALL!

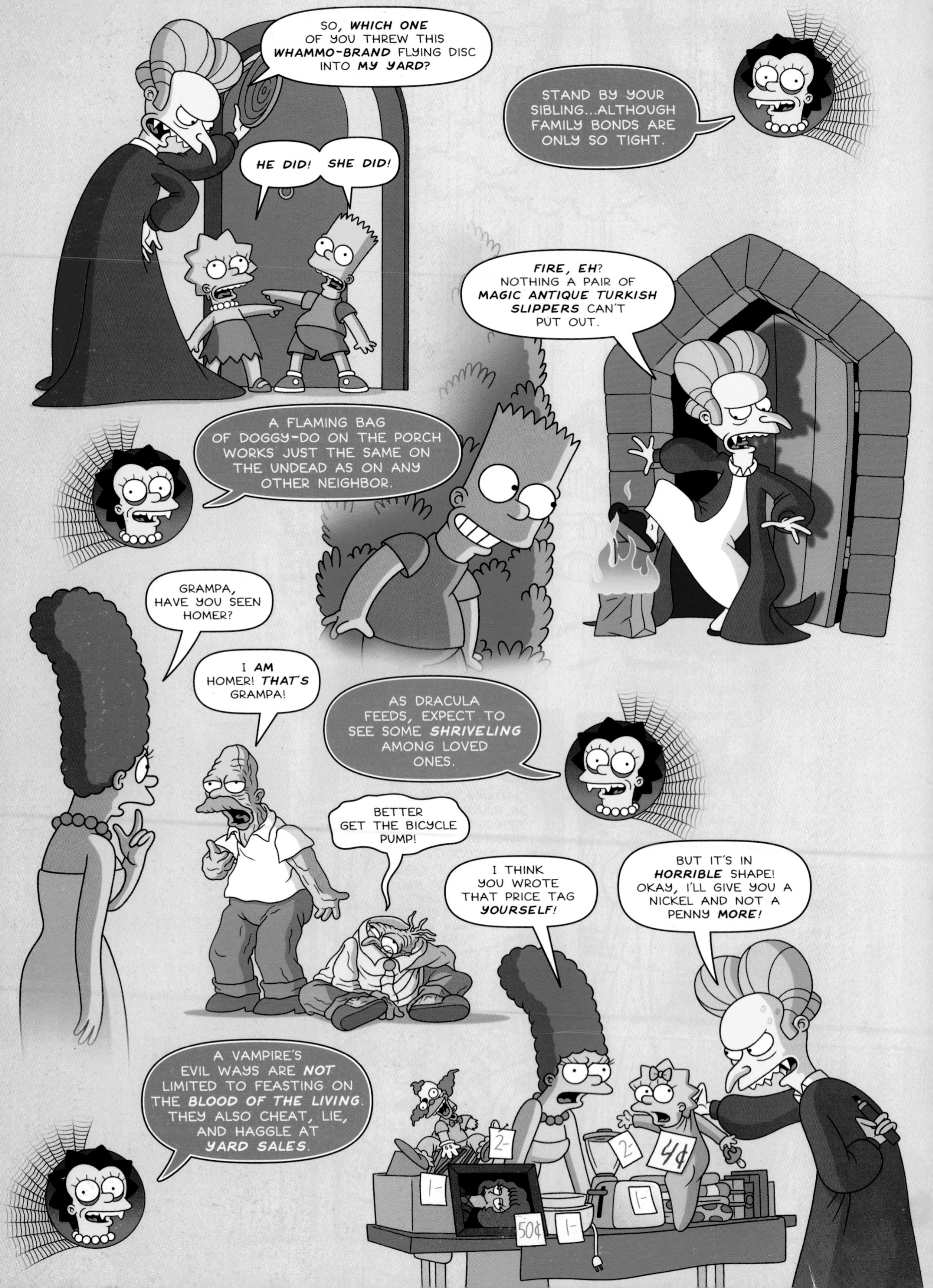
SO, WHICH ONE OF YOU THREW THIS WHAMMO-BRAND FLYING DISC INTO MY YARD?
HE DID!
SHE DID!
STAND BY YOUR SIBLING...ALTHOUGH FAMILY BONDS ARE ONLY SO TIGHT.
FIRE, EH? NOTHING A PAIR OF MAGIC ANTIQUE TURKISH SLIPPERS CAN'T PUT OUT.
A FLAMING BAG OF DOGGY-DO ON THE PORCH WORKS JUST THE SAME ON THE UNDEAD AS ON ANY OTHER NEIGHBOR.
GRAMPA, HAVE YOU SEEN HOMER?
I AM HOMER! THAT'S GRAMPA!
AS DRACULA FEEDS, EXPECT TO SEE SOME SHRIVELING AMONG LOVED ONES.
BETTER GET THE BICYCLE PUMP!
I THINK YOU WROTE THAT PRICE TAG YOURSELF!
BUT IT'S IN HORRIBLE SHAPE! OKAY, I'LL GIVE YOU A NICKEL AND NOT A PENNY MORE!
A VAMPIRE'S EVIL WAYS ARE NOT LIMITED TO FEASTING ON THE BLOOD OF THE LIVING. THEY ALSO CHEAT, LIE, AND HAGGLE AT YARD SALES.
2-
2-
4¢
1-
1-
50¢
1-

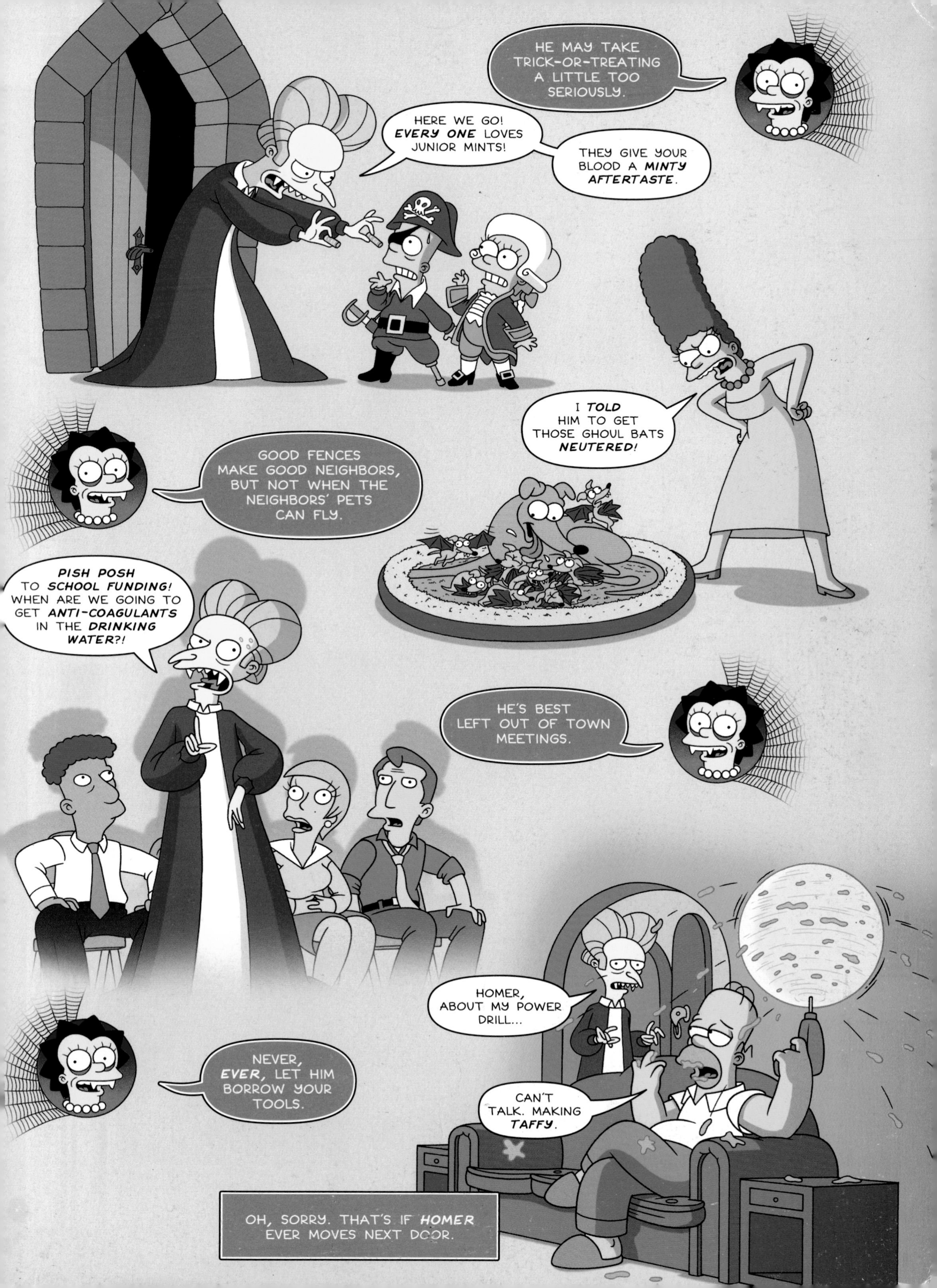
HE MAY TAKE TRICK-OR-TREATING A LITTLE TOO SERIOUSLY.
HERE WE GO! EVERY ONE LOVES JUNIOR MINTS!
THEY GIVE YOUR BLOOD A MINTY AFTERTASTE.
GOOD FENCES MAKE GOOD NEIGHBORS, BUT NOT WHEN THE NEIGHBORS' PETS CAN FLY.
I TOLD HIM TO GET THOSE GHOUL BATS NEUTERED!
PISH POSH TO SCHOOL FUNDING! WHEN ARE WE GOING TO GET ANTI-COAGULANTS IN THE DRINKING WATER?!
HE'S BEST LEFT OUT OF TOWN MEETINGS.
NEVER, EVER, LET HIM BORROW YOUR TOOLS.
HOMER, ABOUT MY POWER DRILL...
CAN'T TALK. MAKING TAFFY.
OH, SORRY. THAT'S IF HOMER EVER MOVES NEXT DOOR.

THEY WON'T STAY DEAD, AND THEY WON'T SHUT UP

MATT GROENING'S

NIGHT OF THE LIVING NED

They keep coming back in a bloodthirsty lust for
HUMAN FLESH and UNNATURAL GOOD CHEER...

Pits the DEAD against the LIVING in an
UNHOLY struggle for SURVIVAL
and NEIGHBORLINESS!

*"You'll say
'Okilly-dokilly!'...
to mind-numbing horror!"*
— GENE SHALIT

NIGHT OF THE LIVING NED A HOLY TERROR PRODUCTION

STARRING NED FLANDERS • ROD FLANDERS • TODD FLANDERS • HOMER SIMPSON • RAINIER WOLFCASTLE

TIMOTHY LOVEJOY • KRUSTY THE CLOWN and re ... MAUDE FLANDERS as "CHOMPY!"

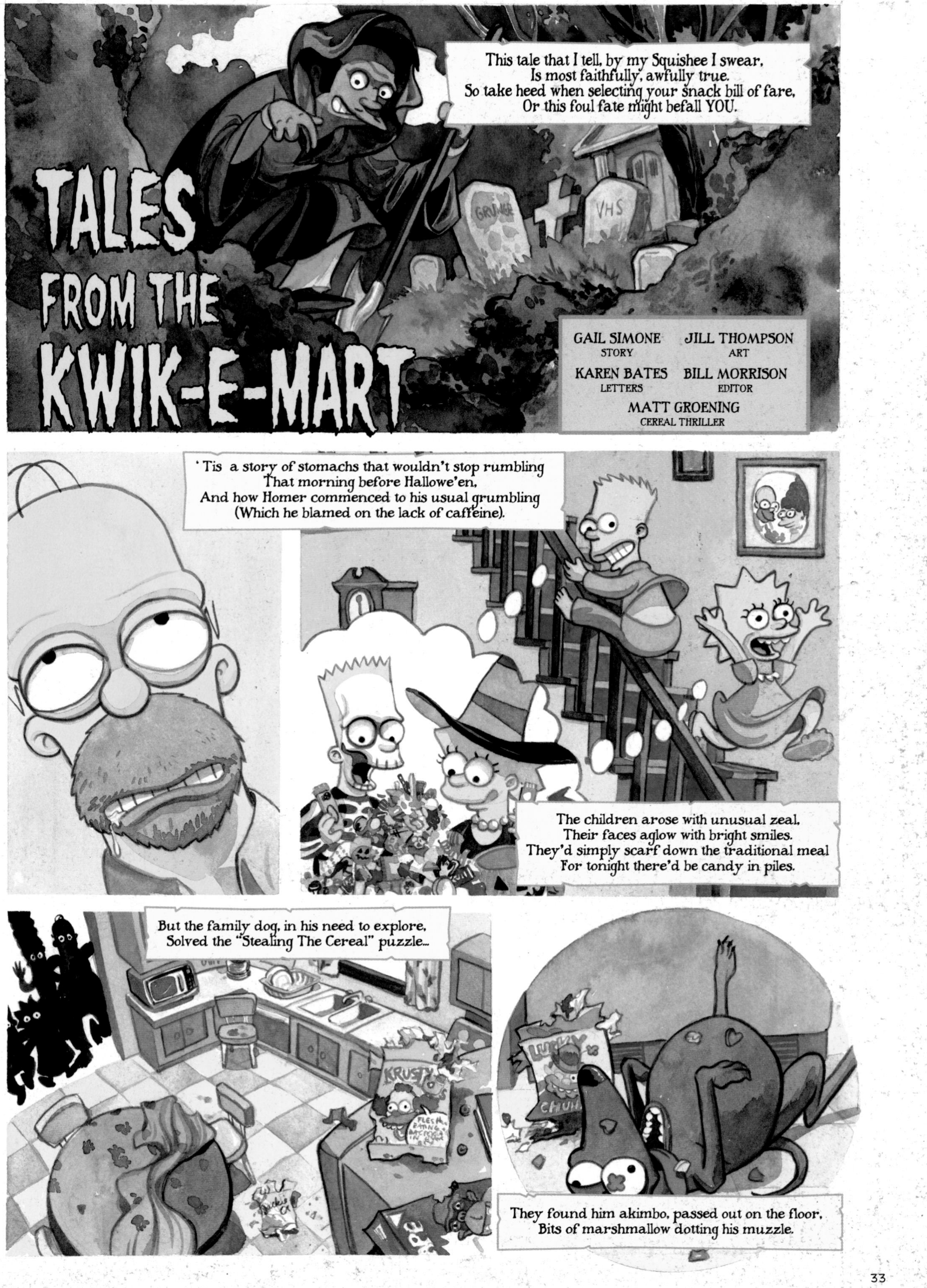
This tale that I tell, by my Squishee I swear,
Is most faithfully, awfully true.
So take heed when selecting your snack bill of fare,
Or this foul fate might befall YOU.
TALES FROM THE KWIK-E-MART
GRUNGE
VHS
GAIL SIMONE STORY
JILL THOMPSON ART
KAREN BATES LETTERS
BILL MORRISON EDITOR
MATT GROENING CEREAL THRILLER
'Tis a story of stomachs that wouldn't stop rumbling
That morning before Hallowe'en,
And how Homer commenced to his usual grumbling
(Which he blamed on the lack of caffeine).
The children arose with unusual zeal,
Their faces aglow with bright smiles.
They'd simply scarf down the traditional meal
For tonight there'd be candy in piles.
But the family dog, in his need to explore,
Solved the "Stealing The Cereal" puzzle...
KRUSTY
They found him akimbo, passed out on the floor,
Bits of marshmallow dotting his muzzle.

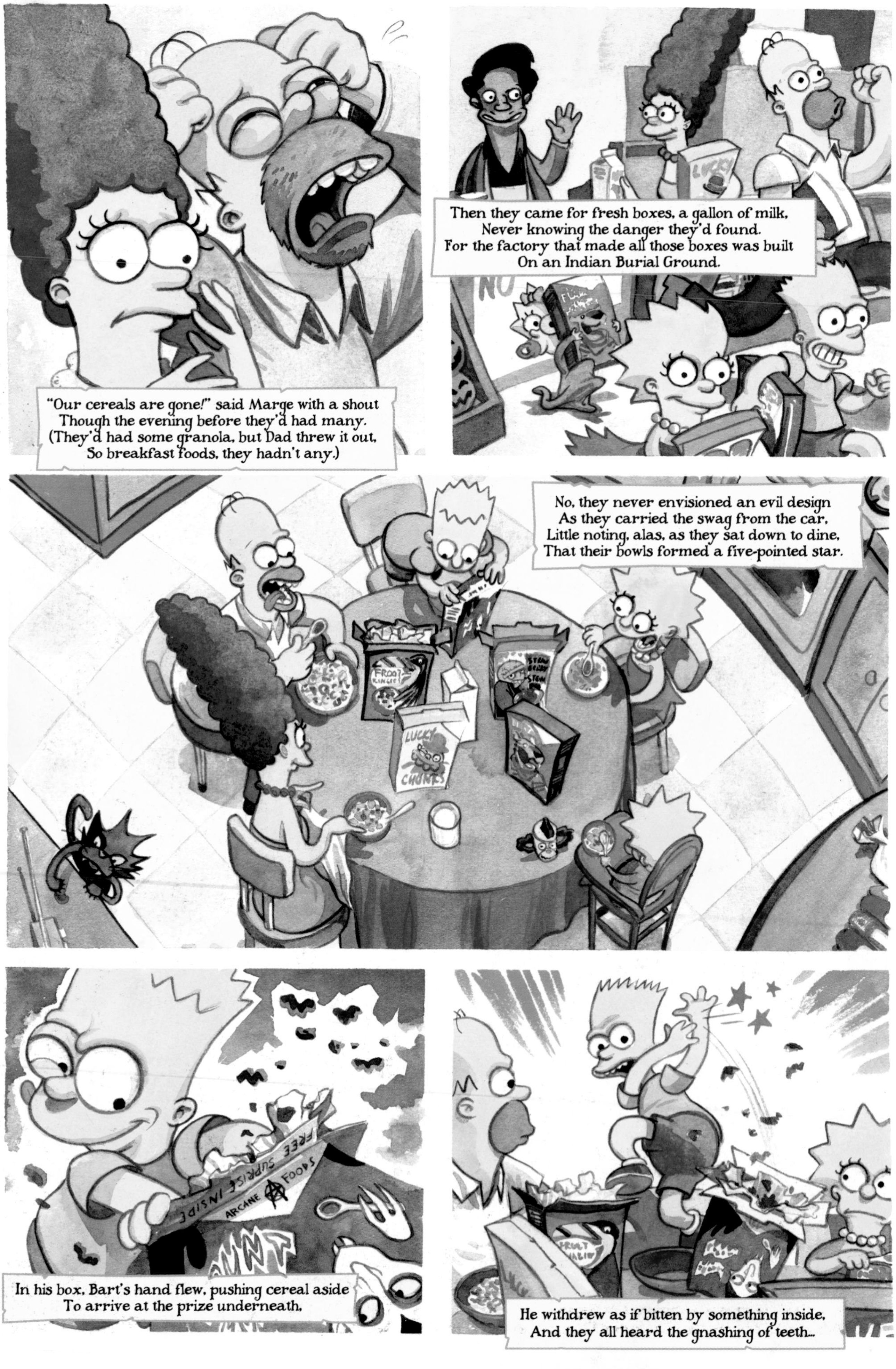
"Our cereals are gone!" said Marge with a shout
Though the evening before they'd had many.
(They'd had some granola, but Dad threw it out,
So breakfast foods, they hadn't any.)
Then they came for fresh boxes, a gallon of milk,
Never knowing the danger they'd found.
For the factory that made all those boxes was built
On an Indian Burial Ground.
No, they never envisioned an evil design
As they carried the swag from the car,
Little noting, alas, as they sat down to dine,
That their bowls formed a five-pointed star.
FREE SURPRISE INSIDE
ARCANE FOODS
In his box, Bart's hand flew, pushing cereal aside
To arrive at the prize underneath.
He withdrew as if bitten by something inside,
And they all heard the gnashing of teeth...

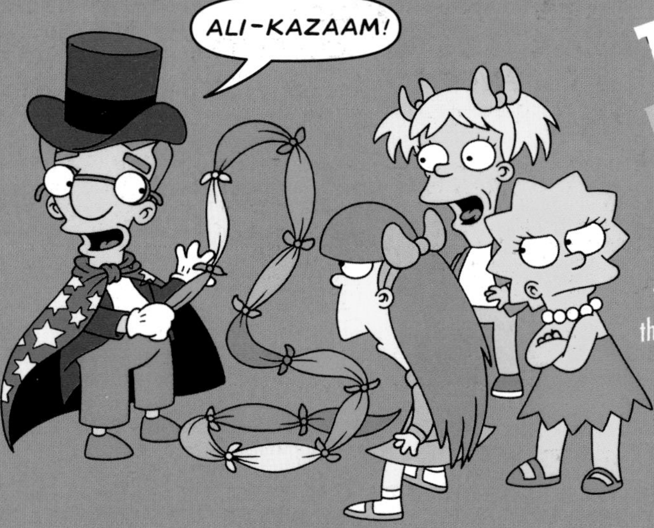
ALI-KAZAAM!

The Great Krustini's Halloween Magic Kit!

WHO KNOWS WHERE ALL THOSE COLORED HANKIES CAME FROM?

YOU WILL!

Tickle 'em with the Ever-Expanding Goiter Stunt!

Wow 'em with the East Mexican Picnic Mystery!

THANKS TO KRUSTY'S
HALLOWEEN MAGIC KIT
YOU TOO CAN PULL RESPECT OUT OF A HAT!

MADAME KRUSTY'S PERPLEXULATIN' PROGNOSTICATIN' KRYSTAL BALL!

Used by weathermen, day traders, and high-ranking members of our intelligence community!

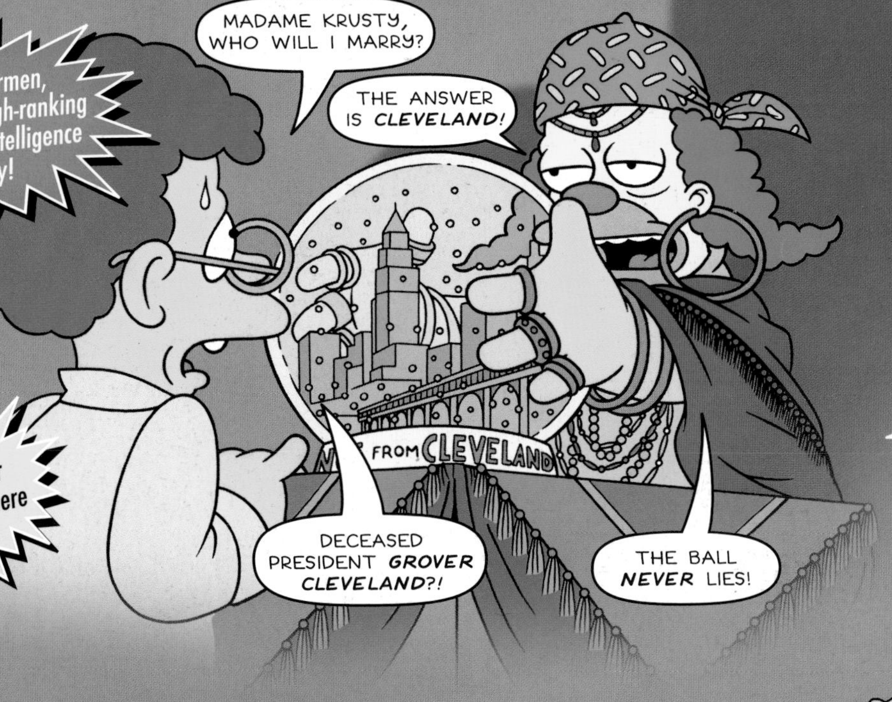
MADAME KRUSTY, WHO WILL I MARRY?
THE ANSWER IS *CLEVELAND!*
FROM CLEVELAND
DECEASED PRESIDENT **GROVER CLEVELAND?!**
THE BALL **NEVER** LIES!

SECRETS OF THE UNIVERSE REVEALED!

Be the first kid on your block to know where you'll die!

Also available in "Cincinnati," "Minneapolis," and "1998 Seoul Olympics!"

Bubble, bubble,
your bath fun will double with

KRUSTY'S WITCH'S BREW TUB MIX!

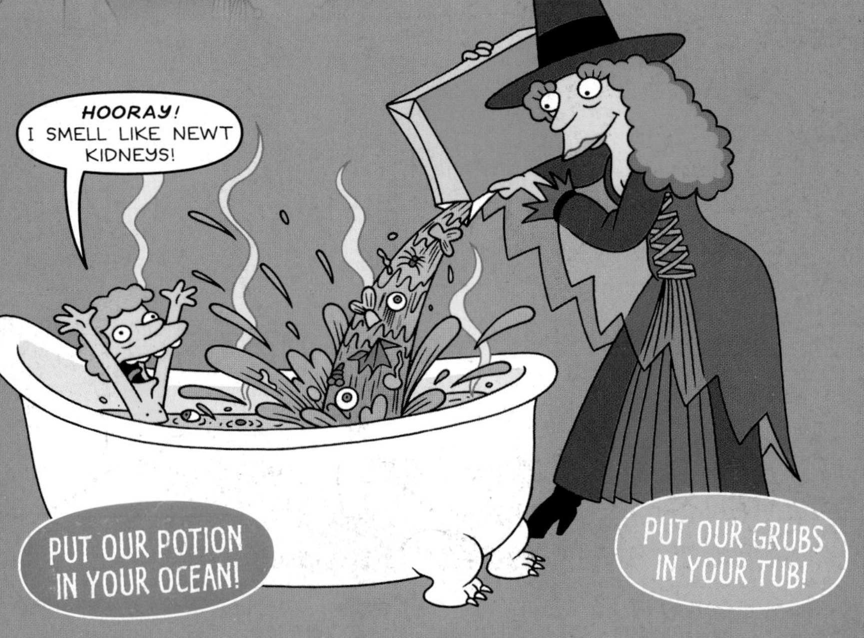
HOORAY! I SMELL LIKE NEWT KIDNEYS!
PUT OUR POTION IN YOUR OCEAN!
PUT OUR GRUBS IN YOUR TUB!

CAUTION: *Fish scales may scrape tub enamel.*

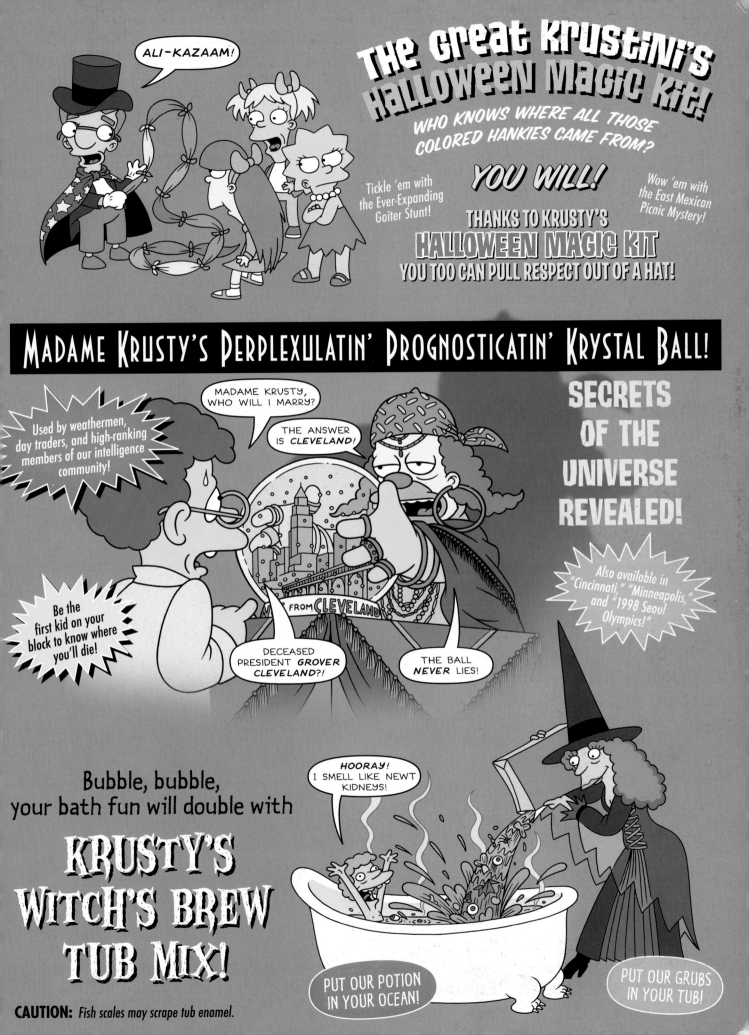

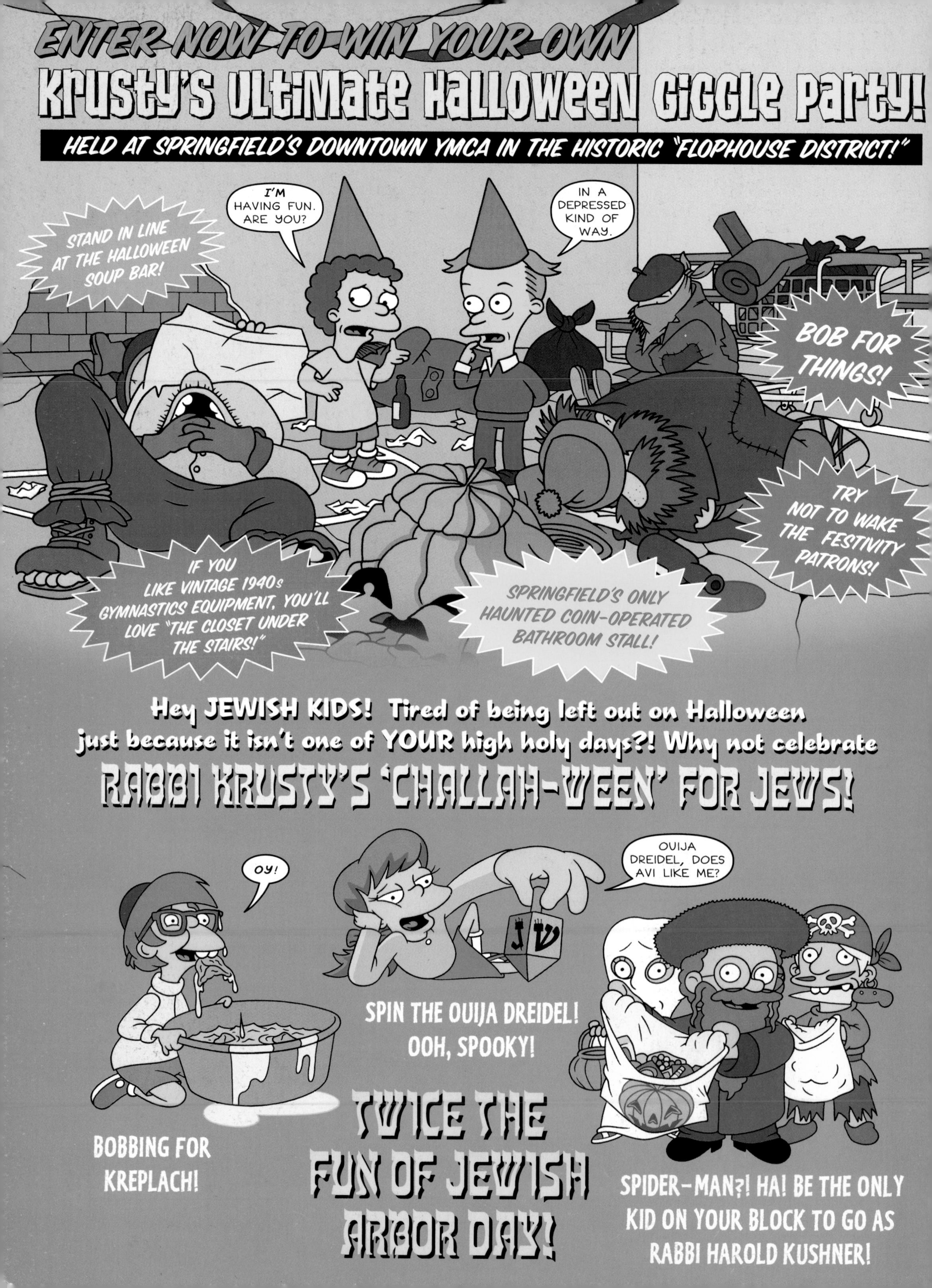
ENTER NOW TO WIN YOUR OWN
KRUSTY'S ULTIMATE HALLOWEEN GIGGLE PARTY!
HELD AT SPRINGFIELD'S DOWNTOWN YMCA IN THE HISTORIC "FLOPHOUSE DISTRICT!"
STAND IN LINE AT THE HALLOWEEN SOUP BAR!
I'M HAVING FUN. ARE YOU?
IN A DEPRESSED KIND OF WAY.
BOB FOR THINGS!
TRY NOT TO WAKE THE FESTIVITY PATRONS!
IF YOU LIKE VINTAGE 1940s GYMNASTICS EQUIPMENT, YOU'LL LOVE "THE CLOSET UNDER THE STAIRS!"
SPRINGFIELD'S ONLY HAUNTED COIN-OPERATED BATHROOM STALL!
Hey JEWISH KIDS! Tired of being left out on Halloween just because it isn't one of YOUR high holy days?! Why not celebrate
RABBI KRUSTY'S 'CHALLAH-WEEN' FOR JEWS!
OY!
OUIJA DREIDEL, DOES AVI LIKE ME?
BOBBING FOR KREPLACH!
SPIN THE OUIJA DREIDEL! OOH, SPOOKY!
TWICE THE FUN OF JEWISH ARBOR DAY!
SPIDER-MAN?! HA! BE THE ONLY KID ON YOUR BLOCK TO GO AS RABBI HAROLD KUSHNER!

KRUSTY'S JUNIOR JAILBIRD ATOMIC VANDAL KIT!

TAKE YOUR JUVENILE DELINQUENCY TO NEW HEIGHTS!

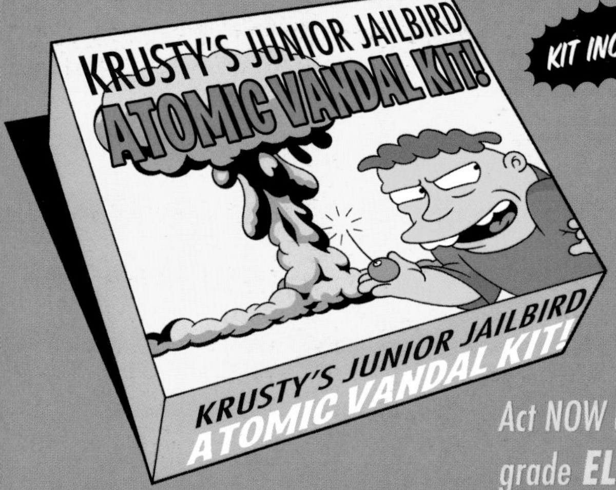
KRUSTY'S JUNIOR JAILBIRD
ATOMIC VANDAL KIT!
KRUSTY'S JUNIOR JAILBIRD
ATOMIC VANDAL KIT!

KIT INCLUDES:

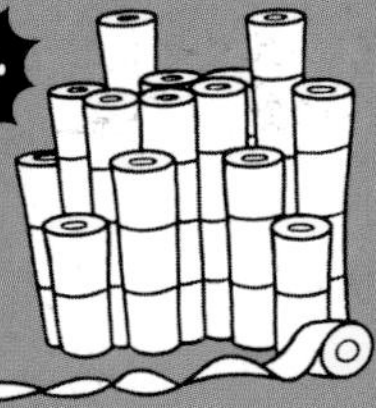

FORTY ROLLS
of toilet paper.
Now in decorator colors!

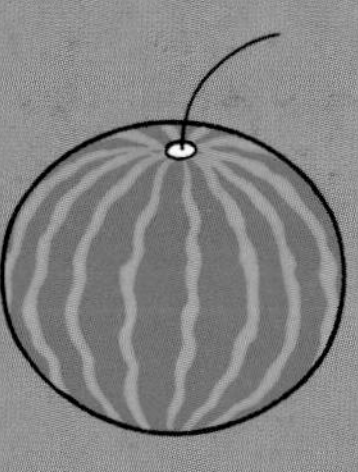

CHERRY BOMB?
Try *WATERMELON BOMB!*

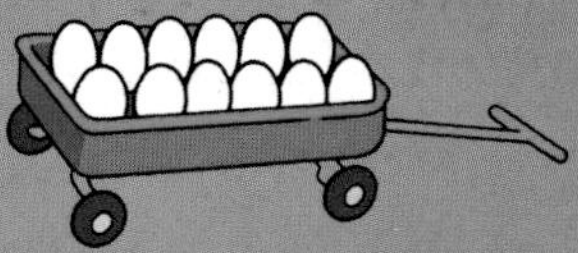

Like to whip eggs at houses?
Try a dozen ostrich eggs!*
That's right, OSTRICH EGGS!**

Act NOW and receive **SIXTEEN POUNDS** of circus grade **ELEPHANT WASTE** as a **BONUS!** Yegads!!

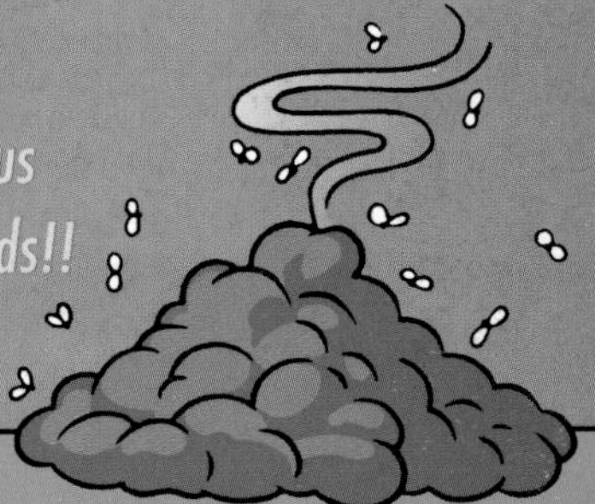

* When lobbing ostrich eggs, always make sure to lift with your legs.

** CAUTION! Some eggs may contain fully-formed ostrich babies with powerful beaks and claws. (Protective eyewear should be worn.)

KRUSTY THE CLOWN'S KRAZY-KOLORED KANDY KORN!!

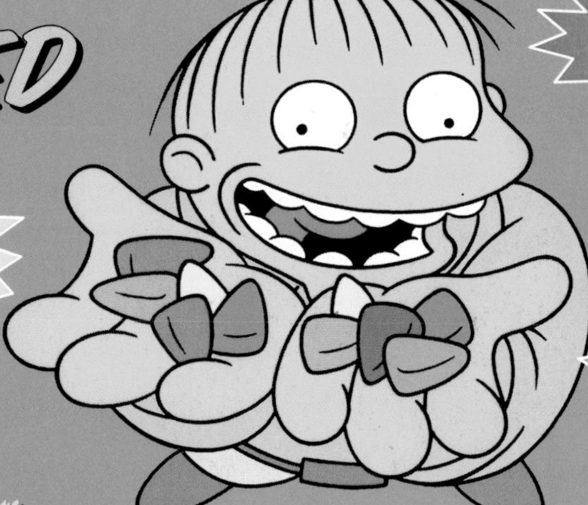
YOWZA-LICIOUS!
FULL OF VITAMIN K!
SOME ARE JUST PAINTED PINTO BEANS!

SPOOKULATING! HORRIFYING! SERGEANT O'KRUSTY'S GRAY MARKET POLICE EVIDENCE GRAB BAG!

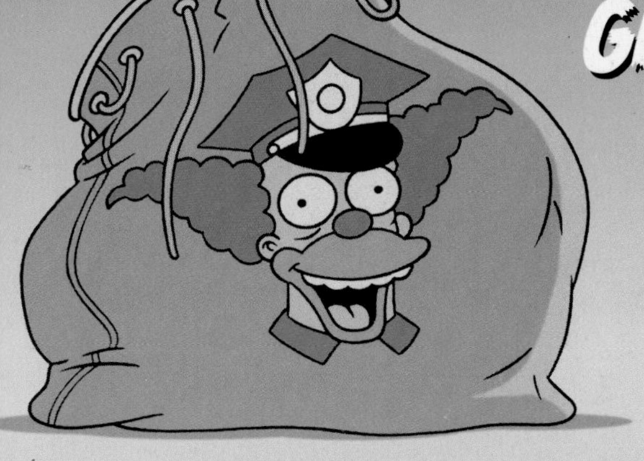

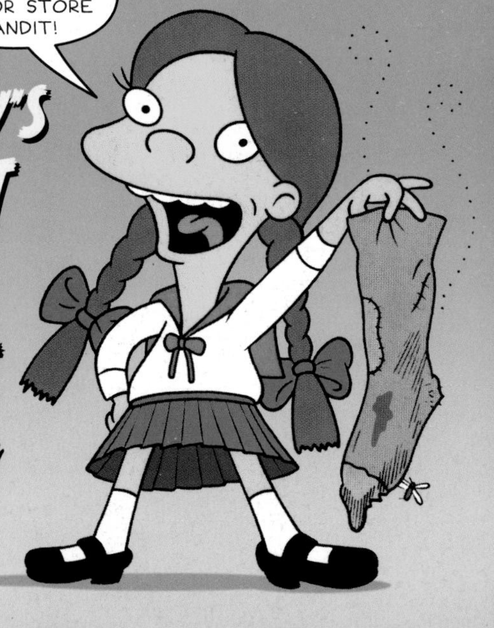
I GOT A SOCK FROM A LIQUOR STORE BANDIT!

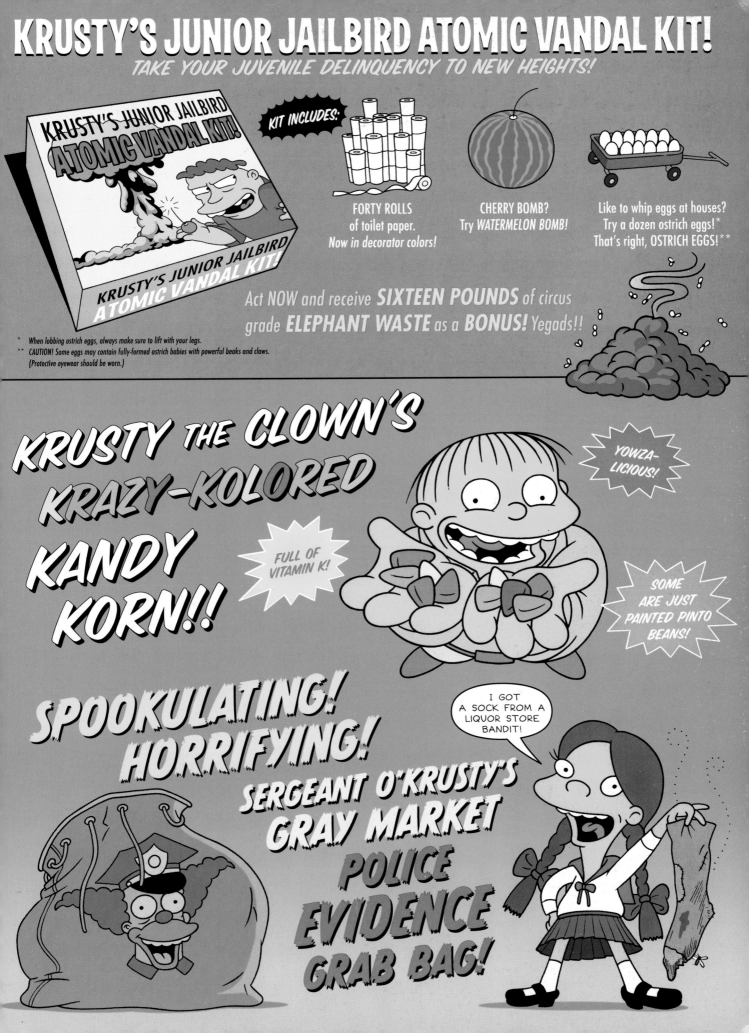

COMIC BOOK GUY'S
Best Costumes Ever - Part 2

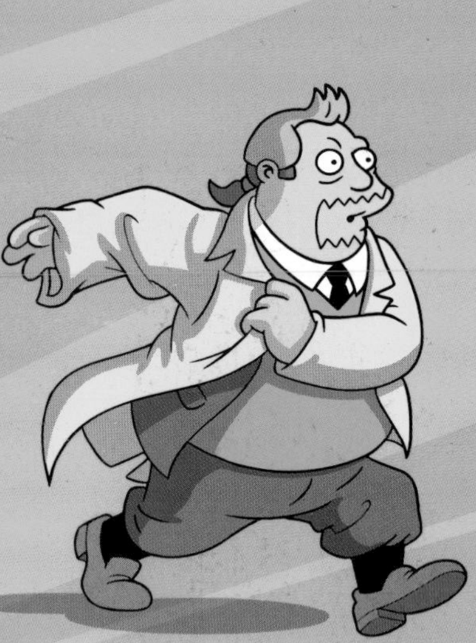

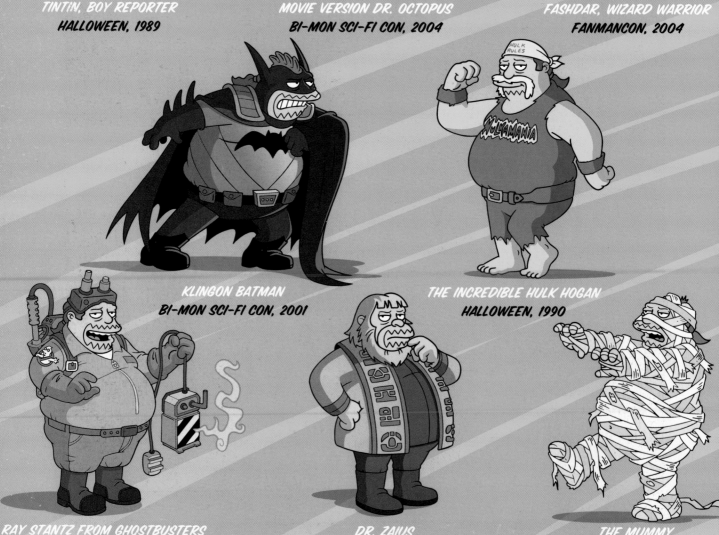

TINTIN, BOY REPORTER
HALLOWEEN, 1989

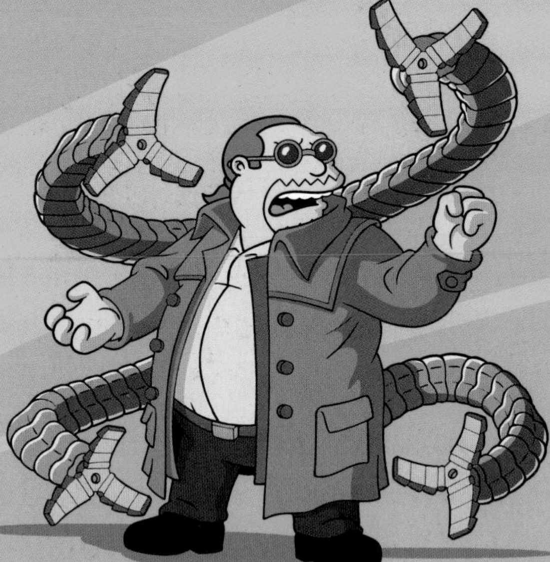

MOVIE VERSION DR. OCTOPUS
BI-MON SCI-FI CON, 2004

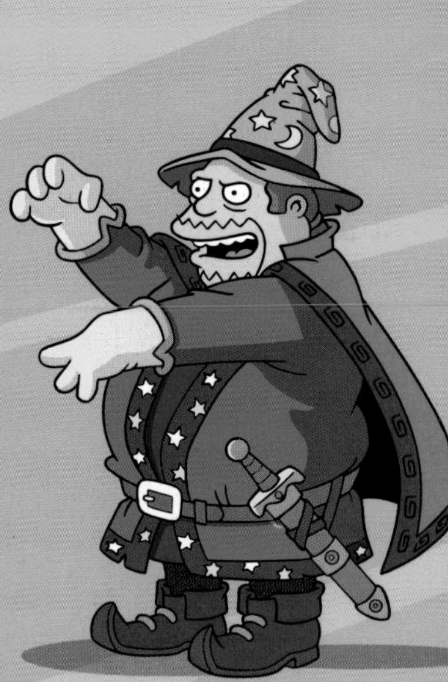

FASHDAR, WIZARD WARRIOR
FANMANCON, 2004

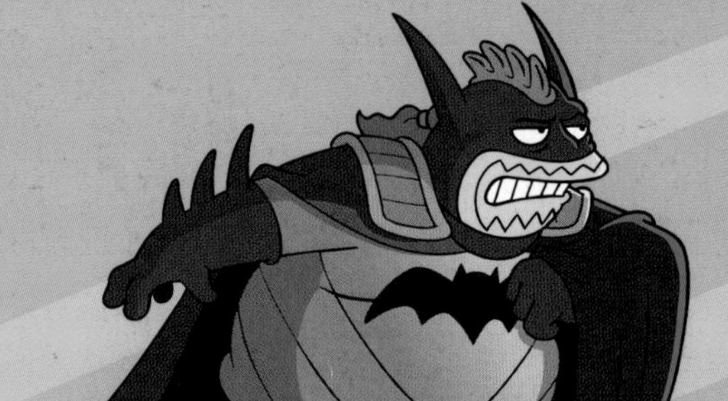

KLINGON BATMAN
BI-MON SCI-FI CON, 2001

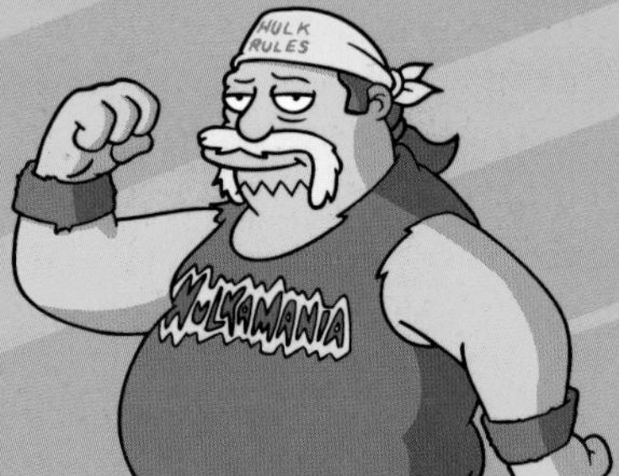
HULK RULES
HULKAMANIA

THE INCREDIBLE HULK HOGAN
HALLOWEEN, 1990

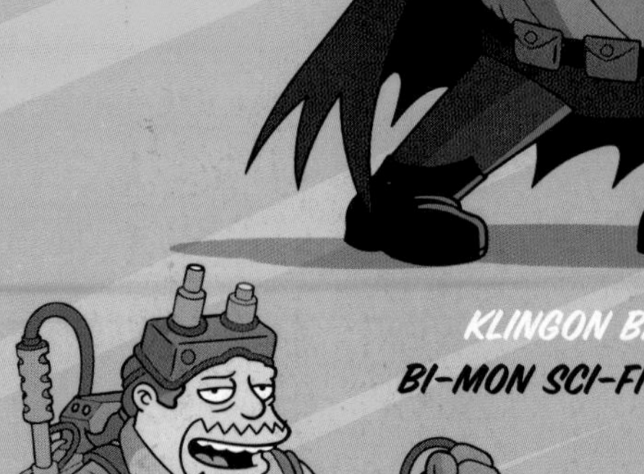

RAY STANTZ FROM GHOSTBUSTERS
AYKROYD CON, 1996

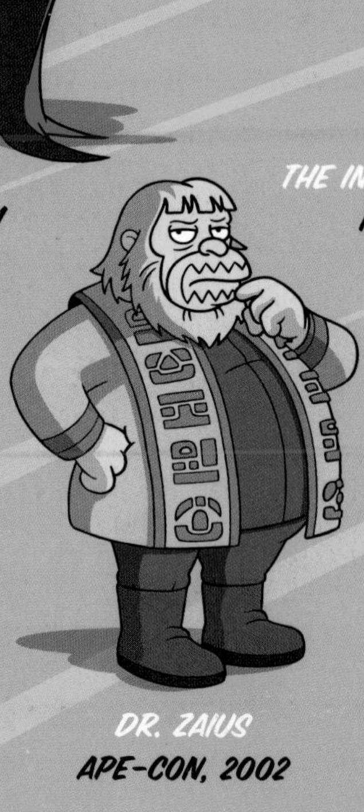

DR. ZAIUS
APE-CON, 2002

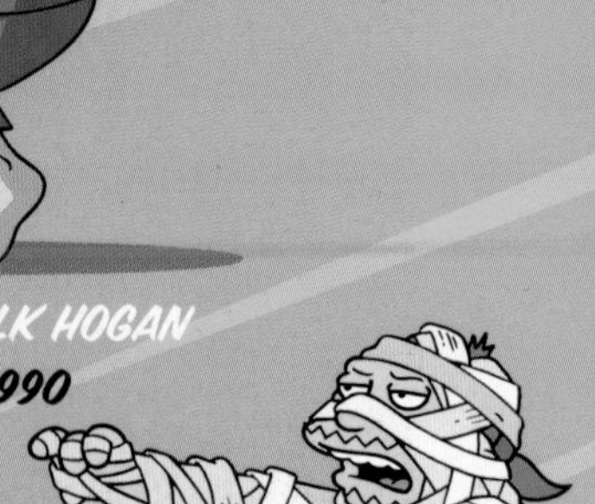

THE MUMMY
MUMMY CON, 1998

THE POWER PLANT OF PAIN

OOPS! HOW CLUMSY OF ME! I SEEM TO HAVE *ACCIDENTALLY* SPILLED ANOTHER CANISTER. CLEAN THAT UP, SMITHERS! HEH, HEH. WELL, *ROTTEN READERS*, ONCE AGAIN IT'S TIME FOR *RANCID RHYMES* AND *PUTRID POETRY*. TONIGHT, WE PRY OPEN A *DICTIONARY* OF THE *DISGUSTING* TO REVEAL AN AWFUL ALPHA*BETTE NOIR!* THIS *INTERMINABLE TOME* OF THE *LOWBROW LITERATI* IS CALLED...

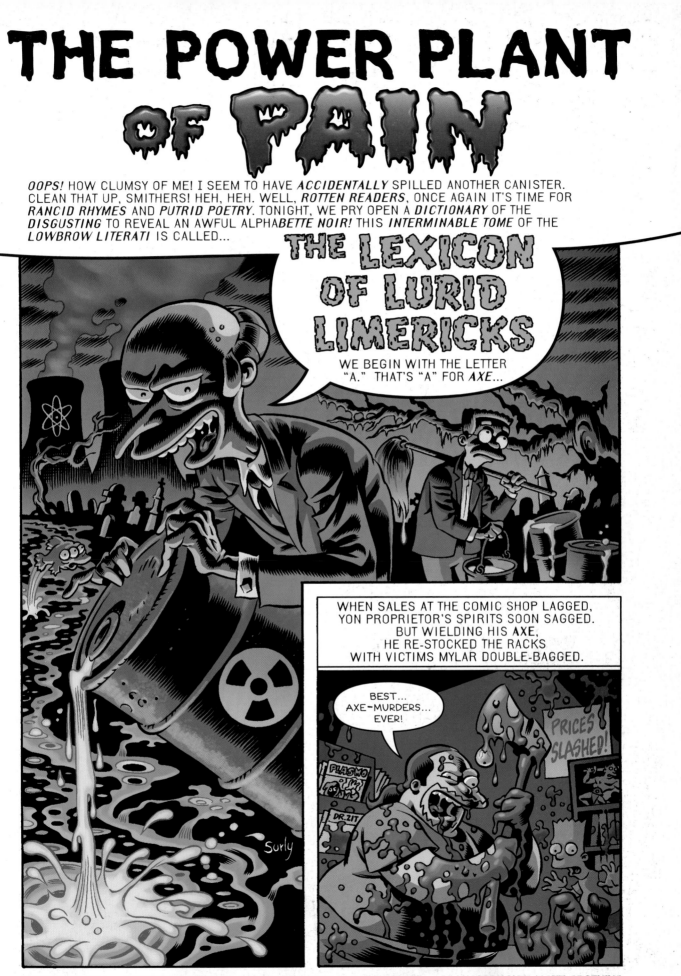

THE LEXICON OF LURID LIMERICKS

WE BEGIN WITH THE LETTER "A." THAT'S "A" FOR *AXE*...

WHEN SALES AT THE COMIC SHOP LAGGED,
YON PROPRIETOR'S SPIRITS SOON SAGGED.
BUT WIELDING HIS **AXE**,
HE RE-STOCKED THE RACKS
WITH VICTIMS MYLAR DOUBLE-BAGGED.

BEST... AXE-MURDERS... EVER!

PRICES SLASHED!

HILARY BARTA
CO-SCRIPT/ART

STEPHEN SULLIVAN
CO-SCRIPT

DAVE STEWART
COLORS

KAREN BATES
LETTERS

BILL MORRISON
EDITOR

MATT GROENING
THE ALPHABETIZER

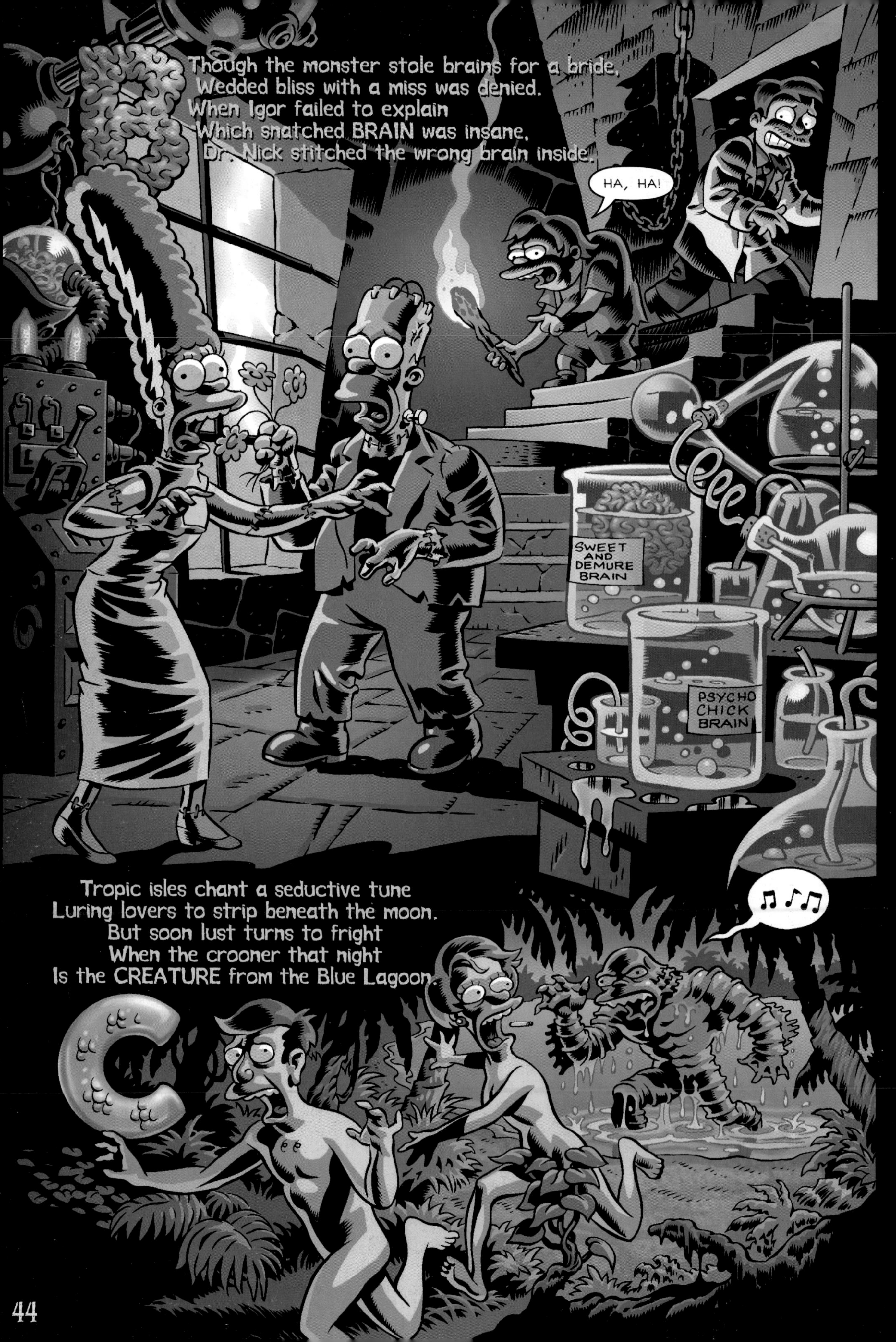
Though the monster stole brains for a bride,
Wedded bliss with a miss was denied.
When Igor failed to explain
Which snatched BRAIN was insane,
Dr. Nick stitched the wrong brain inside.
HA, HA!
SWEET AND DEMURE BRAIN
PSYCHO CHICK BRAIN
Tropic isles chant a seductive tune
Luring lovers to strip beneath the moon.
But soon lust turns to fright
When the crooner that night
Is the CREATURE from the Blue Lagoon.

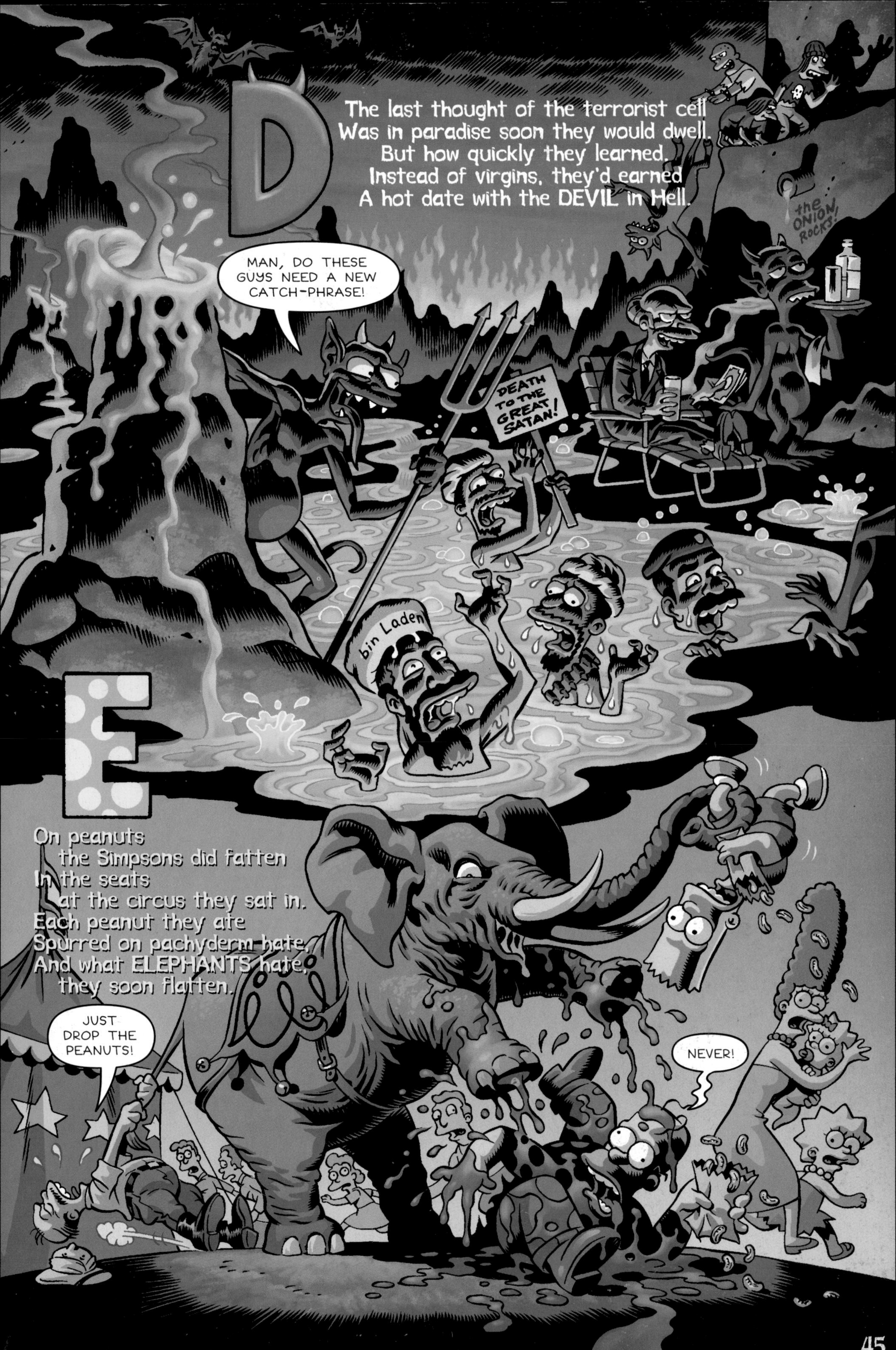
D
The last thought of the terrorist cell
Was in paradise soon they would dwell.
But how quickly they learned.
Instead of virgins, they'd earned
A hot date with the DEVIL in Hell.
the ONION ROCKS!
MAN, DO THESE GUYS NEED A NEW CATCH-PHRASE!
DEATH TO THE GREAT SATAN!
bin Laden
E
On peanuts
the Simpsons did fatten
In the seats
at the circus they sat in.
Each peanut they ate
Spurred on pachyderm hate,
And what ELEPHANTS hate,
they soon flatten.
JUST DROP THE PEANUTS!
NEVER!

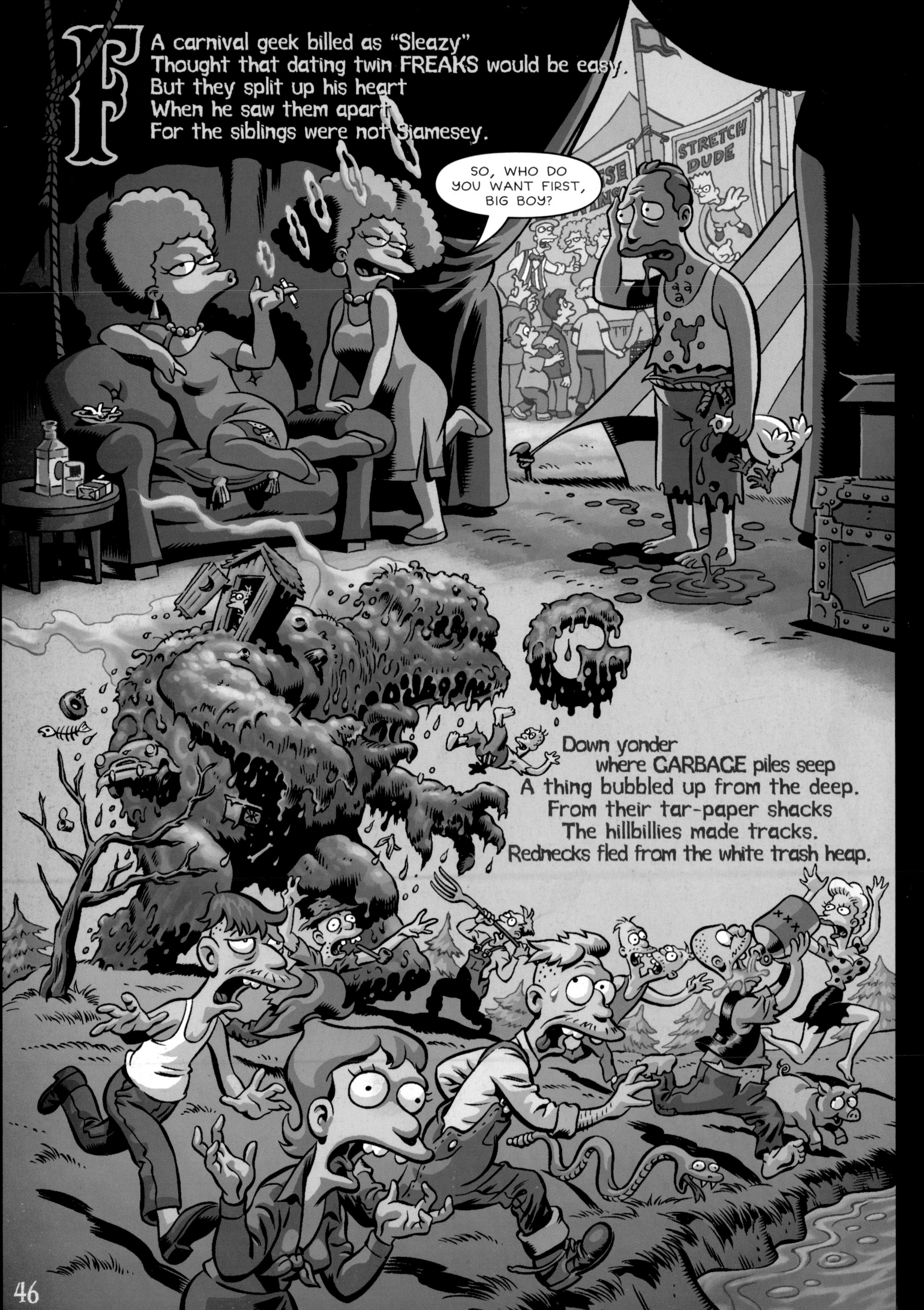
F
A carnival geek billed as "Sleazy"
Thought that dating twin FREAKS would be easy.
But they split up his heart
When he saw them apart
For the siblings were not Siamesey.
SO, WHO DO YOU WANT FIRST, BIG BOY?
STRETCH DUDE
G
Down yonder
where GARBAGE piles seep
A thing bubbled up from the deep.
From their tar-paper shacks
The hillbillies made tracks.
Rednecks fled from the white trash heap.

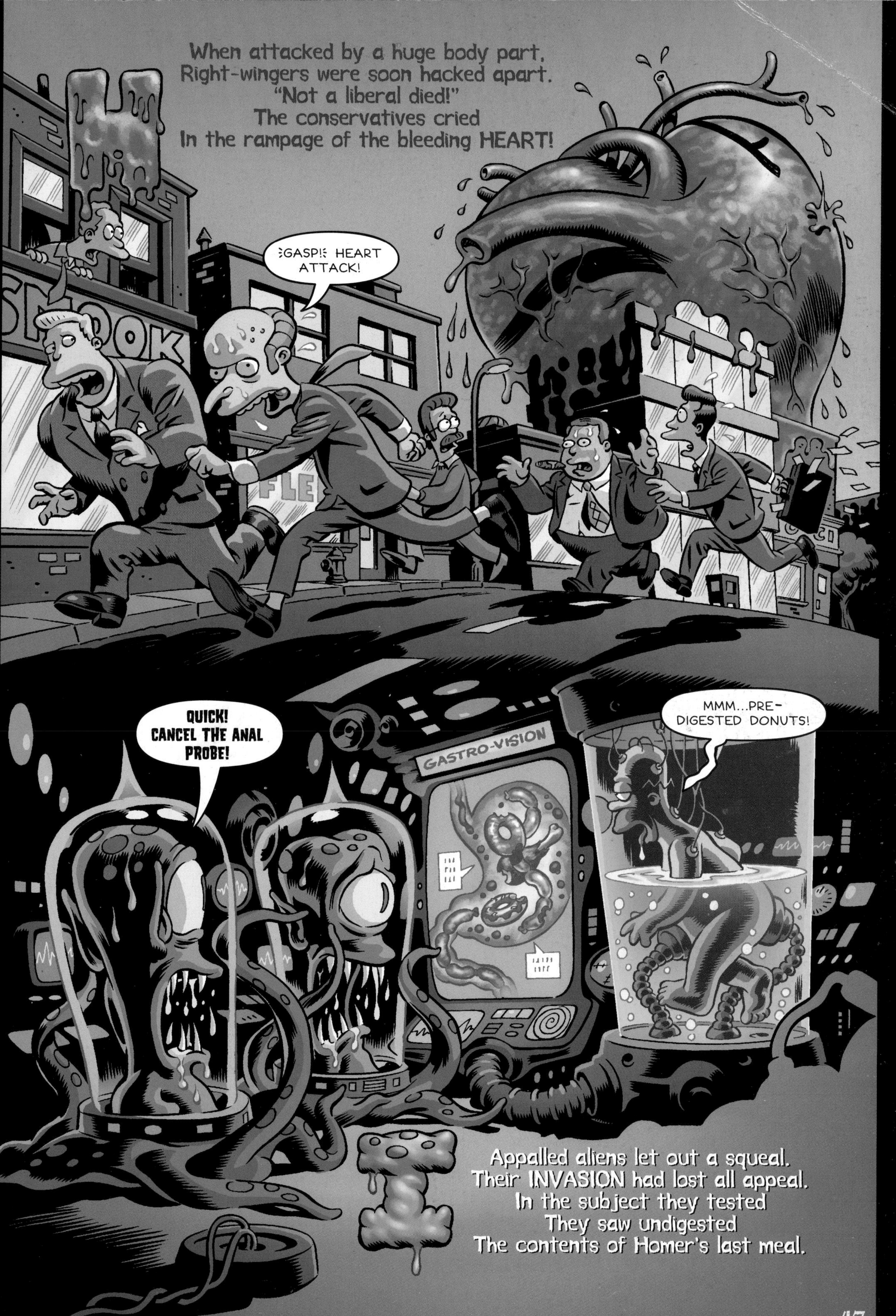
When attacked by a huge body part,
Right-wingers were soon hacked apart.
"Not a liberal died!"
The conservatives cried
In the rampage of the bleeding HEART!
:GASP!: HEART ATTACK!
QUICK! CANCEL THE ANAL PROBE!
GASTRO-VISION
MMM...PRE-DIGESTED DONUTS!
Appalled aliens let out a squeal.
Their INVASION had lost all appeal.
In the subject they tested
They saw undigested
The contents of Homer's last meal.

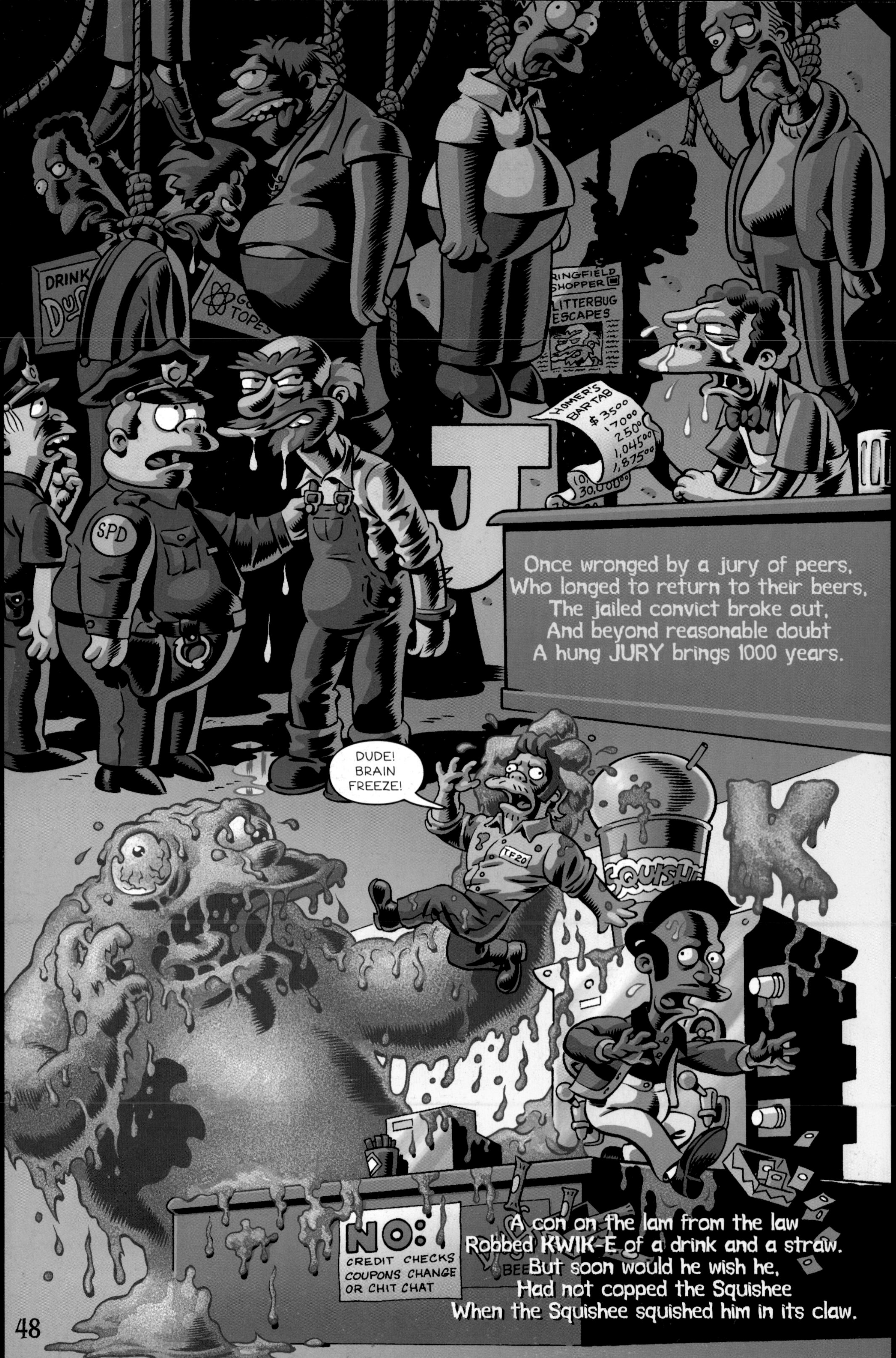

RINGFIELD SHOPPER
LITTERBUG ESCAPES
HOMER'S BAR TAB $35.00 170.00 250.00 1,045.00 1,875.00 30,000.00
SPD
Once wronged by a jury of peers,
Who longed to return to their beers,
The jailed convict broke out,
And beyond reasonable doubt
A hung JURY brings 1000 years.
DUDE! BRAIN FREEZE!
TF20
SQUISHE
NO:
CREDIT CHECKS
COUPONS CHANGE
OR CHIT CHAT
A con on the lam from the law
Robbed KWIK-E of a drink and a straw.
But soon would he wish he,
Had not copped the Squishee
When the Squishee squished him in its claw.

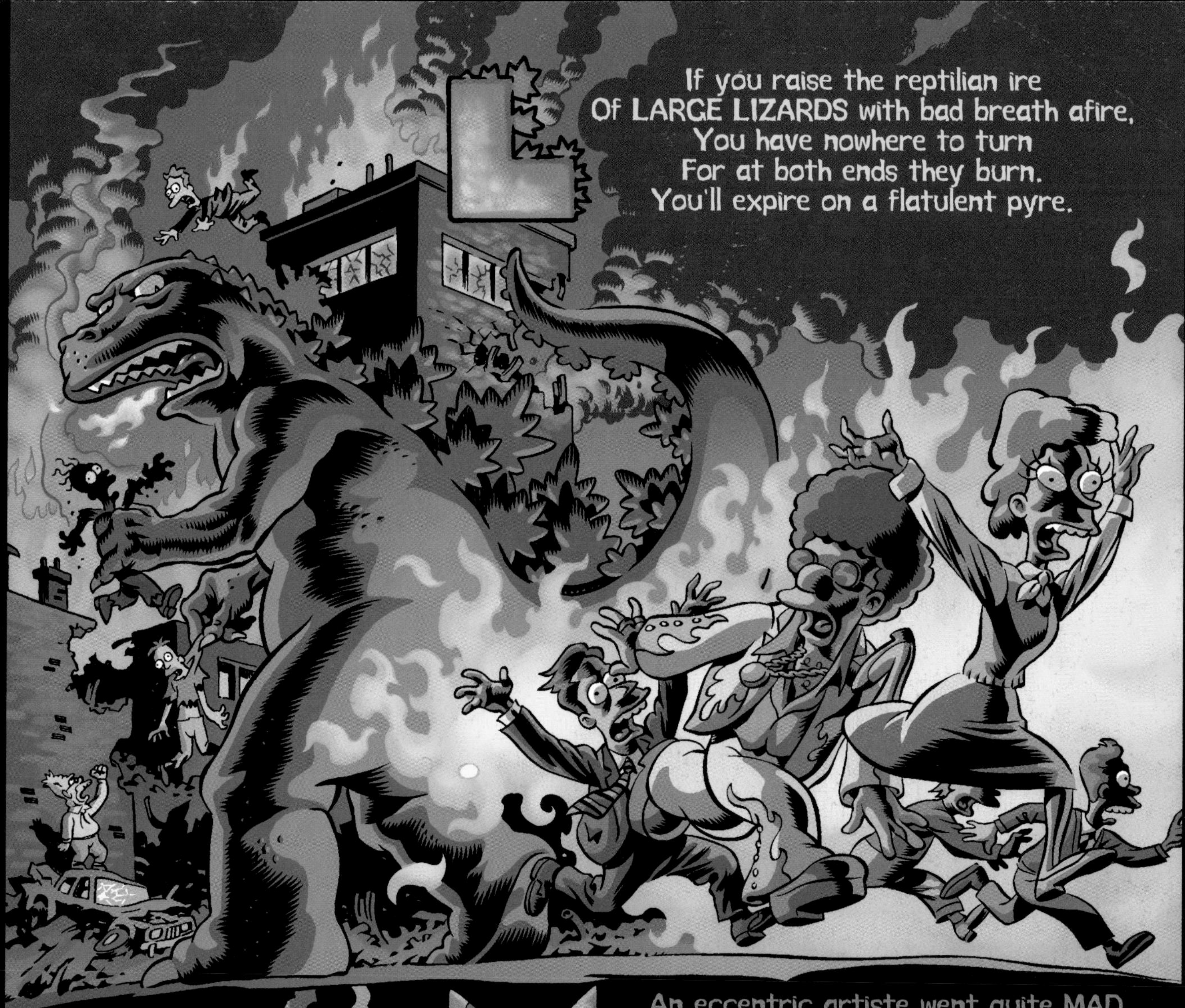
L
If you raise the reptilian ire
Of LARGE LIZARDS with bad breath afire,
You have nowhere to turn
For at both ends they burn.
You'll expire on a flatulent pyre.

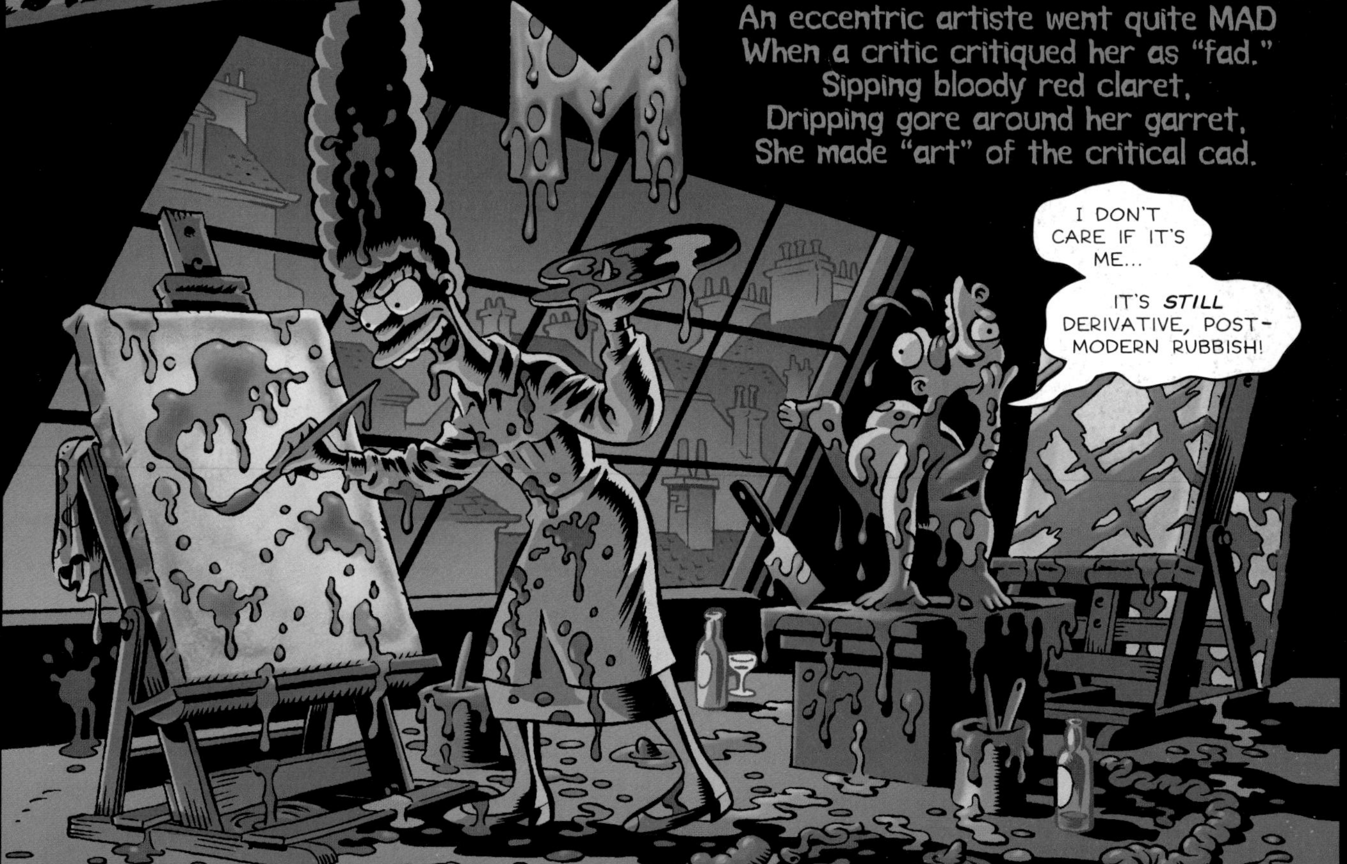
M
An eccentric artiste went quite MAD
When a critic critiqued her as "fad."
Sipping bloody red claret,
Dripping gore around her garret,
She made "art" of the critical cad.
I DON'T CARE IF IT'S ME...
IT'S *STILL* DERIVATIVE, POST-MODERN RUBBISH!

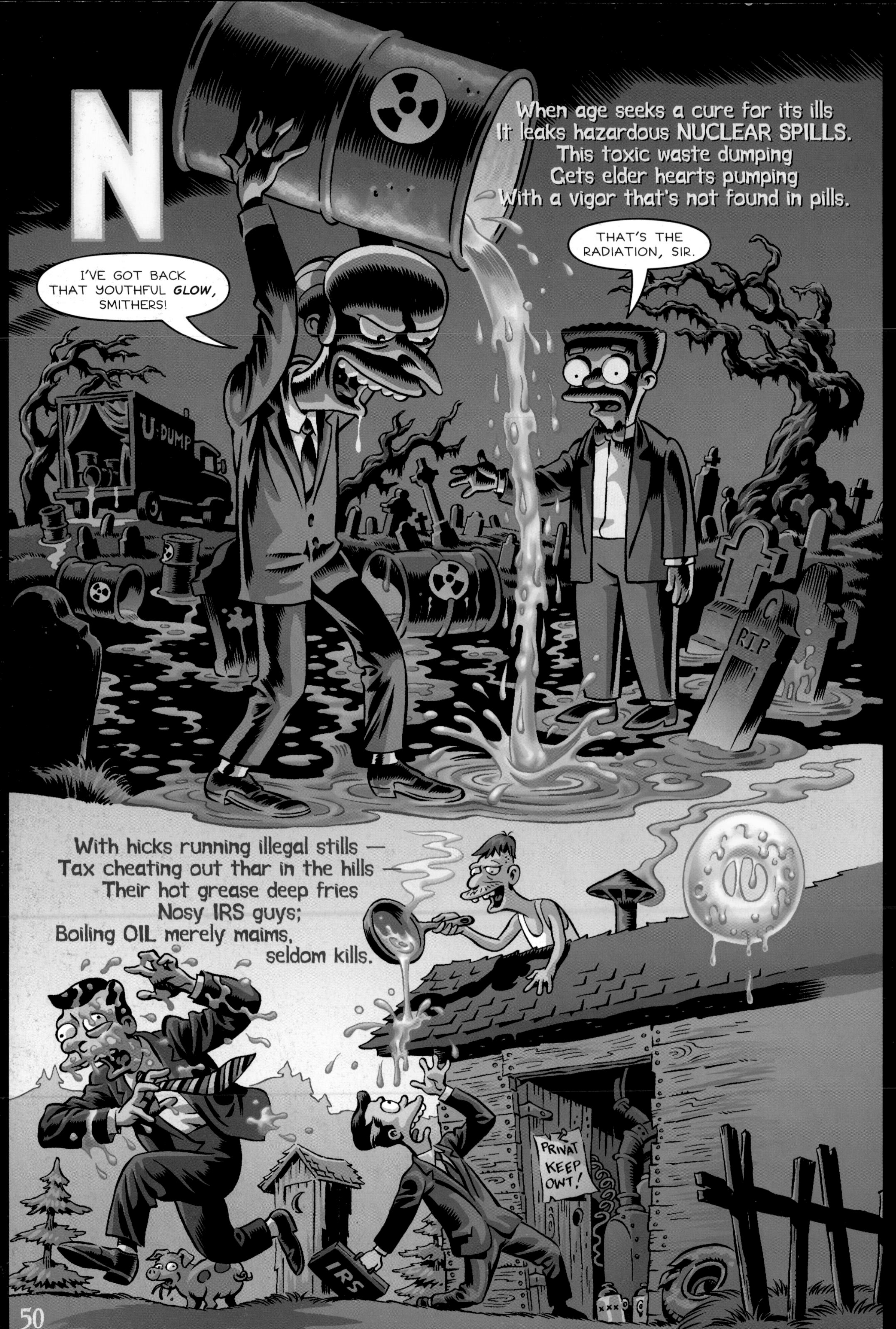
N
When age seeks a cure for its ills
It leaks hazardous NUCLEAR SPILLS.
This toxic waste dumping
Gets elder hearts pumping
With a vigor that's not found in pills.
I'VE GOT BACK THAT YOUTHFUL GLOW, SMITHERS!
THAT'S THE RADIATION, SIR.
U-DUMP
R.I.P.
With hicks running illegal stills —
Tax cheating out thar in the hills —
Their hot grease deep fries
Nosy IRS guys;
Boiling OIL merely maims,
seldom kills.
PRIVAT KEEP OWT!
IRS

Oozing through a dimensional PORTAL
Drooling goo, thirsty dark gods did chortle.
They found four yahoos
So bloated from booze
Each got sloshed on the blood of a mortal.

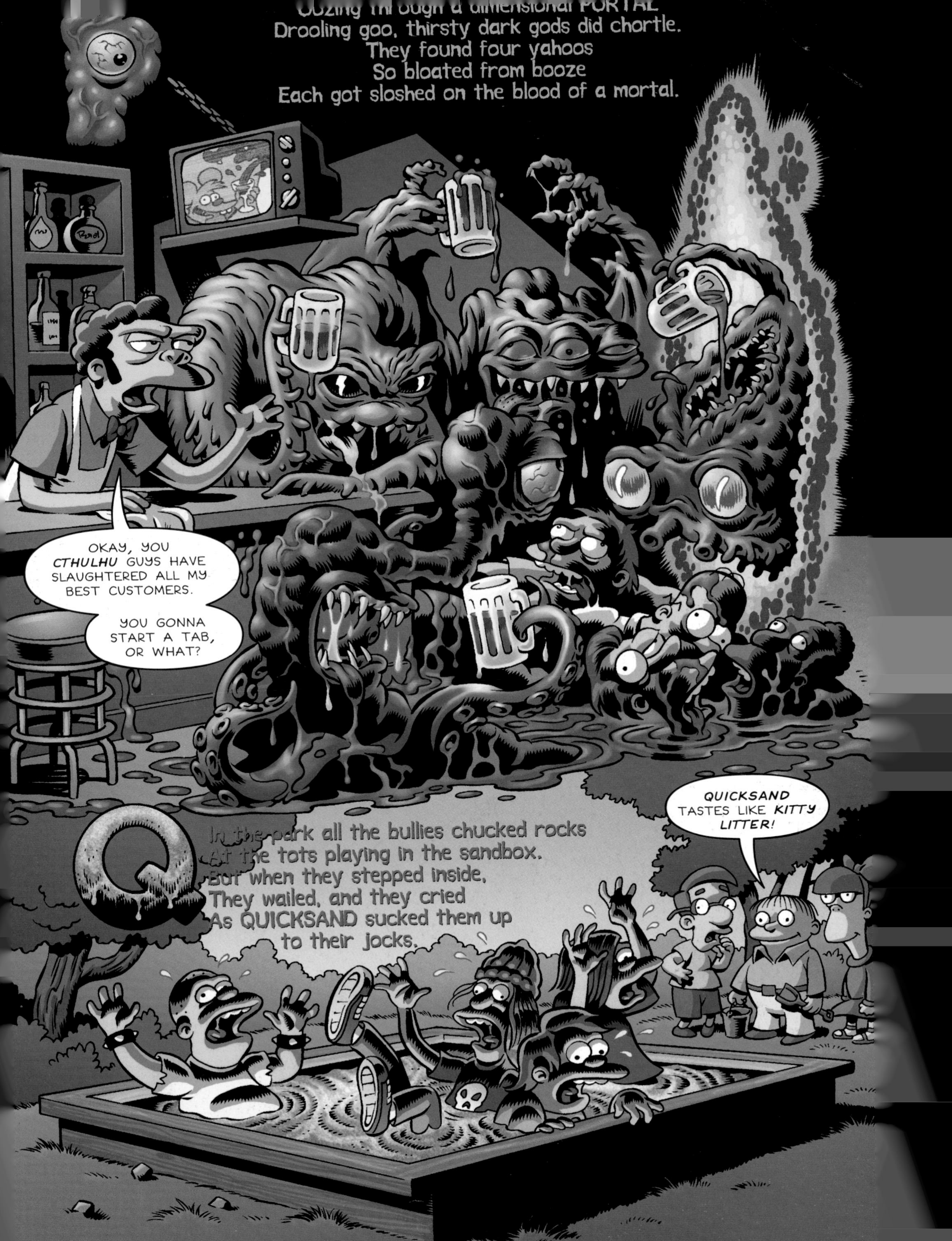

OKAY, YOU CTHULHU GUYS HAVE SLAUGHTERED ALL MY BEST CUSTOMERS.
YOU GONNA START A TAB, OR WHAT?
QUICKSAND TASTES LIKE KITTY LITTER!

Q

In the park all the bullies chucked rocks
At the tots playing in the sandbox.
But when they stepped inside,
They wailed, and they cried
As QUICKSAND sucked them up
to their jocks.

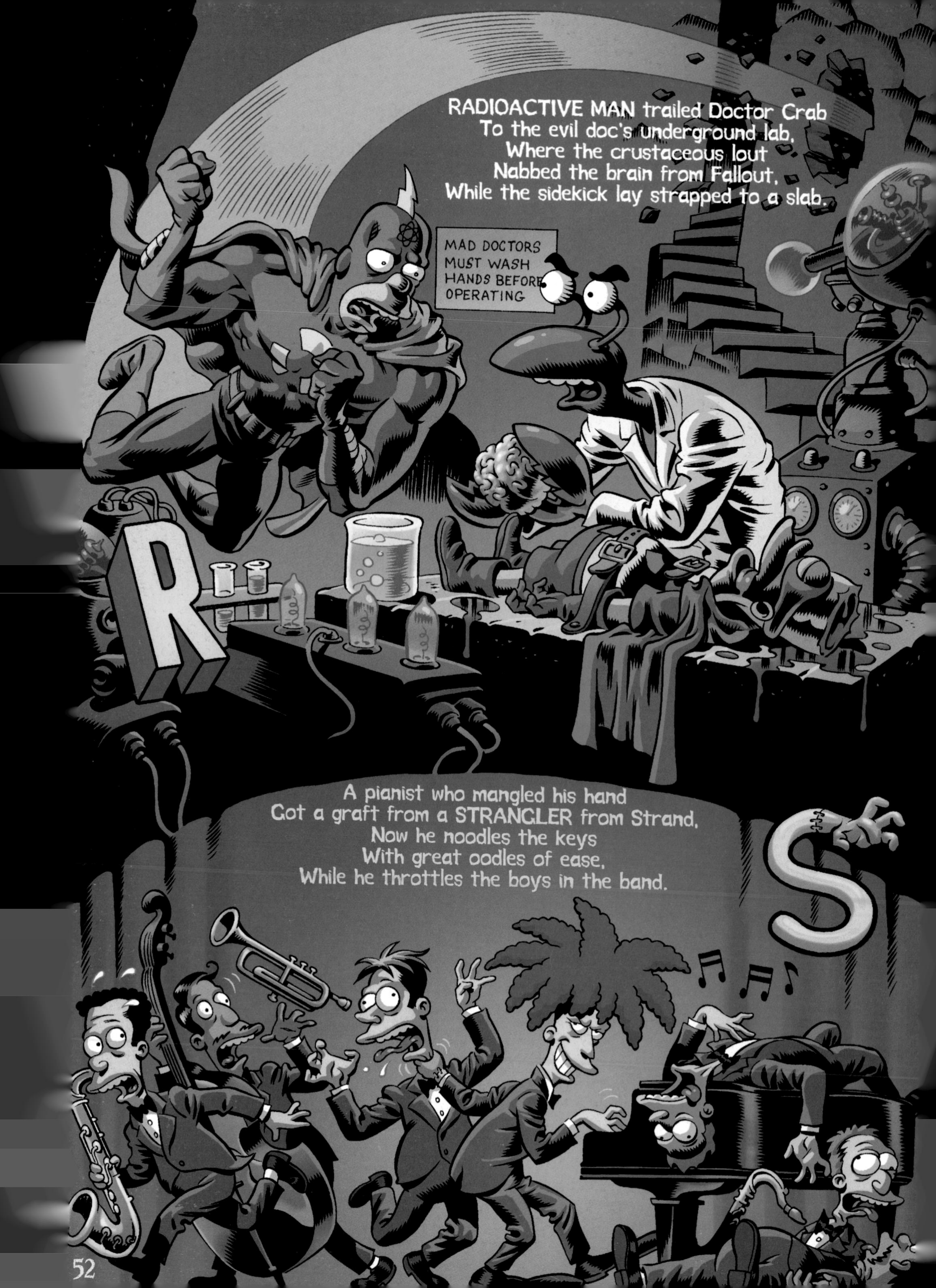
RADIOACTIVE MAN trailed Doctor Crab
To the evil doc's underground lab,
Where the crustaceous lout
Nabbed the brain from Fallout,
While the sidekick lay strapped to a slab.
MAD DOCTORS MUST WASH HANDS BEFORE OPERATING
R
A pianist who mangled his hand
Got a graft from a STRANGLER from Strand,
Now he noodles the keys
With great oodles of ease,
While he throttles the boys in the band.
S

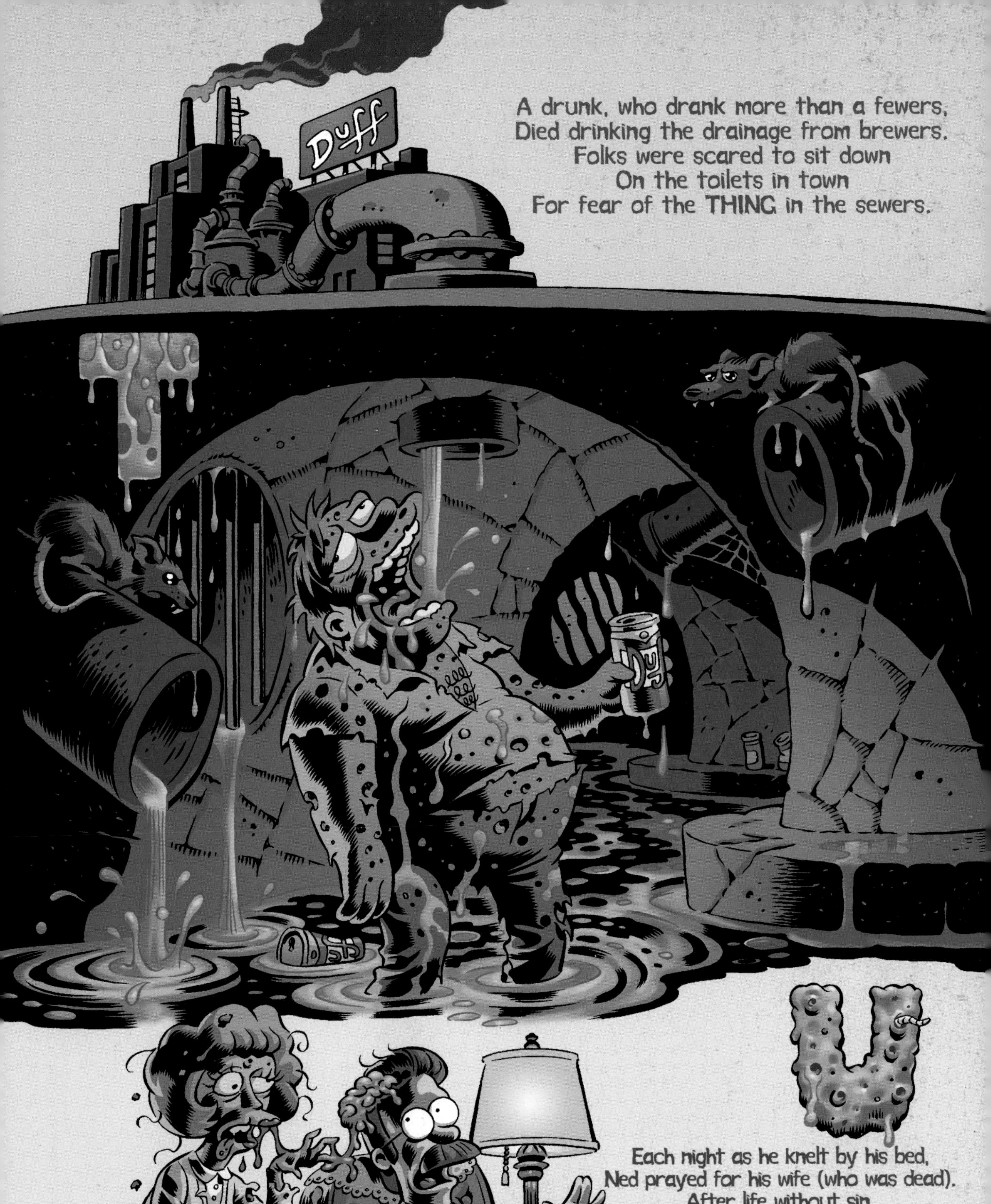
Duff

A drunk, who drank more than a fewers,
Died drinking the drainage from brewers.
Folks were scared to sit down
On the toilets in town
For fear of the **THING** in the sewers.

U

Each night as he knelt by his bed,
Ned prayed for his wife (who was dead).
After life without sin,
Heaven should let her in,
But she came back as **UNDEAD** instead.

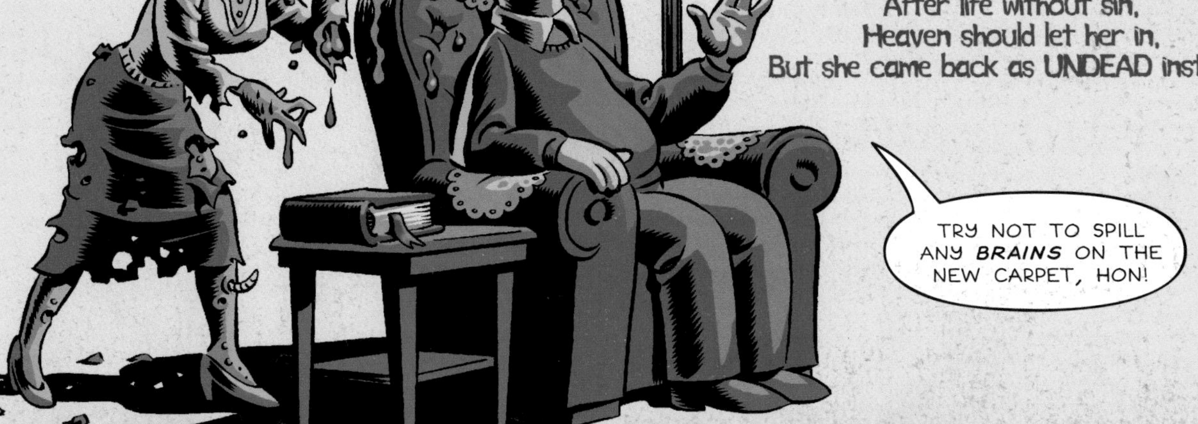
TRY NOT TO SPILL ANY *BRAINS* ON THE NEW CARPET, HON!

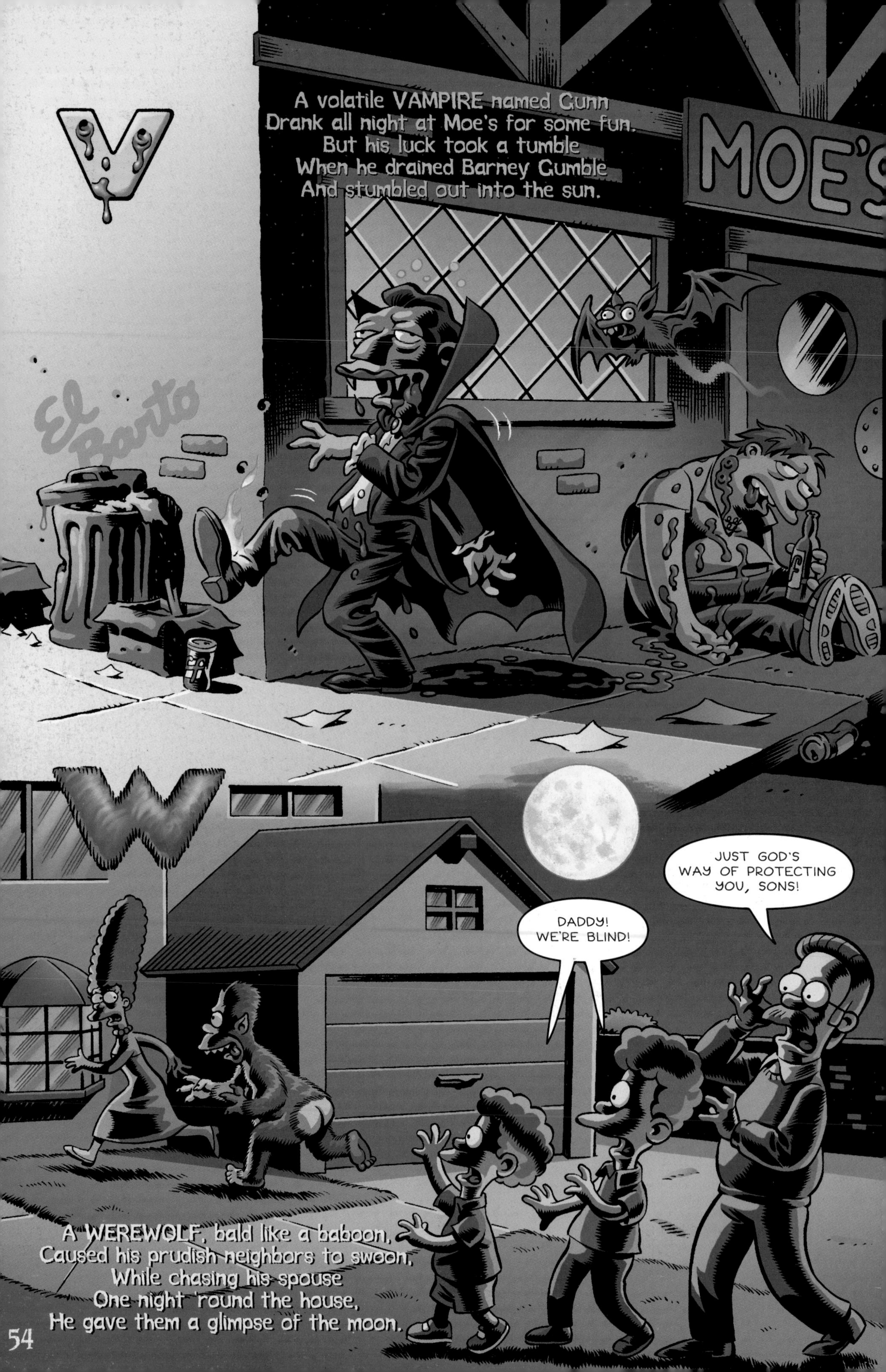
V
A volatile VAMPIRE named Gunn
Drank all night at Moe's for some fun.
But his luck took a tumble
When he drained Barney Gumble
And stumbled out into the sun.
MOE'S
El Barto
W
DADDY! WE'RE BLIND!
JUST GOD'S WAY OF PROTECTING YOU, SONS!
A WEREWOLF, bald like a baboon,
Caused his prudish neighbors to swoon,
While chasing his spouse
One night 'round the house,
He gave them a glimpse of the moon.

X

Like a scene from "The Lord of the Flies,"
The teen hoodlums in school terrorize.
But they stopped kicking asses
When they broke the thick glasses
Of the boy with the X-RAY eyes.

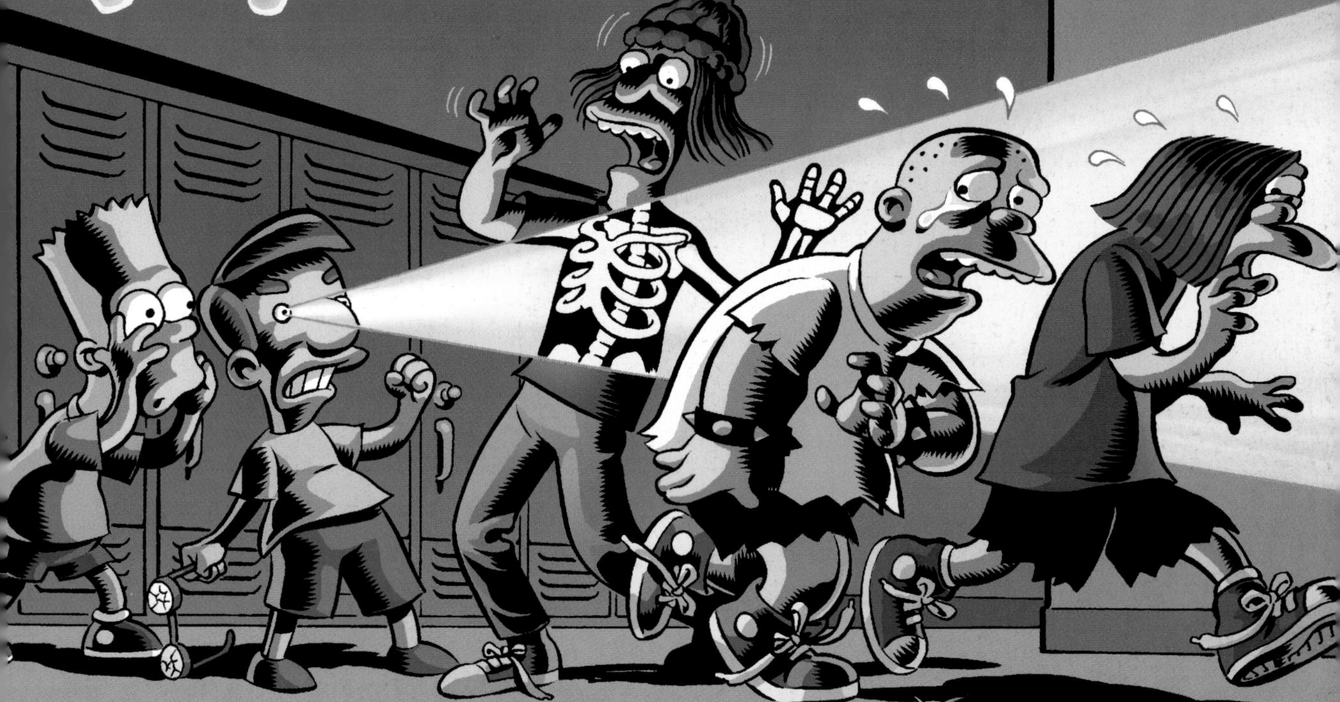

Y

Hiking mountainous slopes in Tibet, he
Met up with a wandering YETI.
But the snowman of white
Craved Italian that night,
So he wound up as Yeti spaghetti.

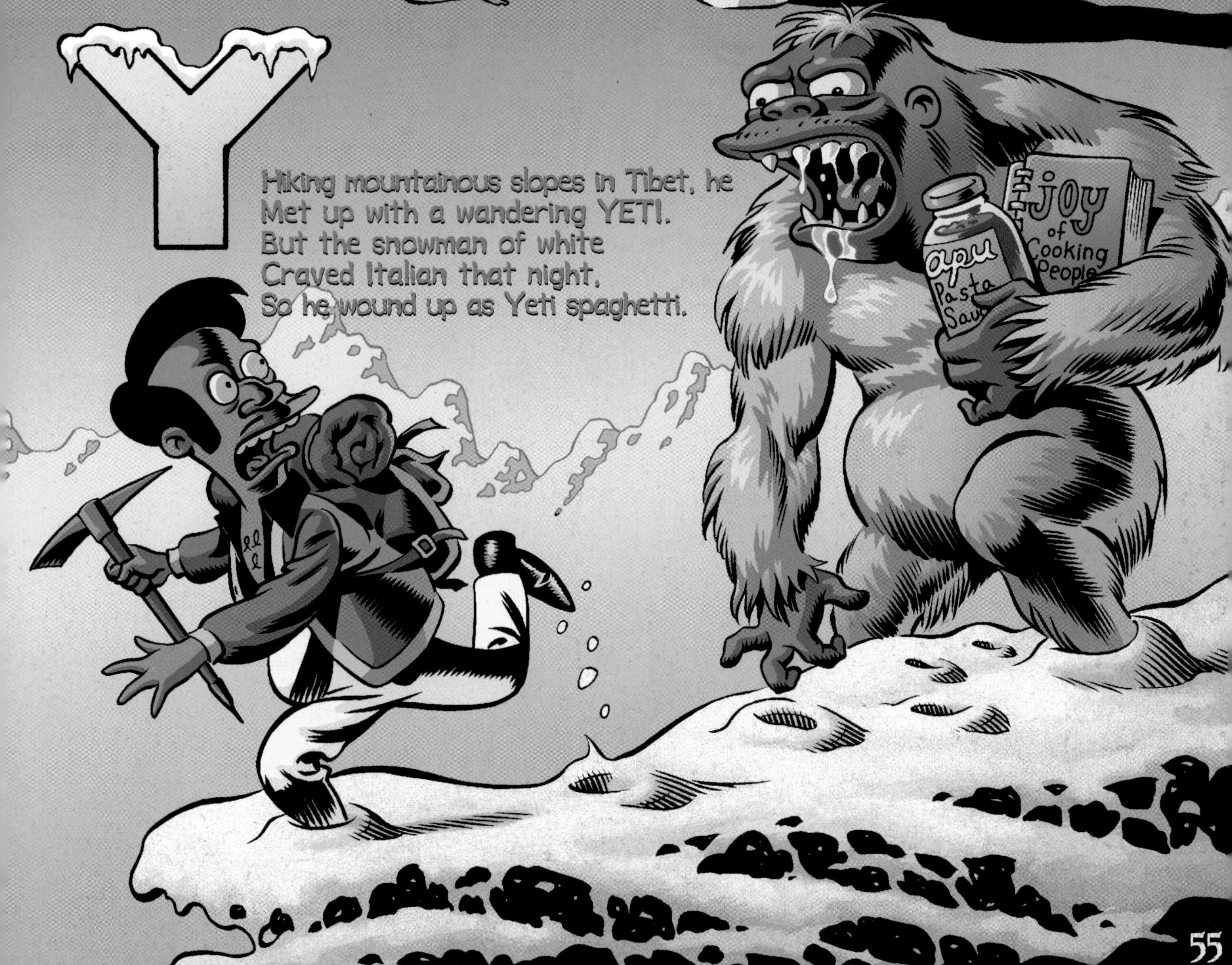
joy of Cooking People
apu Pasta Sau

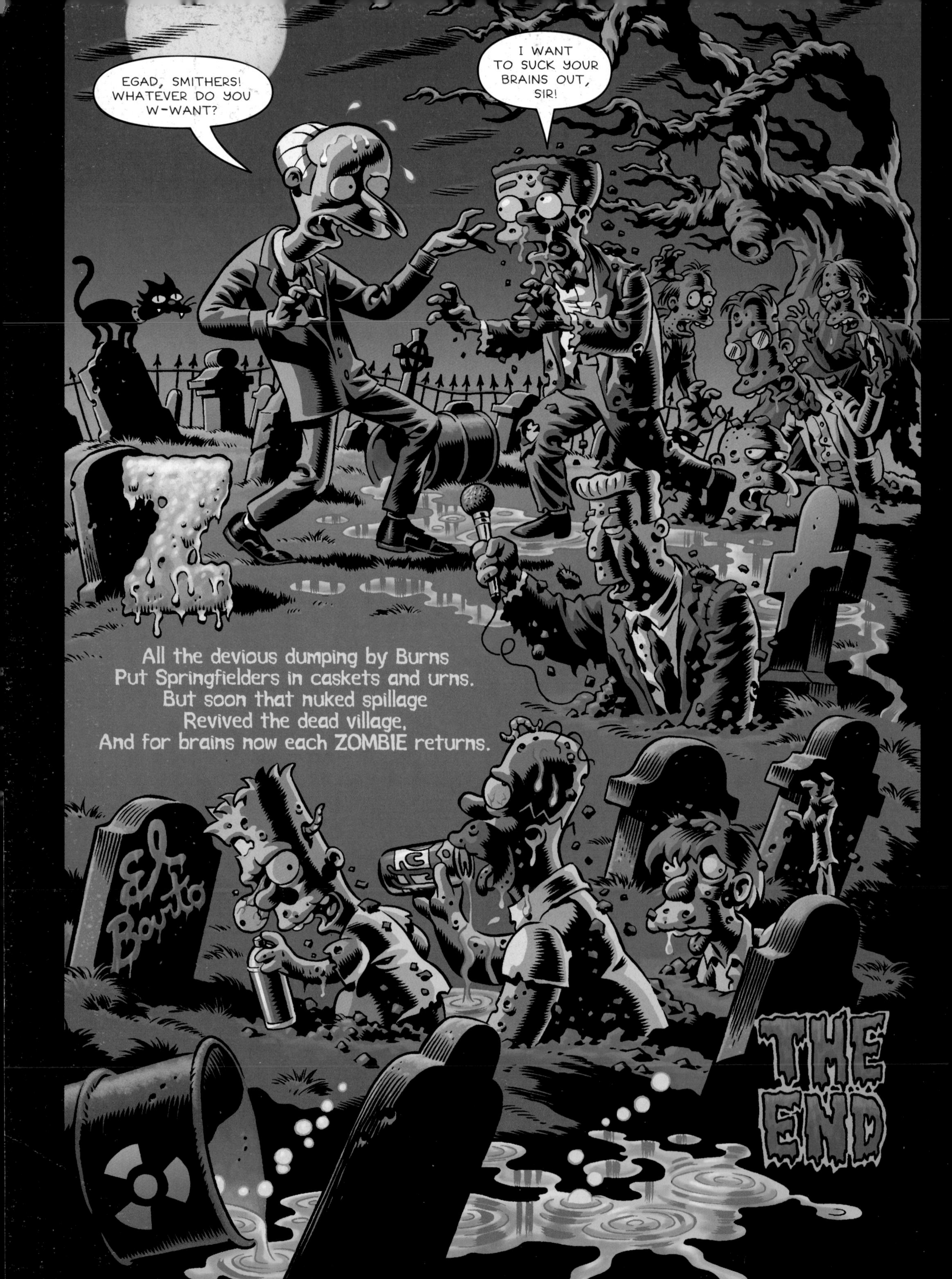
EGAD, SMITHERS! WHATEVER DO YOU W-WANT?
I WANT TO SUCK YOUR BRAINS OUT, SIR!
Z
All the devious dumping by Burns
Put Springfielders in caskets and urns.
But soon that nuked spillage
Revived the dead village,
And for brains now each ZOMBIE returns.
El Barto
THE END

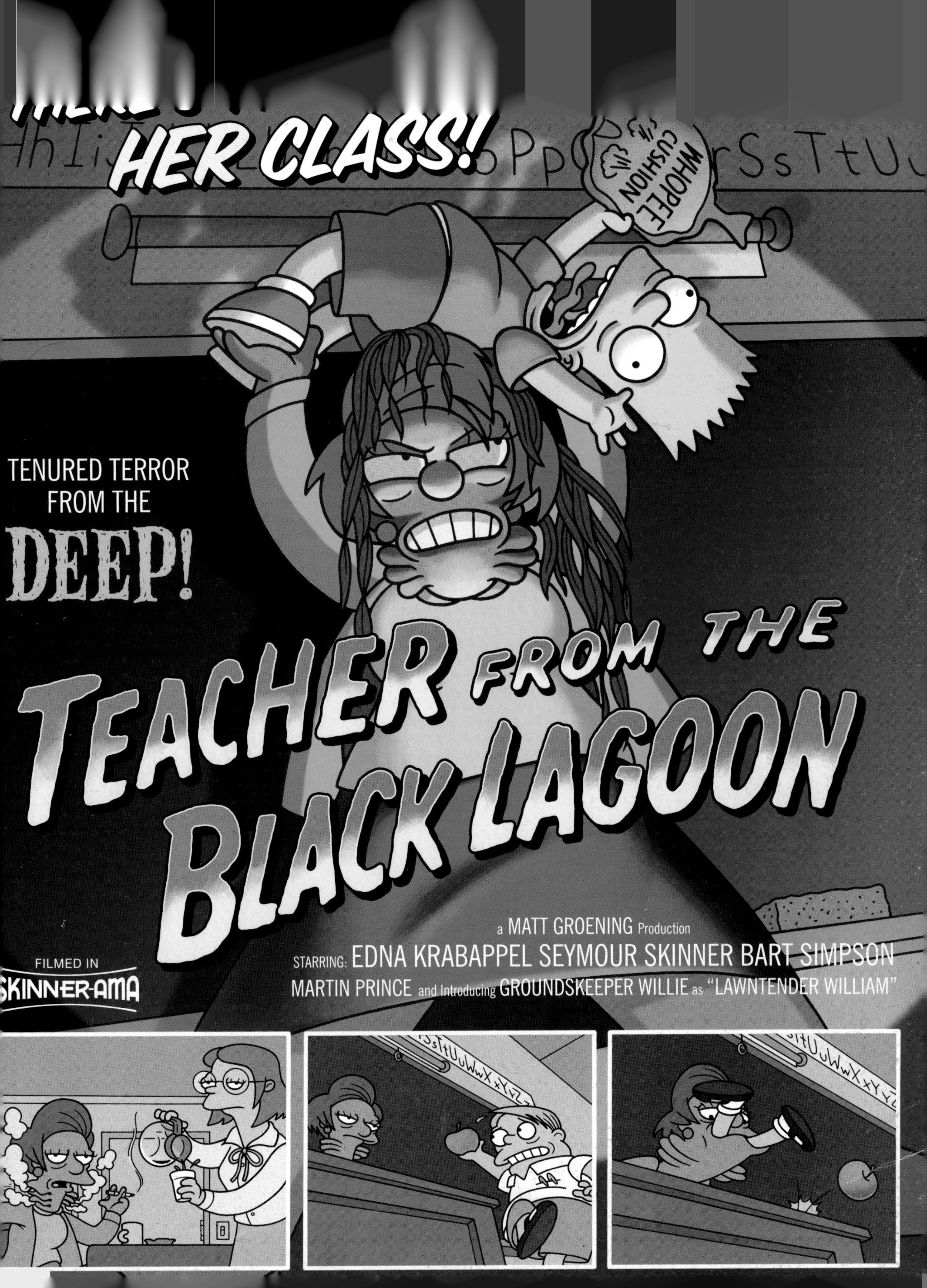

HER CLASS!
WHOPEE CUSHION
TENURED TERROR FROM THE
DEEP!
TEACHER FROM THE BLACK LAGOON
a MATT GROENING Production
STARRING: EDNA KRABAPPEL SEYMOUR SKINNER BART SIMPSON
MARTIN PRINCE and Introducing GROUNDSKEEPER WILLIE as "LAWNTENDER WILLIAM"
FILMED IN
SKINNER-AMA

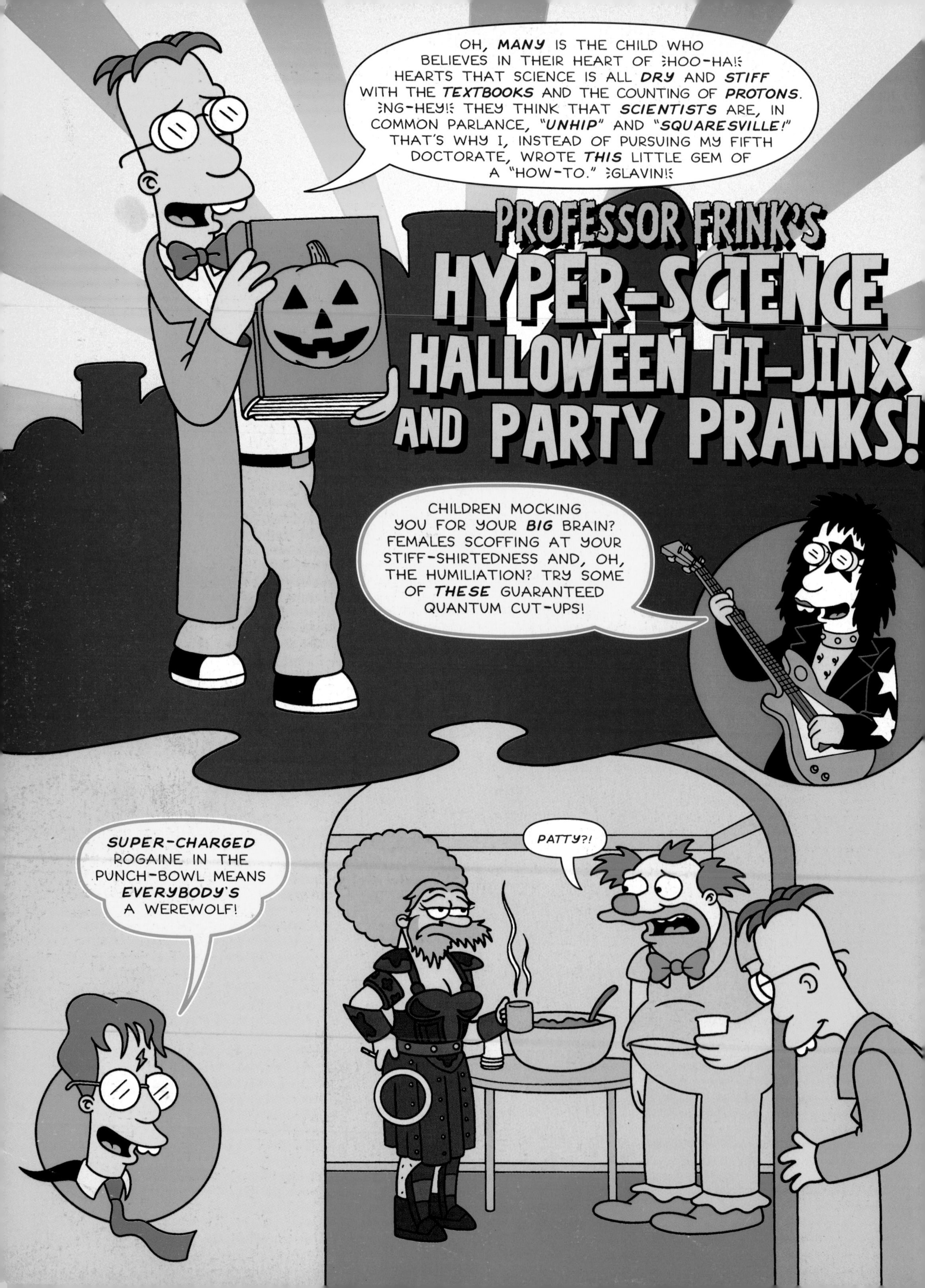
OH, MANY IS THE CHILD WHO BELIEVES IN THEIR HEART OF ⦚HOO-HA!⦚ HEARTS THAT SCIENCE IS ALL DRY AND STIFF WITH THE TEXTBOOKS AND THE COUNTING OF PROTONS. ⦚NG-HEY!⦚ THEY THINK THAT SCIENTISTS ARE, IN COMMON PARLANCE, "UNHIP" AND "SQUARESVILLE!" THAT'S WHY I, INSTEAD OF PURSUING MY FIFTH DOCTORATE, WROTE THIS LITTLE GEM OF A "HOW-TO." ⦚GLAVIN!⦚
PROFESSOR FRINK'S
HYPER-SCIENCE HALLOWEEN HI-JINX AND PARTY PRANKS!
CHILDREN MOCKING YOU FOR YOUR BIG BRAIN? FEMALES SCOFFING AT YOUR STIFF-SHIRTEDNESS AND, OH, THE HUMILIATION? TRY SOME OF THESE GUARANTEED QUANTUM CUT-UPS!
SUPER-CHARGED ROGAINE IN THE PUNCH-BOWL MEANS EVERYBODY'S A WEREWOLF!
PATTY?!

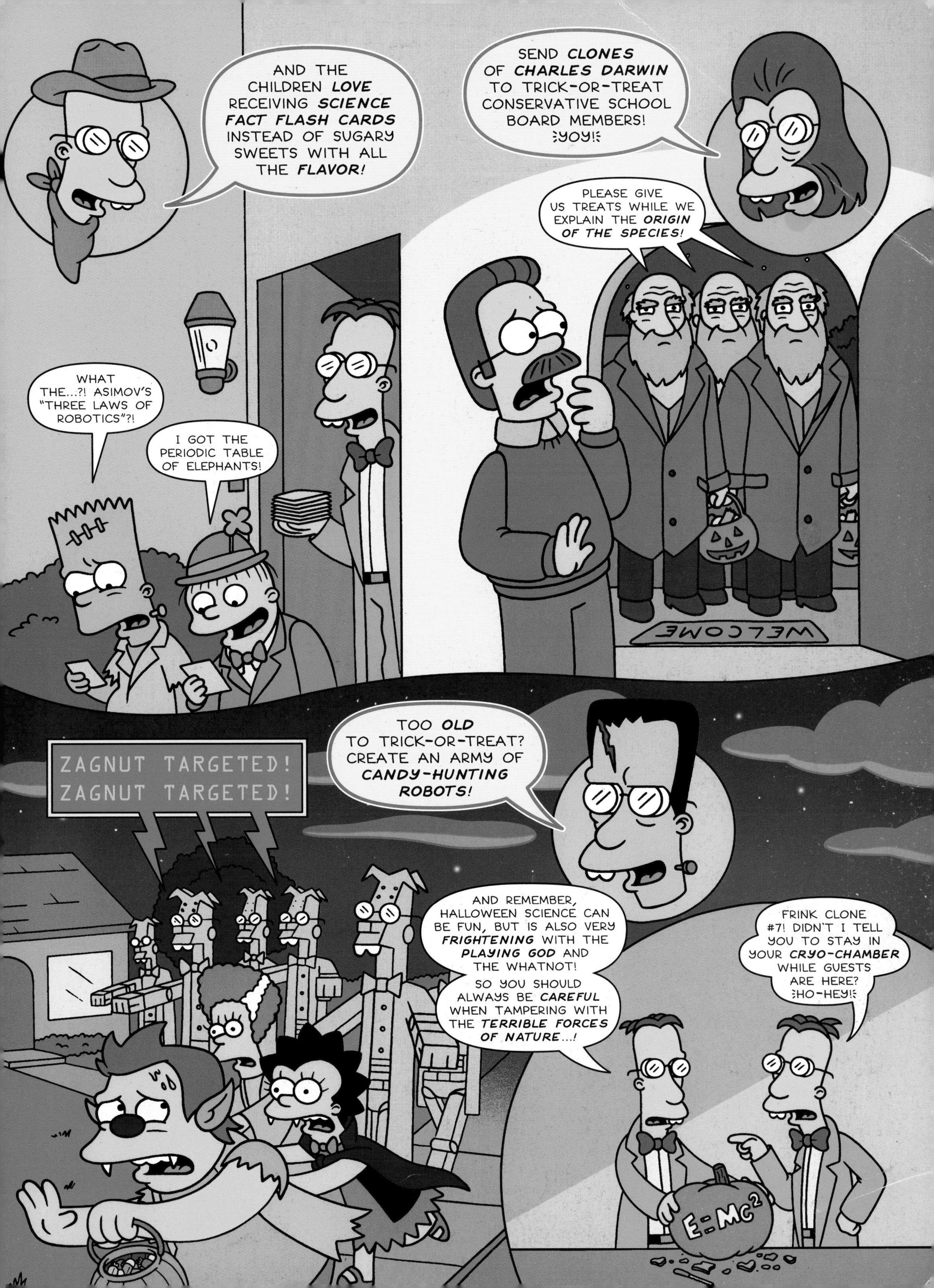
AND THE CHILDREN LOVE RECEIVING SCIENCE FACT FLASH CARDS INSTEAD OF SUGARY SWEETS WITH ALL THE FLAVOR!
WHAT THE...?! ASIMOV'S "THREE LAWS OF ROBOTICS"?!
I GOT THE PERIODIC TABLE OF ELEPHANTS!
SEND CLONES OF CHARLES DARWIN TO TRICK-OR-TREAT CONSERVATIVE SCHOOL BOARD MEMBERS! YOY!
PLEASE GIVE US TREATS WHILE WE EXPLAIN THE ORIGIN OF THE SPECIES!
WELCOME
TOO OLD TO TRICK-OR-TREAT? CREATE AN ARMY OF CANDY-HUNTING ROBOTS!
ZAGNUT TARGETED! ZAGNUT TARGETED!
AND REMEMBER, HALLOWEEN SCIENCE CAN BE FUN, BUT IS ALSO VERY FRIGHTENING WITH THE PLAYING GOD AND THE WHATNOT!
SO YOU SHOULD ALWAYS BE CAREFUL WHEN TAMPERING WITH THE TERRIBLE FORCES OF NATURE...!
FRINK CLONE #7! DIDN'T I TELL YOU TO STAY IN YOUR CRYO-CHAMBER WHILE GUESTS ARE HERE? HO-HEY!
E=MC2

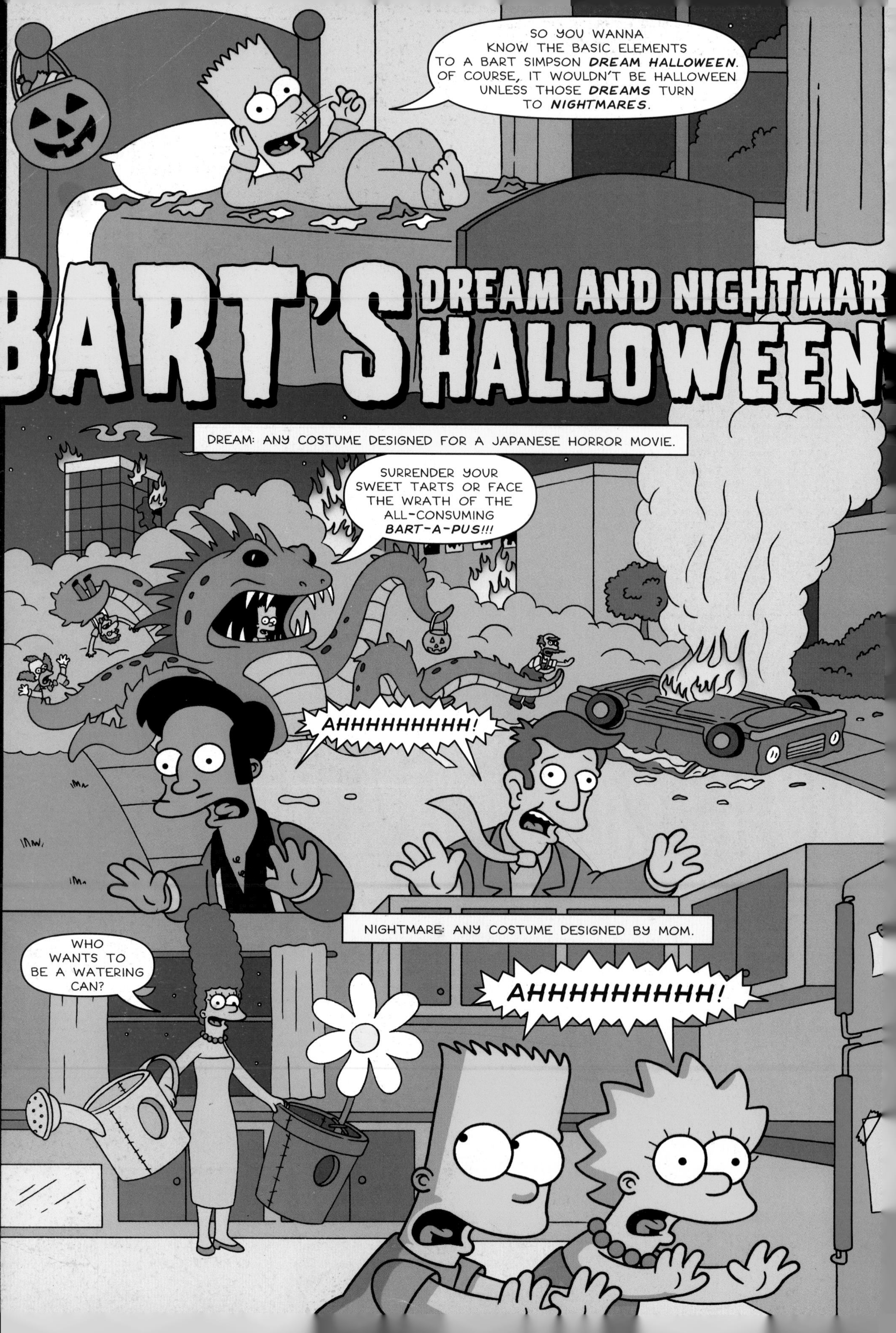

SO YOU WANNA KNOW THE BASIC ELEMENTS TO A BART SIMPSON DREAM HALLOWEEN. OF COURSE, IT WOULDN'T BE HALLOWEEN UNLESS THOSE DREAMS TURN TO NIGHTMARES.
BART'S DREAM AND NIGHTMAR HALLOWEEN
DREAM: ANY COSTUME DESIGNED FOR A JAPANESE HORROR MOVIE.
SURRENDER YOUR SWEET TARTS OR FACE THE WRATH OF THE ALL-CONSUMING BART-A-PUS!!!
AHHHHHHHHHH!
NIGHTMARE: ANY COSTUME DESIGNED BY MOM.
WHO WANTS TO BE A WATERING CAN?
AHHHHHHHHHH!

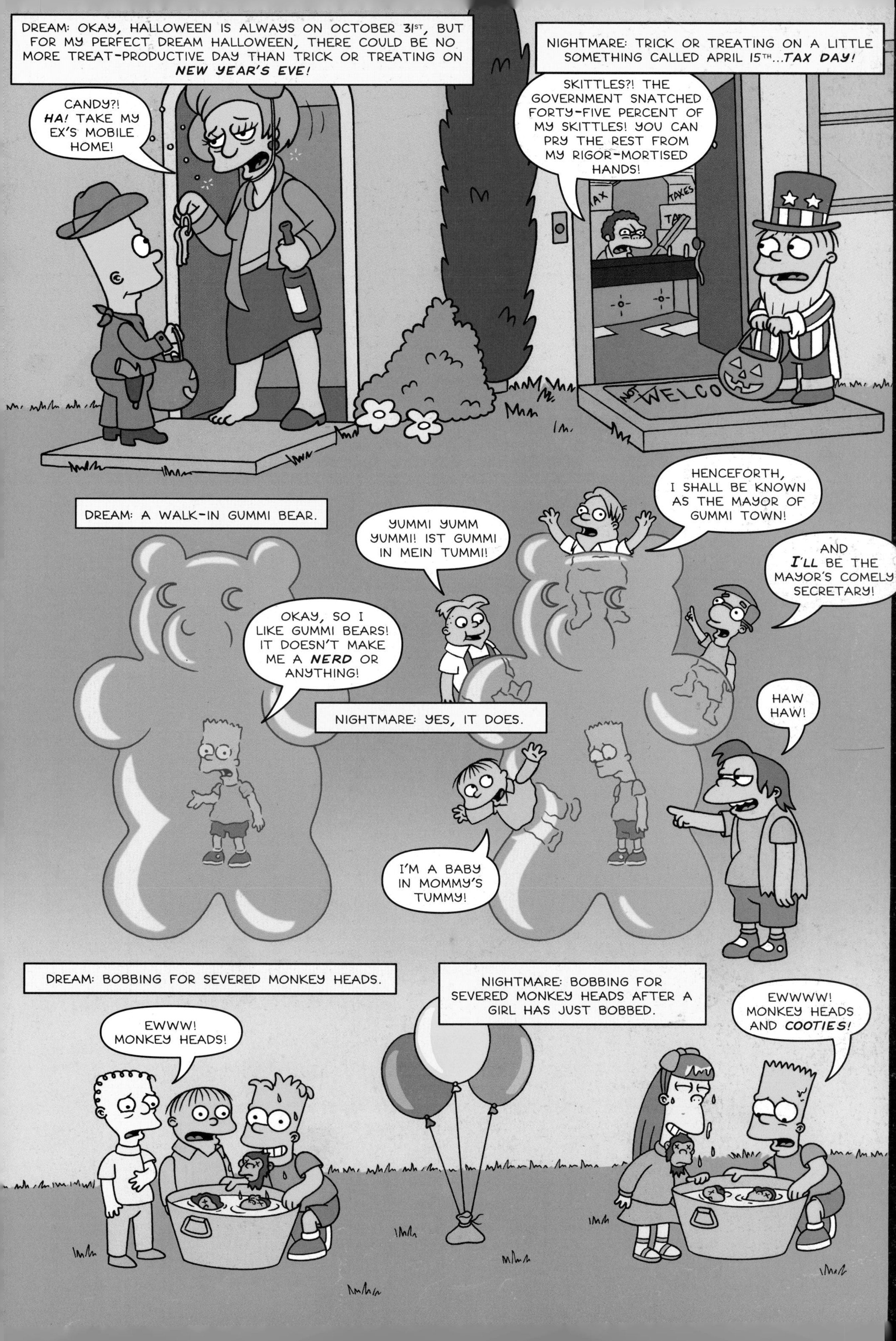

DREAM: OKAY, HALLOWEEN IS ALWAYS ON OCTOBER 31ST, BUT FOR MY PERFECT DREAM HALLOWEEN, THERE COULD BE NO MORE TREAT-PRODUCTIVE DAY THAN TRICK OR TREATING ON NEW YEAR'S EVE!
CANDY?! HA! TAKE MY EX'S MOBILE HOME!
NIGHTMARE: TRICK OR TREATING ON A LITTLE SOMETHING CALLED APRIL 15TH...TAX DAY!
SKITTLES?! THE GOVERNMENT SNATCHED FORTY-FIVE PERCENT OF MY SKITTLES! YOU CAN PRY THE REST FROM MY RIGOR-MORTISED HANDS!
TAX
TAXES
WELCO
DREAM: A WALK-IN GUMMI BEAR.
OKAY, SO I LIKE GUMMI BEARS! IT DOESN'T MAKE ME A NERD OR ANYTHING!
NIGHTMARE: YES, IT DOES.
YUMMI YUMM YUMMI! IST GUMMI IN MEIN TUMMI!
HENCEFORTH, I SHALL BE KNOWN AS THE MAYOR OF GUMMI TOWN!
AND I'LL BE THE MAYOR'S COMELY SECRETARY!
HAW HAW!
I'M A BABY IN MOMMY'S TUMMY!
DREAM: BOBBING FOR SEVERED MONKEY HEADS.
EWWW! MONKEY HEADS!
NIGHTMARE: BOBBING FOR SEVERED MONKEY HEADS AFTER A GIRL HAS JUST BOBBED.
EWWWW! MONKEY HEADS AND COOTIES!

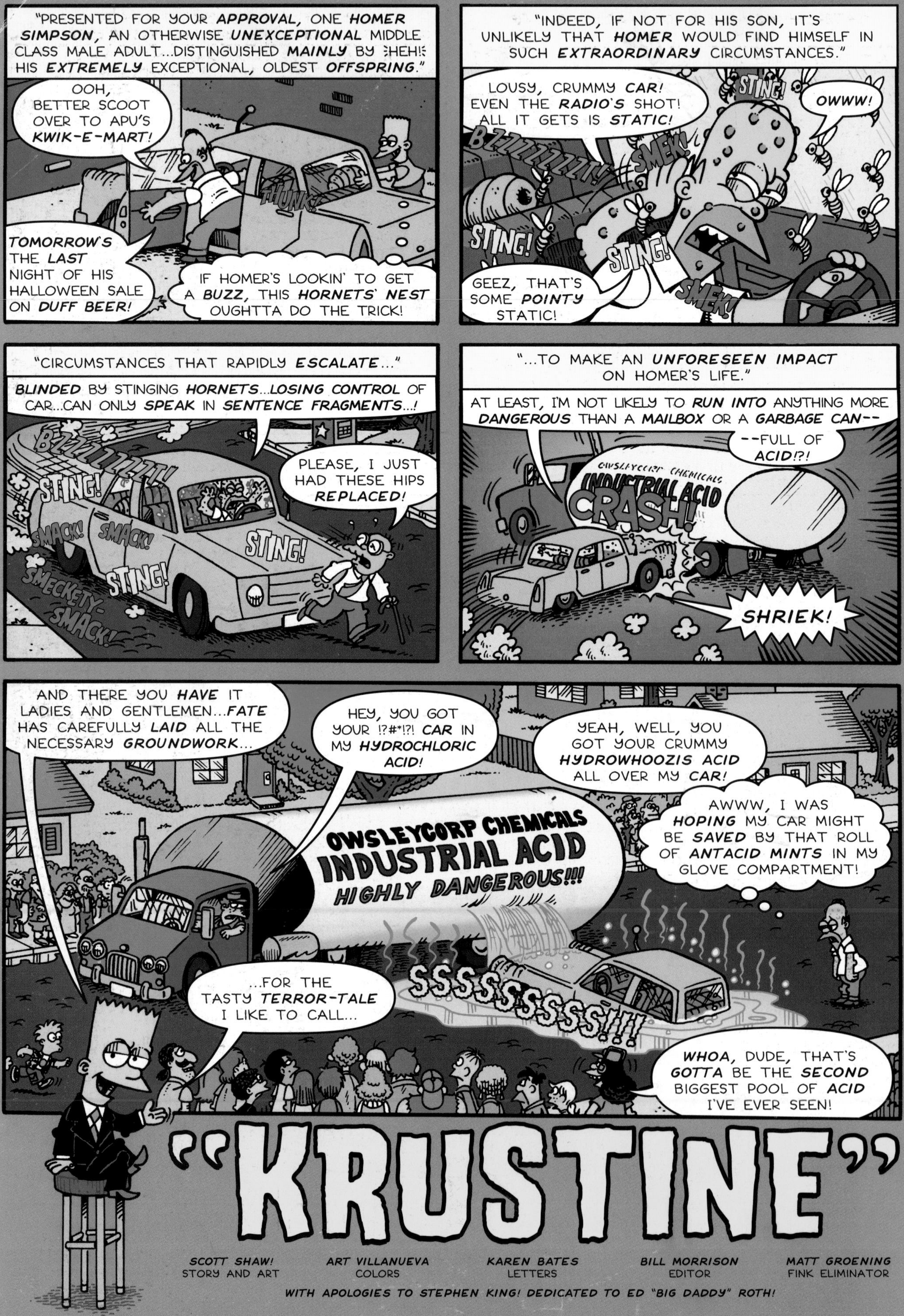
"PRESENTED FOR YOUR APPROVAL, ONE HOMER SIMPSON, AN OTHERWISE UNEXCEPTIONAL MIDDLE CLASS MALE ADULT...DISTINGUISHED MAINLY BY :HEH!: HIS EXTREMELY EXCEPTIONAL, OLDEST OFFSPRING."
OOH, BETTER SCOOT OVER TO APU'S KWIK-E-MART!
THUNK!
TOMORROW'S THE LAST NIGHT OF HIS HALLOWEEN SALE ON DUFF BEER!
IF HOMER'S LOOKIN' TO GET A BUZZ, THIS HORNETS' NEST OUGHTTA DO THE TRICK!
"INDEED, IF NOT FOR HIS SON, IT'S UNLIKELY THAT HOMER WOULD FIND HIMSELF IN SUCH EXTRAORDINARY CIRCUMSTANCES."
LOUSY, CRUMMY CAR! EVEN THE RADIO'S SHOT! ALL IT GETS IS STATIC!
STING!
OWWW!
BZZZZZZZZZT!
SMEK!
STING!
STING!
SMEK!
GEEZ, THAT'S SOME POINTY STATIC!
"CIRCUMSTANCES THAT RAPIDLY ESCALATE..."
BLINDED BY STINGING HORNETS...LOSING CONTROL OF CAR...CAN ONLY SPEAK IN SENTENCE FRAGMENTS...!
BZZZZZZZZT!
STING!
SMACK!
SMACK!
STING!
STING!
SMECKETY-SMACK!
PLEASE, I JUST HAD THESE HIPS REPLACED!
"...TO MAKE AN UNFORESEEN IMPACT ON HOMER'S LIFE."
AT LEAST, I'M NOT LIKELY TO RUN INTO ANYTHING MORE DANGEROUS THAN A MAILBOX OR A GARBAGE CAN--
--FULL OF ACID!?!
OWSLEYCORP CHEMICALS
INDUSTRIAL ACID
CRASH!
SHRIEK!
AND THERE YOU HAVE IT LADIES AND GENTLEMEN...FATE HAS CAREFULLY LAID ALL THE NECESSARY GROUNDWORK...
HEY, YOU GOT YOUR !?#*!?! CAR IN MY HYDROCHLORIC ACID!
YEAH, WELL, YOU GOT YOUR CRUMMY HYDROWHOOZIS ACID ALL OVER MY CAR!
AWWW, I WAS HOPING MY CAR MIGHT BE SAVED BY THAT ROLL OF ANTACID MINTS IN MY GLOVE COMPARTMENT!
OWSLEYCORP CHEMICALS
INDUSTRIAL ACID
HIGHLY DANGEROUS!!!
SSSSSSSSSSSS!!!
...FOR THE TASTY TERROR-TALE I LIKE TO CALL...
WHOA, DUDE, THAT'S GOTTA BE THE SECOND BIGGEST POOL OF ACID I'VE EVER SEEN!

"KRUSTINE"

SCOTT SHAW! STORY AND ART · **ART VILLANUEVA** COLORS · **KAREN BATES** LETTERS · **BILL MORRISON** EDITOR · **MATT GROENING** FINK ELIMINATOR

WITH APOLOGIES TO STEPHEN KING! DEDICATED TO ED "BIG DADDY" ROTH!

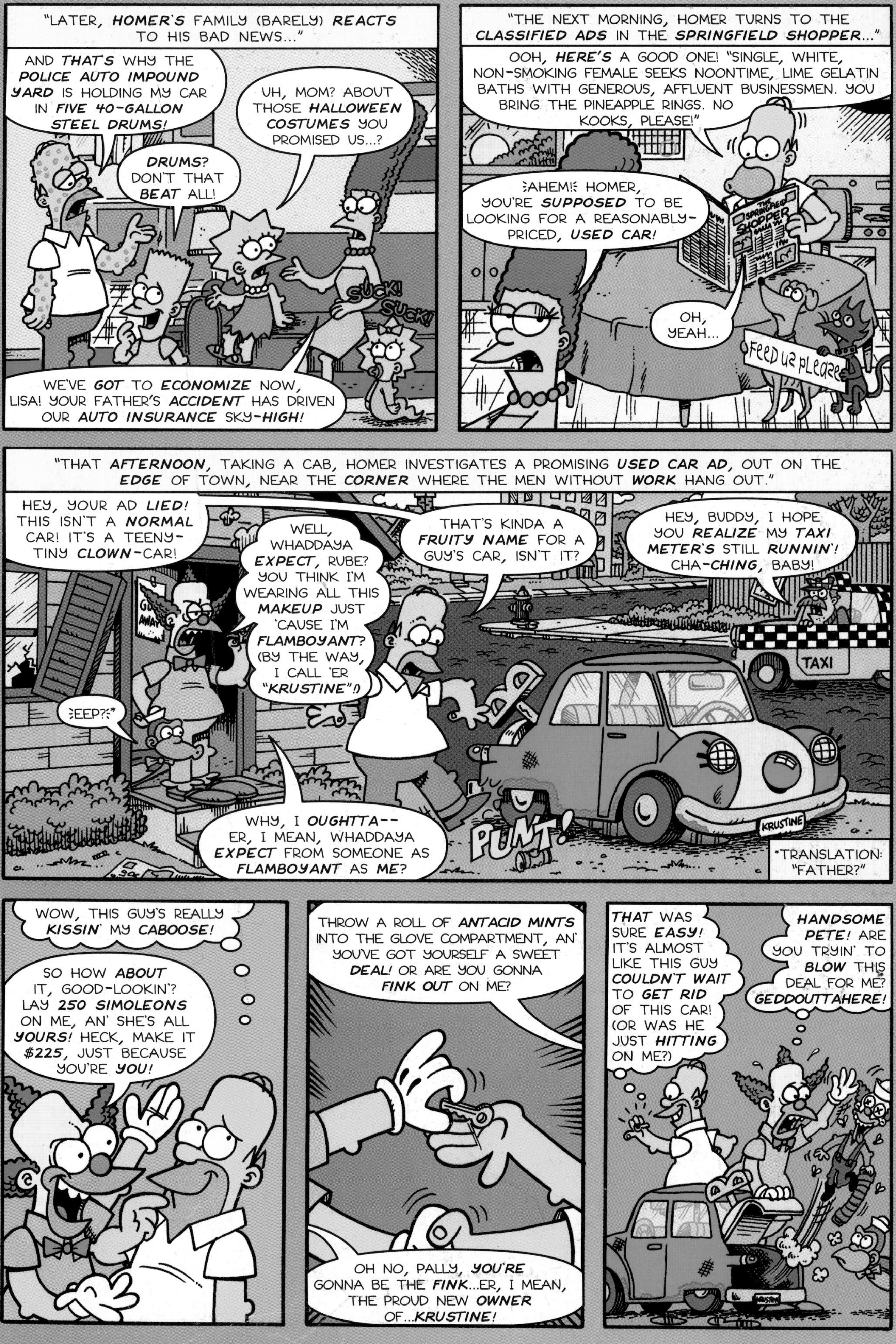
"LATER, HOMER'S FAMILY (BARELY) REACTS TO HIS BAD NEWS..."
AND THAT'S WHY THE POLICE AUTO IMPOUND YARD IS HOLDING MY CAR IN FIVE 40-GALLON STEEL DRUMS!
DRUMS? DON'T THAT BEAT ALL!
UH, MOM? ABOUT THOSE HALLOWEEN COSTUMES YOU PROMISED US...?
SUCK! SUCK!
WE'VE GOT TO ECONOMIZE NOW, LISA! YOUR FATHER'S ACCIDENT HAS DRIVEN OUR AUTO INSURANCE SKY-HIGH!
"THE NEXT MORNING, HOMER TURNS TO THE CLASSIFIED ADS IN THE SPRINGFIELD SHOPPER..."
OOH, HERE'S A GOOD ONE! "SINGLE, WHITE, NON-SMOKING FEMALE SEEKS NOONTIME, LIME GELATIN BATHS WITH GENEROUS, AFFLUENT BUSINESSMEN. YOU BRING THE PINEAPPLE RINGS. NO KOOKS, PLEASE!"
AHEM! HOMER, YOU'RE SUPPOSED TO BE LOOKING FOR A REASONABLY-PRICED, USED CAR!
OH, YEAH...
THE SPRINGFIELD SHOPPER
FEED US PLEASE
"THAT AFTERNOON, TAKING A CAB, HOMER INVESTIGATES A PROMISING USED CAR AD, OUT ON THE EDGE OF TOWN, NEAR THE CORNER WHERE THE MEN WITHOUT WORK HANG OUT."
HEY, YOUR AD LIED! THIS ISN'T A NORMAL CAR! IT'S A TEENY-TINY CLOWN-CAR!
WELL, WHADDAYA EXPECT, RUBE? YOU THINK I'M WEARING ALL THIS MAKEUP JUST 'CAUSE I'M FLAMBOYANT? (BY THE WAY, I CALL 'ER "KRUSTINE"!)
THAT'S KINDA A FRUITY NAME FOR A GUY'S CAR, ISN'T IT?
HEY, BUDDY, I HOPE YOU REALIZE MY TAXI METER'S STILL RUNNIN'! CHA-CHING, BABY!
TAXI
EEP?*
WHY, I OUGHTTA-- ER, I MEAN, WHADDAYA EXPECT FROM SOMEONE AS FLAMBOYANT AS ME?
PUNT!
KRUSTINE
*TRANSLATION: "FATHER?"
WOW, THIS GUY'S REALLY KISSIN' MY CABOOSE!
SO HOW ABOUT IT, GOOD-LOOKIN'? LAY 250 SIMOLEONS ON ME, AN' SHE'S ALL YOURS! HECK, MAKE IT $225, JUST BECAUSE YOU'RE YOU!
THROW A ROLL OF ANTACID MINTS INTO THE GLOVE COMPARTMENT, AN' YOU'VE GOT YOURSELF A SWEET DEAL! OR ARE YOU GONNA FINK OUT ON ME?
OH NO, PALLY, YOU'RE GONNA BE THE FINK...ER, I MEAN, THE PROUD NEW OWNER OF...KRUSTINE!
THAT WAS SURE EASY! IT'S ALMOST LIKE THIS GUY COULDN'T WAIT TO GET RID OF THIS CAR! (OR WAS HE JUST HITTING ON ME?)
HANDSOME PETE! ARE YOU TRYIN' TO BLOW THIS DEAL FOR ME? GEDDOUTTAHERE!
KRUSTINE

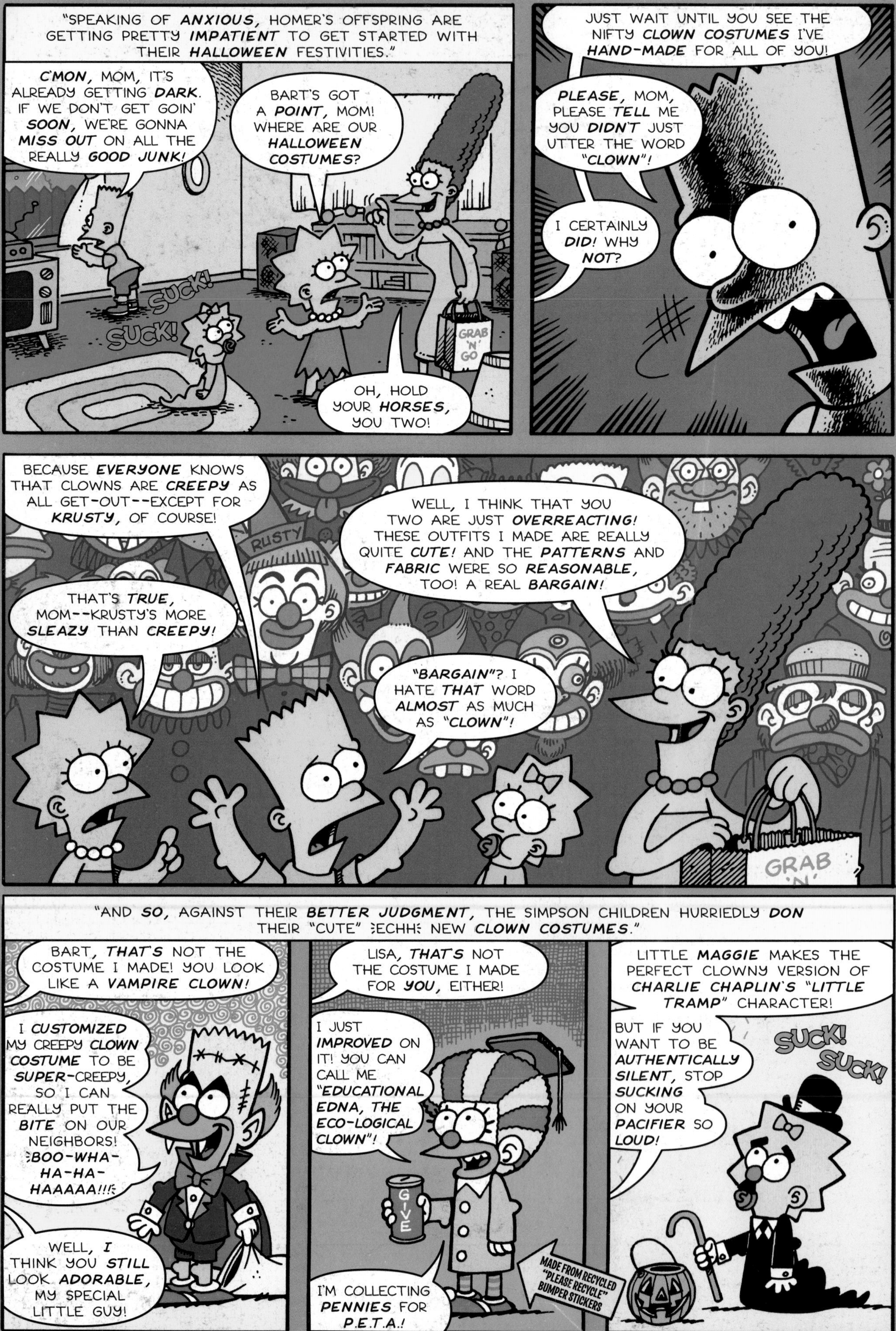
"SPEAKING OF ANXIOUS, HOMER'S OFFSPRING ARE GETTING PRETTY IMPATIENT TO GET STARTED WITH THEIR HALLOWEEN FESTIVITIES."
C'MON, MOM, IT'S ALREADY GETTING DARK. IF WE DON'T GET GOIN' SOON, WE'RE GONNA MISS OUT ON ALL THE REALLY GOOD JUNK!
BART'S GOT A POINT, MOM! WHERE ARE OUR HALLOWEEN COSTUMES?
SUCK!
SUCK!
GRAB 'N' GO
OH, HOLD YOUR HORSES, YOU TWO!
JUST WAIT UNTIL YOU SEE THE NIFTY CLOWN COSTUMES I'VE HAND-MADE FOR ALL OF YOU!
PLEASE, MOM, PLEASE TELL ME YOU DIDN'T JUST UTTER THE WORD "CLOWN"!
I CERTAINLY DID! WHY NOT?
BECAUSE EVERYONE KNOWS THAT CLOWNS ARE CREEPY AS ALL GET-OUT--EXCEPT FOR KRUSTY, OF COURSE!
RUSTY
WELL, I THINK THAT YOU TWO ARE JUST OVERREACTING! THESE OUTFITS I MADE ARE REALLY QUITE CUTE! AND THE PATTERNS AND FABRIC WERE SO REASONABLE, TOO! A REAL BARGAIN!
THAT'S TRUE, MOM--KRUSTY'S MORE SLEAZY THAN CREEPY!
"BARGAIN"? I HATE THAT WORD ALMOST AS MUCH AS "CLOWN"!
GRAB 'N'
"AND SO, AGAINST THEIR BETTER JUDGMENT, THE SIMPSON CHILDREN HURRIEDLY DON THEIR "CUTE" :ECHH: NEW CLOWN COSTUMES."
BART, THAT'S NOT THE COSTUME I MADE! YOU LOOK LIKE A VAMPIRE CLOWN!
I CUSTOMIZED MY CREEPY CLOWN COSTUME TO BE SUPER-CREEPY, SO I CAN REALLY PUT THE BITE ON OUR NEIGHBORS! :BOO-WHA-HA-HA-HAAAAA!!!:
WELL, I THINK YOU STILL LOOK ADORABLE, MY SPECIAL LITTLE GUY!
LISA, THAT'S NOT THE COSTUME I MADE FOR YOU, EITHER!
I JUST IMPROVED ON IT! YOU CAN CALL ME "EDUCATIONAL EDNA, THE ECO-LOGICAL CLOWN"!
GIVE
I'M COLLECTING PENNIES FOR P.E.T.A.!
MADE FROM RECYCLED "PLEASE RECYCLE" BUMPER STICKERS
LITTLE MAGGIE MAKES THE PERFECT CLOWNY VERSION OF CHARLIE CHAPLIN'S "LITTLE TRAMP" CHARACTER!
BUT IF YOU WANT TO BE AUTHENTICALLY SILENT, STOP SUCKING ON YOUR PACIFIER SO LOUD!
SUCK!
SUCK!

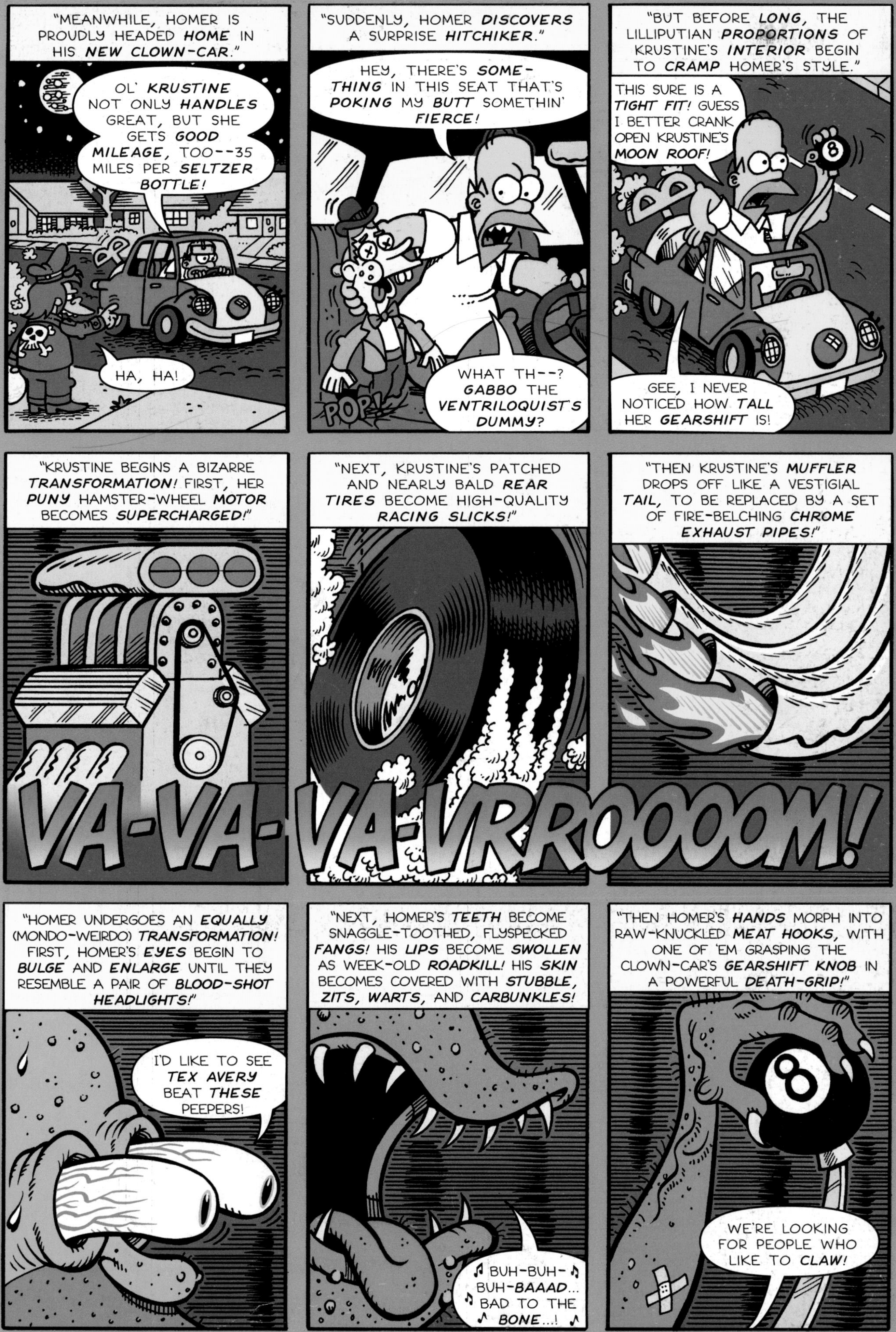
"MEANWHILE, HOMER IS PROUDLY HEADED HOME IN HIS NEW CLOWN-CAR."
OL' KRUSTINE NOT ONLY HANDLES GREAT, BUT SHE GETS GOOD MILEAGE, TOO--35 MILES PER SELTZER BOTTLE!
HA, HA!
"SUDDENLY, HOMER DISCOVERS A SURPRISE HITCHIKER."
HEY, THERE'S SOMETHING IN THIS SEAT THAT'S POKING MY BUTT SOMETHIN' FIERCE!
POP!
WHAT TH--? GABBO THE VENTRILOQUIST'S DUMMY?
"BUT BEFORE LONG, THE LILLIPUTIAN PROPORTIONS OF KRUSTINE'S INTERIOR BEGIN TO CRAMP HOMER'S STYLE."
THIS SURE IS A TIGHT FIT! GUESS I BETTER CRANK OPEN KRUSTINE'S MOON ROOF!
GEE, I NEVER NOTICED HOW TALL HER GEARSHIFT IS!
"KRUSTINE BEGINS A BIZARRE TRANSFORMATION! FIRST, HER PUNY HAMSTER-WHEEL MOTOR BECOMES SUPERCHARGED!"
"NEXT, KRUSTINE'S PATCHED AND NEARLY BALD REAR TIRES BECOME HIGH-QUALITY RACING SLICKS!"
"THEN KRUSTINE'S MUFFLER DROPS OFF LIKE A VESTIGIAL TAIL, TO BE REPLACED BY A SET OF FIRE-BELCHING CHROME EXHAUST PIPES!"
VA-VA-VA-VRROOOOM!
"HOMER UNDERGOES AN EQUALLY (MONDO-WEIRDO) TRANSFORMATION! FIRST, HOMER'S EYES BEGIN TO BULGE AND ENLARGE UNTIL THEY RESEMBLE A PAIR OF BLOOD-SHOT HEADLIGHTS!"
I'D LIKE TO SEE TEX AVERY BEAT THESE PEEPERS!
"NEXT, HOMER'S TEETH BECOME SNAGGLE-TOOTHED, FLYSPECKED FANGS! HIS LIPS BECOME SWOLLEN AS WEEK-OLD ROADKILL! HIS SKIN BECOMES COVERED WITH STUBBLE, ZITS, WARTS, AND CARBUNKLES!
♪ BUH-BUH- ♪ BUH-BAAAD... ♪ BAD TO THE ♪ BONE...! ♪
"THEN HOMER'S HANDS MORPH INTO RAW-KNUCKLED MEAT HOOKS, WITH ONE OF 'EM GRASPING THE CLOWN-CAR'S GEARSHIFT KNOB IN A POWERFUL DEATH-GRIP!"
WE'RE LOOKING FOR PEOPLE WHO LIKE TO CLAW!

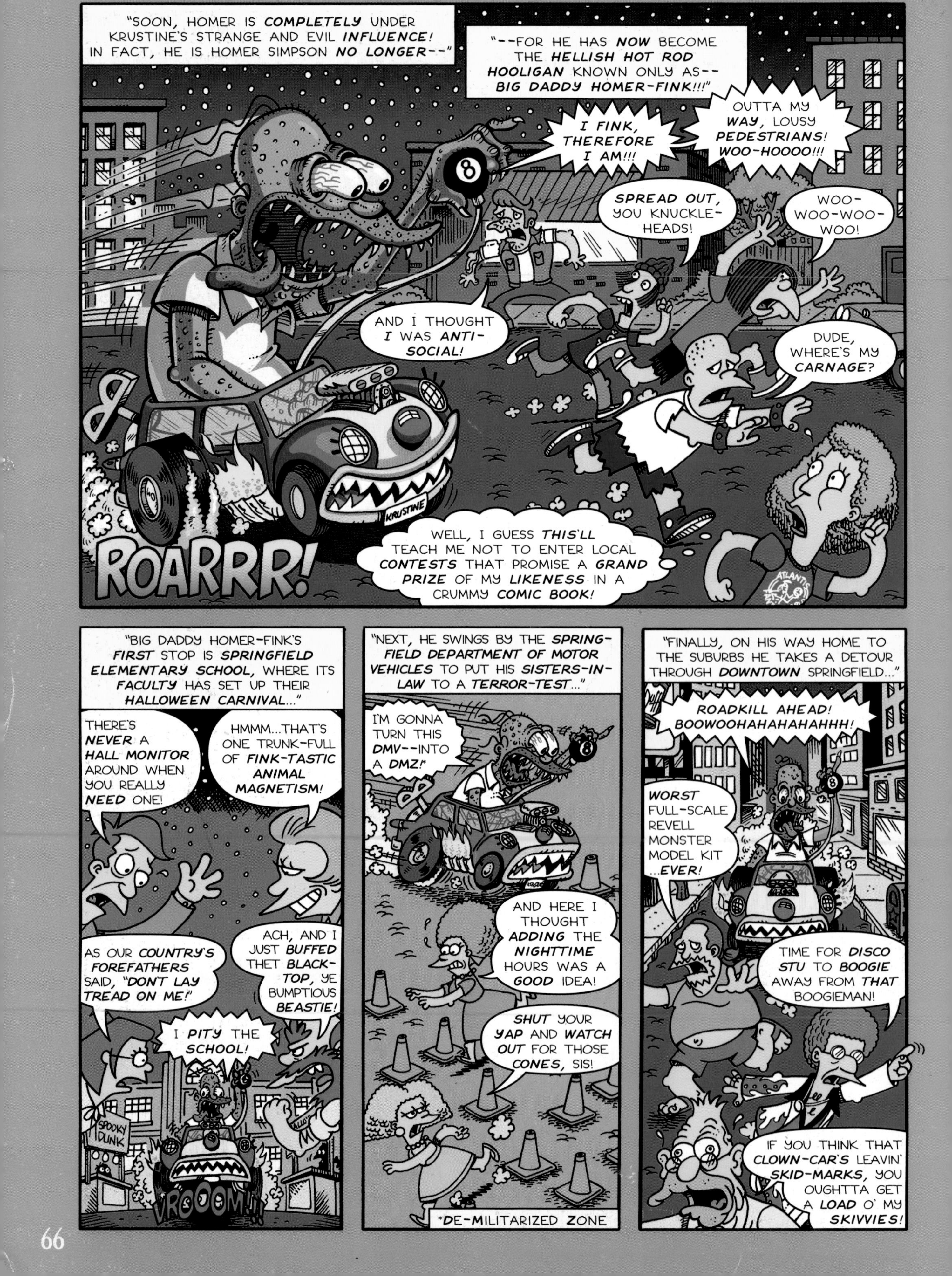
"SOON, HOMER IS COMPLETELY UNDER KRUSTINE'S STRANGE AND EVIL INFLUENCE! IN FACT, HE IS HOMER SIMPSON NO LONGER--"
"--FOR HE HAS NOW BECOME THE HELLISH HOT ROD HOOLIGAN KNOWN ONLY AS--BIG DADDY HOMER-FINK!!!"
I FINK, THEREFORE I AM!!!
OUTTA MY WAY, LOUSY PEDESTRIANS! WOO-HOOOO!!!
SPREAD OUT, YOU KNUCKLE-HEADS!
WOO-WOO-WOO-WOO!
AND I THOUGHT I WAS ANTI-SOCIAL!
DUDE, WHERE'S MY CARNAGE?
KRUSTINE
WELL, I GUESS THIS'LL TEACH ME NOT TO ENTER LOCAL CONTESTS THAT PROMISE A GRAND PRIZE OF MY LIKENESS IN A CRUMMY COMIC BOOK!
ROARRR!
ATLANTIS
"BIG DADDY HOMER-FINK'S FIRST STOP IS SPRINGFIELD ELEMENTARY SCHOOL, WHERE ITS FACULTY HAS SET UP THEIR HALLOWEEN CARNIVAL..."
THERE'S NEVER A HALL MONITOR AROUND WHEN YOU REALLY NEED ONE!
HMMM...THAT'S ONE TRUNK-FULL OF FINK-TASTIC ANIMAL MAGNETISM!
AS OUR COUNTRY'S FOREFATHERS SAID, "DON'T LAY TREAD ON ME!"
ACH, AND I JUST BUFFED THET BLACK-TOP, YE BUMPTIOUS BEASTIE!
I PITY THE SCHOOL!
SPOOKY DUNK
VROOOM!!!
"NEXT, HE SWINGS BY THE SPRINGFIELD DEPARTMENT OF MOTOR VEHICLES TO PUT HIS SISTERS-IN-LAW TO A TERROR-TEST..."
I'M GONNA TURN THIS DMV--INTO A DMZ!*
AND HERE I THOUGHT ADDING THE NIGHTTIME HOURS WAS A GOOD IDEA!
SHUT YOUR YAP AND WATCH OUT FOR THOSE CONES, SIS!
*DE-MILITARIZED ZONE
"FINALLY, ON HIS WAY HOME TO THE SUBURBS HE TAKES A DETOUR THROUGH DOWNTOWN SPRINGFIELD..."
ROADKILL AHEAD! BOOWOOHAHAHAHAHHH!
WORST FULL-SCALE REVELL MONSTER MODEL KIT ...EVER!
TIME FOR DISCO STU TO BOOGIE AWAY FROM THAT BOOGIEMAN!
IF YOU THINK THAT CLOWN-CAR'S LEAVIN' SKID-MARKS, YOU OUGHTTA GET A LOAD O' MY SKIVVIES!

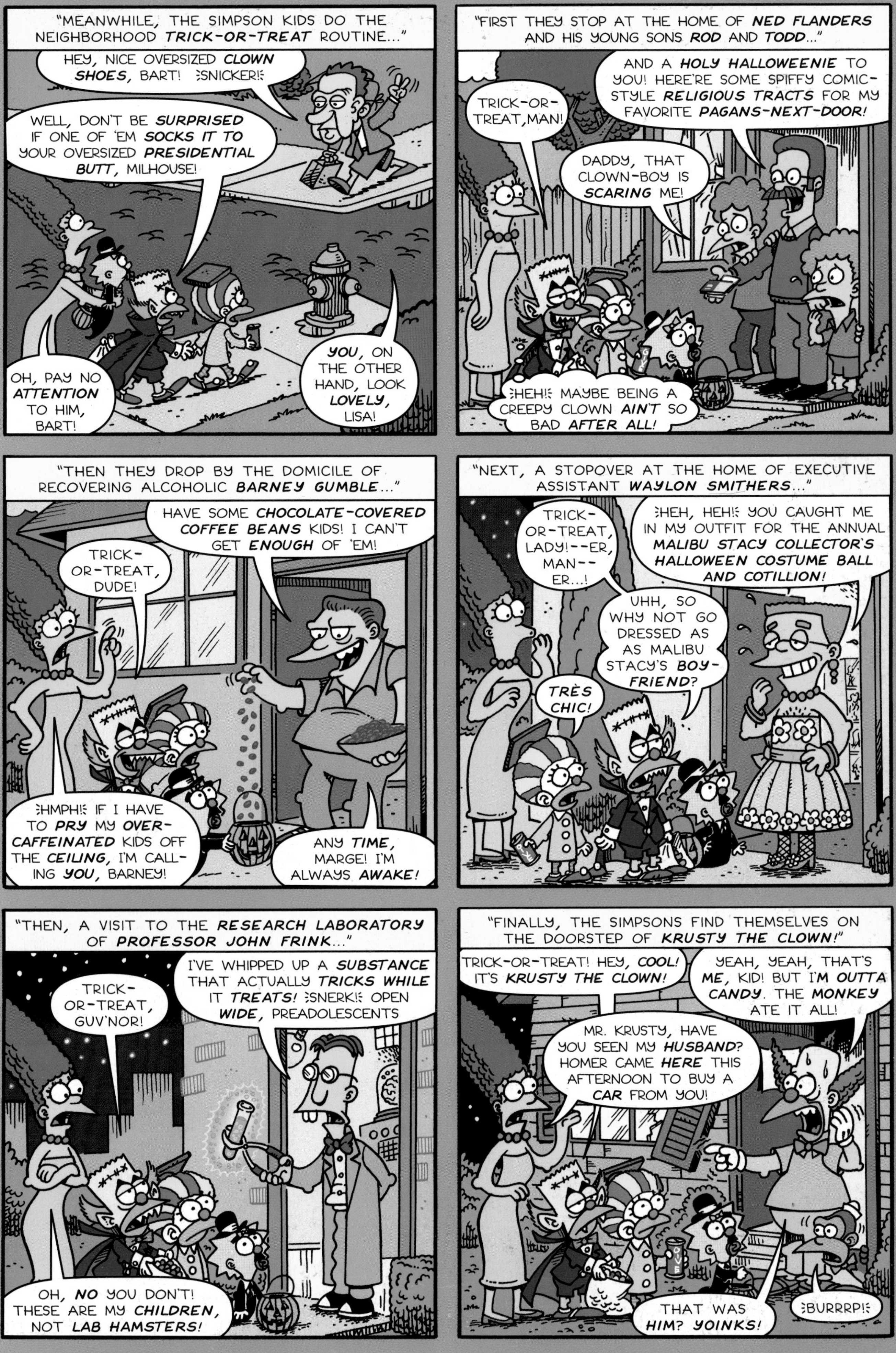
"MEANWHILE, THE SIMPSON KIDS DO THE NEIGHBORHOOD TRICK-OR-TREAT ROUTINE..."
HEY, NICE OVERSIZED CLOWN SHOES, BART! ⁝SNICKER!⁝
WELL, DON'T BE SURPRISED IF ONE OF 'EM SOCKS IT TO YOUR OVERSIZED PRESIDENTIAL BUTT, MILHOUSE!
OH, PAY NO ATTENTION TO HIM, BART!
YOU, ON THE OTHER HAND, LOOK LOVELY, LISA!
"FIRST THEY STOP AT THE HOME OF NED FLANDERS AND HIS YOUNG SONS ROD AND TODD..."
TRICK-OR-TREAT,MAN!
AND A HOLY HALLOWEENIE TO YOU! HERE'RE SOME SPIFFY COMIC-STYLE RELIGIOUS TRACTS FOR MY FAVORITE PAGANS-NEXT-DOOR!
DADDY, THAT CLOWN-BOY IS SCARING ME!
⁝HEH!⁝ MAYBE BEING A CREEPY CLOWN AIN'T SO BAD AFTER ALL!
"THEN THEY DROP BY THE DOMICILE OF RECOVERING ALCOHOLIC BARNEY GUMBLE..."
TRICK-OR-TREAT, DUDE!
HAVE SOME CHOCOLATE-COVERED COFFEE BEANS KIDS! I CAN'T GET ENOUGH OF 'EM!
⁝HMPH!⁝ IF I HAVE TO PRY MY OVER-CAFFEINATED KIDS OFF THE CEILING, I'M CALL-ING YOU, BARNEY!
ANY TIME, MARGE! I'M ALWAYS AWAKE!
"NEXT, A STOPOVER AT THE HOME OF EXECUTIVE ASSISTANT WAYLON SMITHERS..."
TRICK-OR-TREAT, LADY!--ER, MAN--ER...!
⁝HEH, HEH!⁝ YOU CAUGHT ME IN MY OUTFIT FOR THE ANNUAL MALIBU STACY COLLECTOR'S HALLOWEEN COSTUME BALL AND COTILLION!
UHH, SO WHY NOT GO DRESSED AS AS MALIBU STACY'S BOY-FRIEND?
TRÈS CHIC!
"THEN, A VISIT TO THE RESEARCH LABORATORY OF PROFESSOR JOHN FRINK..."
TRICK-OR-TREAT, GUV'NOR!
I'VE WHIPPED UP A SUBSTANCE THAT ACTUALLY TRICKS WHILE IT TREATS! ⁝SNERK!⁝ OPEN WIDE, PREADOLESCENTS
OH, NO YOU DON'T! THESE ARE MY CHILDREN, NOT LAB HAMSTERS!
"FINALLY, THE SIMPSONS FIND THEMSELVES ON THE DOORSTEP OF KRUSTY THE CLOWN!"
TRICK-OR-TREAT! HEY, COOL! IT'S KRUSTY THE CLOWN!
YEAH, YEAH, THAT'S ME, KID! BUT I'M OUTTA CANDY. THE MONKEY ATE IT ALL!
MR. KRUSTY, HAVE YOU SEEN MY HUSBAND? HOMER CAME HERE THIS AFTERNOON TO BUY A CAR FROM YOU!
THAT WAS HIM? YOINKS!
⁝BURRRP!⁝

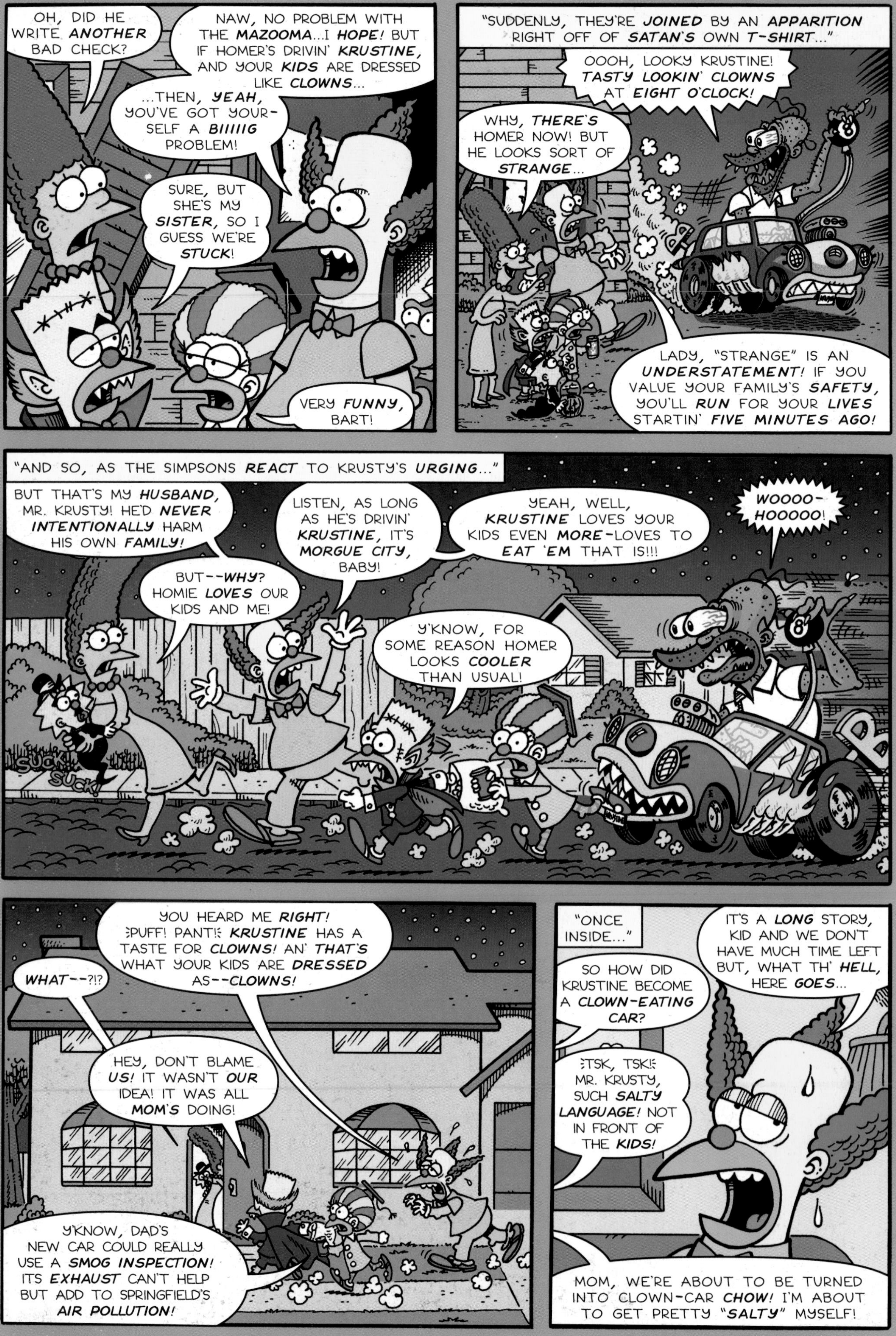

OH, DID HE WRITE ANOTHER BAD CHECK?
NAW, NO PROBLEM WITH THE MAZOOMA...I HOPE! BUT IF HOMER'S DRIVIN' KRUSTINE, AND YOUR KIDS ARE DRESSED LIKE CLOWNS...
...THEN, YEAH, YOU'VE GOT YOURSELF A BIIIIIG PROBLEM!
SURE, BUT SHE'S MY SISTER, SO I GUESS WE'RE STUCK!
VERY FUNNY, BART!
"SUDDENLY, THEY'RE JOINED BY AN APPARITION RIGHT OFF OF SATAN'S OWN T-SHIRT..."
OOOH, LOOKY KRUSTINE! TASTY LOOKIN' CLOWNS AT EIGHT O'CLOCK!
WHY, THERE'S HOMER NOW! BUT HE LOOKS SORT OF STRANGE...
LADY, "STRANGE" IS AN UNDERSTATEMENT! IF YOU VALUE YOUR FAMILY'S SAFETY, YOU'LL RUN FOR YOUR LIVES STARTIN' FIVE MINUTES AGO!
"AND SO, AS THE SIMPSONS REACT TO KRUSTY'S URGING..."
BUT THAT'S MY HUSBAND, MR. KRUSTY! HE'D NEVER INTENTIONALLY HARM HIS OWN FAMILY!
LISTEN, AS LONG AS HE'S DRIVIN' KRUSTINE, IT'S MORGUE CITY, BABY!
BUT--WHY? HOMIE LOVES OUR KIDS AND ME!
YEAH, WELL, KRUSTINE LOVES YOUR KIDS EVEN MORE-LOVES TO EAT 'EM THAT IS!!!
WOOOO-HOOOOO!
Y'KNOW, FOR SOME REASON HOMER LOOKS COOLER THAN USUAL!
SUCK! SUCK!
YOU HEARD ME RIGHT! PUFF! PANT! KRUSTINE HAS A TASTE FOR CLOWNS! AN' THAT'S WHAT YOUR KIDS ARE DRESSED AS--CLOWNS!
WHAT--?!?
HEY, DON'T BLAME US! IT WASN'T OUR IDEA! IT WAS ALL MOM'S DOING!
Y'KNOW, DAD'S NEW CAR COULD REALLY USE A SMOG INSPECTION! ITS EXHAUST CAN'T HELP BUT ADD TO SPRINGFIELD'S AIR POLLUTION!
"ONCE INSIDE..."
SO HOW DID KRUSTINE BECOME A CLOWN-EATING CAR?
IT'S A LONG STORY, KID AND WE DON'T HAVE MUCH TIME LEFT BUT, WHAT TH' HELL, HERE GOES...
TSK, TSK! MR. KRUSTY, SUCH SALTY LANGUAGE! NOT IN FRONT OF THE KIDS!
MOM, WE'RE ABOUT TO BE TURNED INTO CLOWN-CAR CHOW! I'M ABOUT TO GET PRETTY "SALTY" MYSELF!

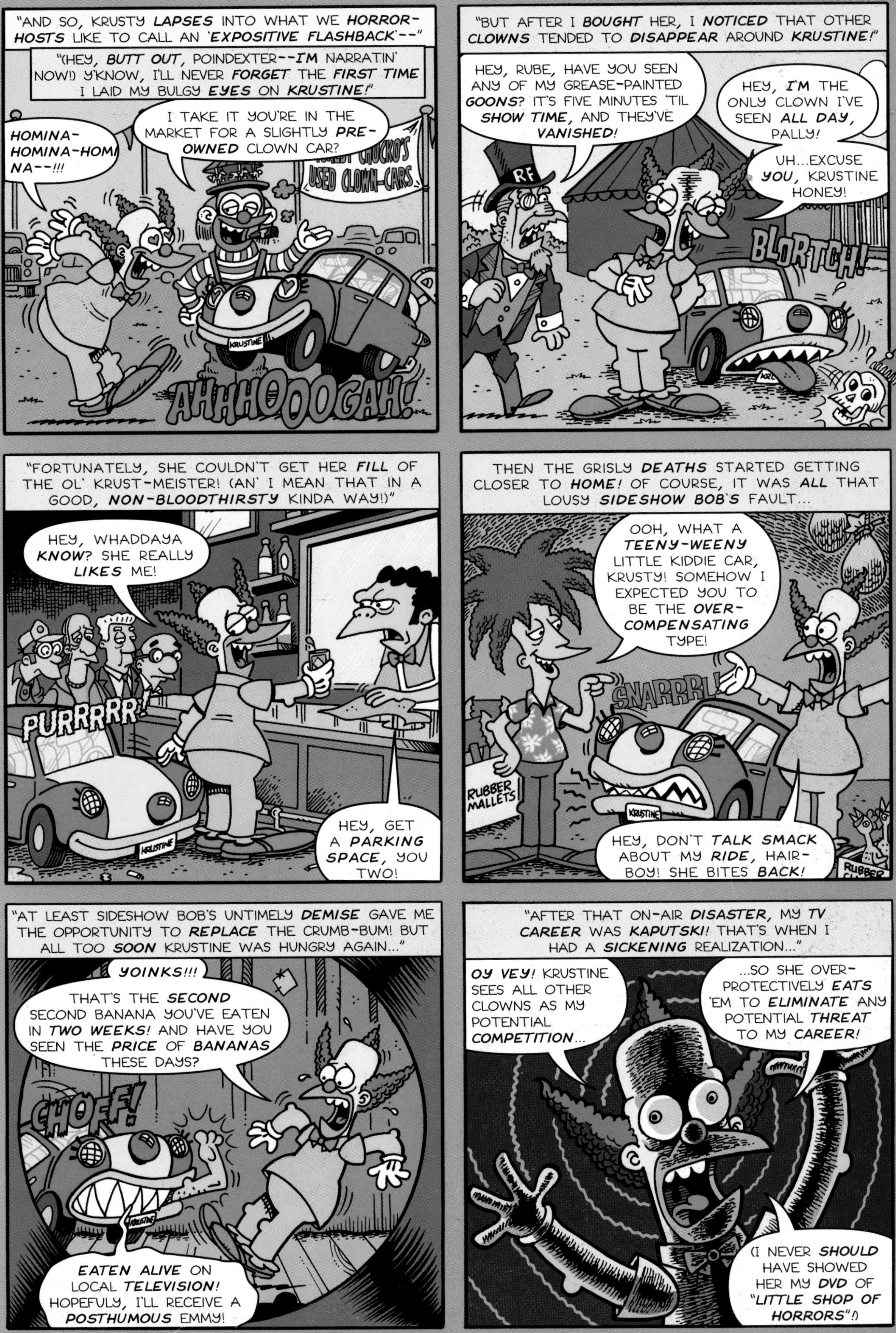
"AND SO, KRUSTY LAPSES INTO WHAT WE HORROR-HOSTS LIKE TO CALL AN 'EXPOSITIVE FLASHBACK'--"
"(HEY, BUTT OUT, POINDEXTER--I'M NARRATIN' NOW!) Y'KNOW, I'LL NEVER FORGET THE FIRST TIME I LAID MY BULGY EYES ON KRUSTINE!"
HOMINA-HOMINA-HOMINA--!!!
I TAKE IT YOU'RE IN THE MARKET FOR A SLIGHTLY PRE-OWNED CLOWN CAR?
CHUCKO'S USED CLOWN-CARS
KRUSTINE
AHHHOOOOGAH!
"BUT AFTER I BOUGHT HER, I NOTICED THAT OTHER CLOWNS TENDED TO DISAPPEAR AROUND KRUSTINE!"
HEY, RUBE, HAVE YOU SEEN ANY OF MY GREASE-PAINTED GOONS? IT'S FIVE MINUTES 'TIL SHOW TIME, AND THEY'VE VANISHED!
RF
HEY, I'M THE ONLY CLOWN I'VE SEEN ALL DAY, PALLY!
UH...EXCUSE YOU, KRUSTINE HONEY!
BLORTCH!
"FORTUNATELY, SHE COULDN'T GET HER FILL OF THE OL' KRUST-MEISTER! (AN' I MEAN THAT IN A GOOD, NON-BLOODTHIRSTY KINDA WAY!)"
HEY, WHADDAYA KNOW? SHE REALLY LIKES ME!
PURRRRR!
KRUSTINE
HEY, GET A PARKING SPACE, YOU TWO!
THEN THE GRISLY DEATHS STARTED GETTING CLOSER TO HOME! OF COURSE, IT WAS ALL THAT LOUSY SIDESHOW BOB'S FAULT...
OOH, WHAT A TEENY-WEENY LITTLE KIDDIE CAR, KRUSTY! SOMEHOW I EXPECTED YOU TO BE THE OVER-COMPENSATING TYPE!
SNARRRL!
RUBBER MALLETS
KRUSTINE
HEY, DON'T TALK SMACK ABOUT MY RIDE, HAIR-BOY! SHE BITES BACK!
"AT LEAST SIDESHOW BOB'S UNTIMELY DEMISE GAVE ME THE OPPORTUNITY TO REPLACE THE CRUMB-BUM! BUT ALL TOO SOON KRUSTINE WAS HUNGRY AGAIN..."
YOINKS!!!
THAT'S THE SECOND SECOND BANANA YOU'VE EATEN IN TWO WEEKS! AND HAVE YOU SEEN THE PRICE OF BANANAS THESE DAYS?
CHOFF!
KRUSTINE
EATEN ALIVE ON LOCAL TELEVISION! HOPEFULLY, I'LL RECEIVE A POSTHUMOUS EMMY!
"AFTER THAT ON-AIR DISASTER, MY TV CAREER WAS KAPUTSKI! THAT'S WHEN I HAD A SICKENING REALIZATION..."
OY VEY! KRUSTINE SEES ALL OTHER CLOWNS AS MY POTENTIAL COMPETITION...
...SO SHE OVER-PROTECTIVELY EATS 'EM TO ELIMINATE ANY POTENTIAL THREAT TO MY CAREER!
(I NEVER SHOULD HAVE SHOWED HER MY DVD OF "LITTLE SHOP OF HORRORS"!)

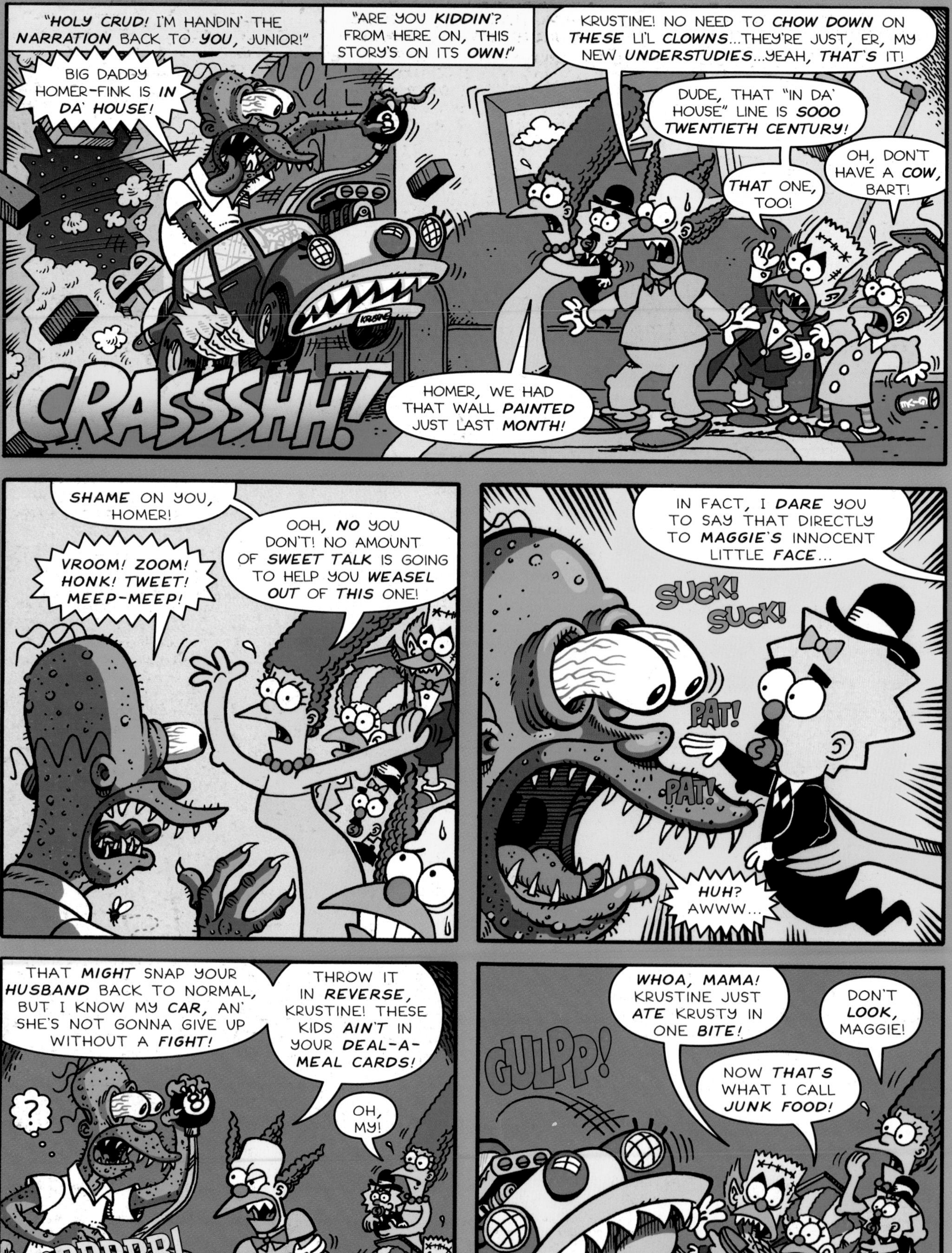
"HOLY CRUD! I'M HANDIN' THE NARRATION BACK TO YOU, JUNIOR!"
"ARE YOU KIDDIN'? FROM HERE ON, THIS STORY'S ON ITS OWN!"
BIG DADDY HOMER-FINK IS IN DA' HOUSE!
KRUSTINE! NO NEED TO CHOW DOWN ON THESE LI'L CLOWNS...THEY'RE JUST, ER, MY NEW UNDERSTUDIES...YEAH, THAT'S IT!
DUDE, THAT "IN DA' HOUSE" LINE IS SOOO TWENTIETH CENTURY!
THAT ONE, TOO!
OH, DON'T HAVE A COW, BART!
KRUSTINE
CRASSSHH!
HOMER, WE HAD THAT WALL PAINTED JUST LAST MONTH!
SHAME ON YOU, HOMER!
VROOM! ZOOM! HONK! TWEET! MEEP-MEEP!
OOH, NO YOU DON'T! NO AMOUNT OF SWEET TALK IS GOING TO HELP YOU WEASEL OUT OF THIS ONE!
IN FACT, I DARE YOU TO SAY THAT DIRECTLY TO MAGGIE'S INNOCENT LITTLE FACE...
SUCK! SUCK!
PAT! PAT!
HUH? AWWW...
THAT MIGHT SNAP YOUR HUSBAND BACK TO NORMAL, BUT I KNOW MY CAR, AN' SHE'S NOT GONNA GIVE UP WITHOUT A FIGHT!
THROW IT IN REVERSE, KRUSTINE! THESE KIDS AIN'T IN YOUR DEAL-A-MEAL CARDS!
?
OH, MY!
GRRRRR!
GULPP!
WHOA, MAMA! KRUSTINE JUST ATE KRUSTY IN ONE BITE!
DON'T LOOK, MAGGIE!
NOW THAT'S WHAT I CALL JUNK FOOD!
SUCK! SUCK!
KRUSTINE
YOINKS!

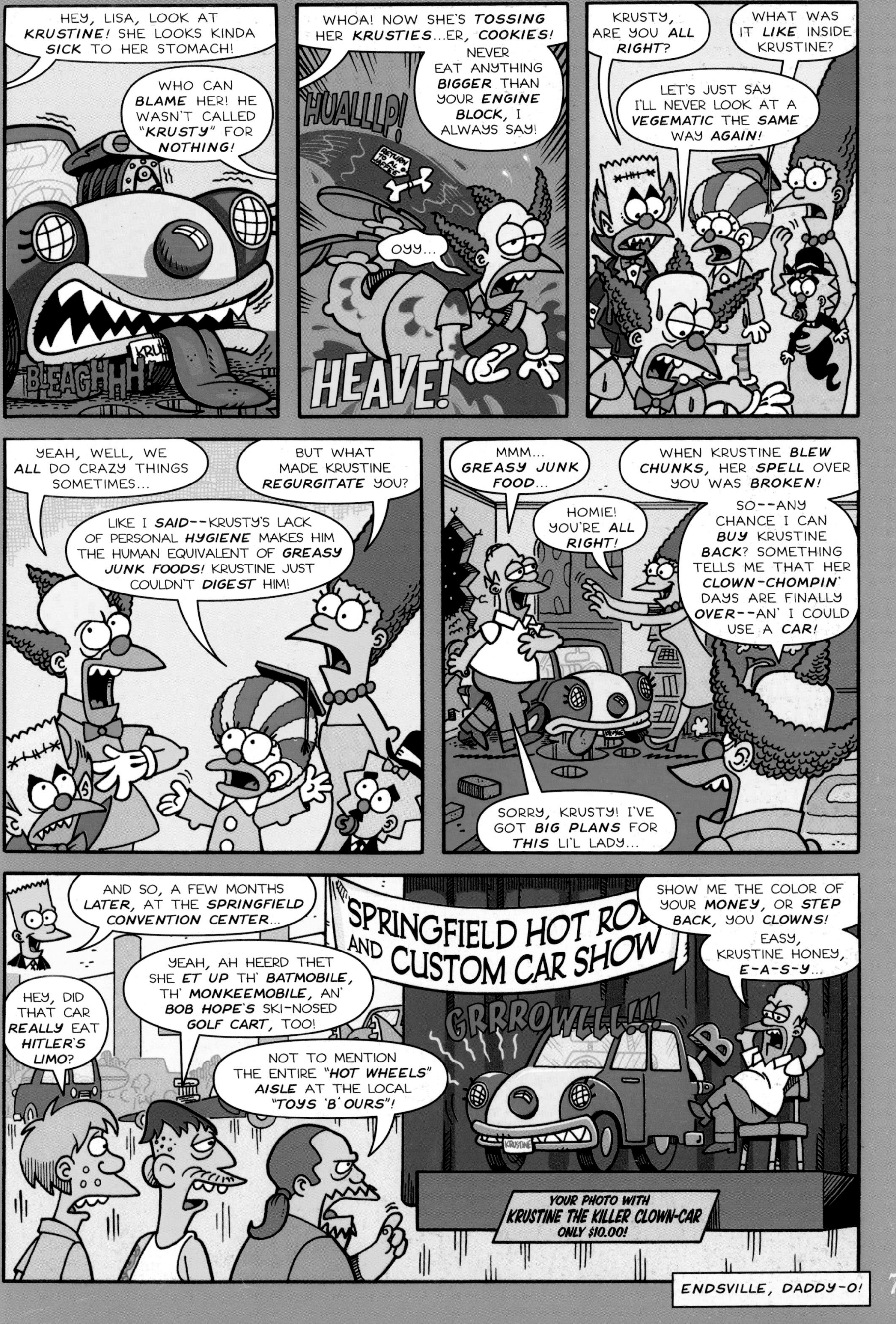
HEY, LISA, LOOK AT KRUSTINE! SHE LOOKS KINDA SICK TO HER STOMACH!
WHO CAN BLAME HER! HE WASN'T CALLED "KRUSTY" FOR NOTHING!
BLEAGHHH
WHOA! NOW SHE'S TOSSING HER KRUSTIES...ER, COOKIES!
NEVER EAT ANYTHING BIGGER THAN YOUR ENGINE BLOCK, I ALWAYS SAY!
HUALLLP!
RETURN TO AL JAFFEE
OYY...
HEAVE!
KRUSTY, ARE YOU ALL RIGHT?
WHAT WAS IT LIKE INSIDE KRUSTINE?
LET'S JUST SAY I'LL NEVER LOOK AT A VEGEMATIC THE SAME WAY AGAIN!
YEAH, WELL, WE ALL DO CRAZY THINGS SOMETIMES...
BUT WHAT MADE KRUSTINE REGURGITATE YOU?
LIKE I SAID--KRUSTY'S LACK OF PERSONAL HYGIENE MAKES HIM THE HUMAN EQUIVALENT OF GREASY JUNK FOODS! KRUSTINE JUST COULDN'T DIGEST HIM!
MMM... GREASY JUNK FOOD...
WHEN KRUSTINE BLEW CHUNKS, HER SPELL OVER YOU WAS BROKEN!
HOMIE! YOU'RE ALL RIGHT!
SO--ANY CHANCE I CAN BUY KRUSTINE BACK? SOMETHING TELLS ME THAT HER CLOWN-CHOMPIN' DAYS ARE FINALLY OVER--AN' I COULD USE A CAR!
SORRY, KRUSTY! I'VE GOT BIG PLANS FOR THIS LI'L LADY...
AND SO, A FEW MONTHS LATER, AT THE SPRINGFIELD CONVENTION CENTER...
SPRINGFIELD HOT ROD AND CUSTOM CAR SHOW
SHOW ME THE COLOR OF YOUR MONEY, OR STEP BACK, YOU CLOWNS!
EASY, KRUSTINE HONEY, E-A-S-Y...
HEY, DID THAT CAR REALLY EAT HITLER'S LIMO?
YEAH, AH HEERD THET SHE ET UP TH' BATMOBILE, TH' MONKEEMOBILE, AN' BOB HOPE'S SKI-NOSED GOLF CART, TOO!
NOT TO MENTION THE ENTIRE "HOT WHEELS" AISLE AT THE LOCAL "TOYS 'B' OURS"!
GRRROWLLLL!!!
KRUSTINE
YOUR PHOTO WITH KRUSTINE THE KILLER CLOWN-CAR ONLY $10.00!
ENDSVILLE, DADDY-O!

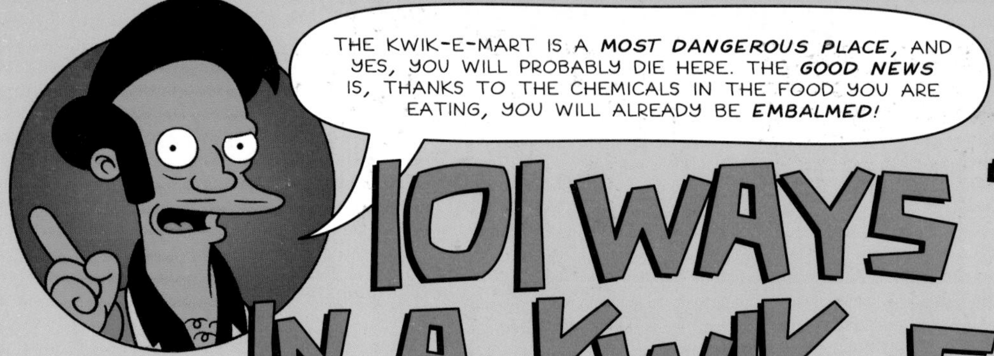
THE KWIK-E-MART IS A MOST DANGEROUS PLACE, AND YES, YOU WILL PROBABLY DIE HERE. THE GOOD NEWS IS, THANKS TO THE CHEMICALS IN THE FOOD YOU ARE EATING, YOU WILL ALREADY BE EMBALMED!

101 WAYS TO DIE IN A KWIK-E-MART

1 A SPLINTER IN AN UNSANDED ROTISSERIE DOG

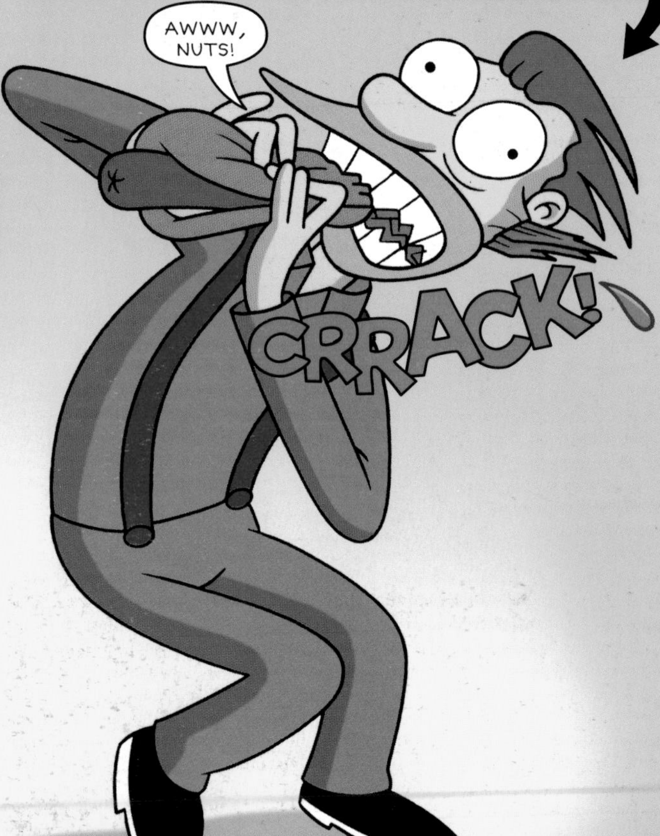
AWWW, NUTS!
CRRACK!

2 BEING THE BOTTOM HALF OF A SEVEN-FOOT-TALL "ADULT"

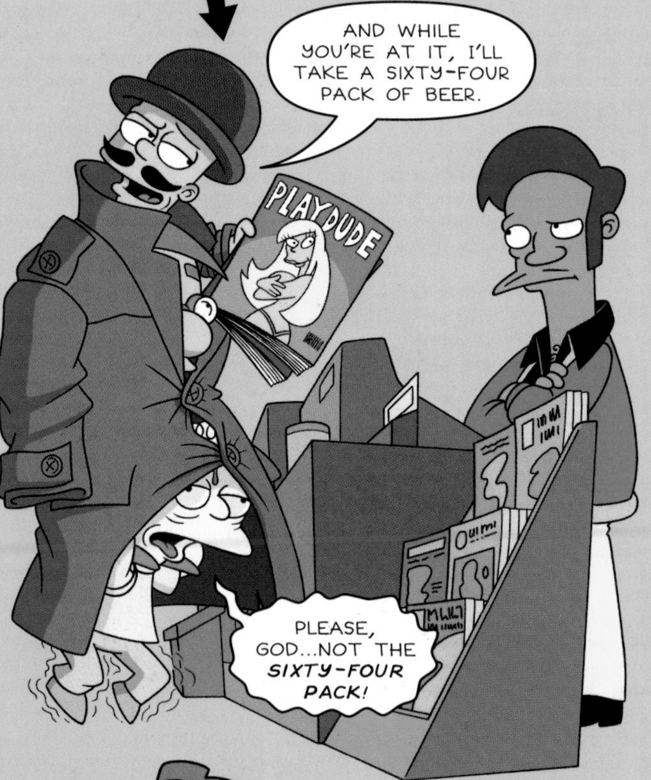
AND WHILE YOU'RE AT IT, I'LL TAKE A SIXTY-FOUR PACK OF BEER.
PLAYDUDE
PLEASE, GOD...NOT THE SIXTY-FOUR PACK!

3 FROM A BULLET*

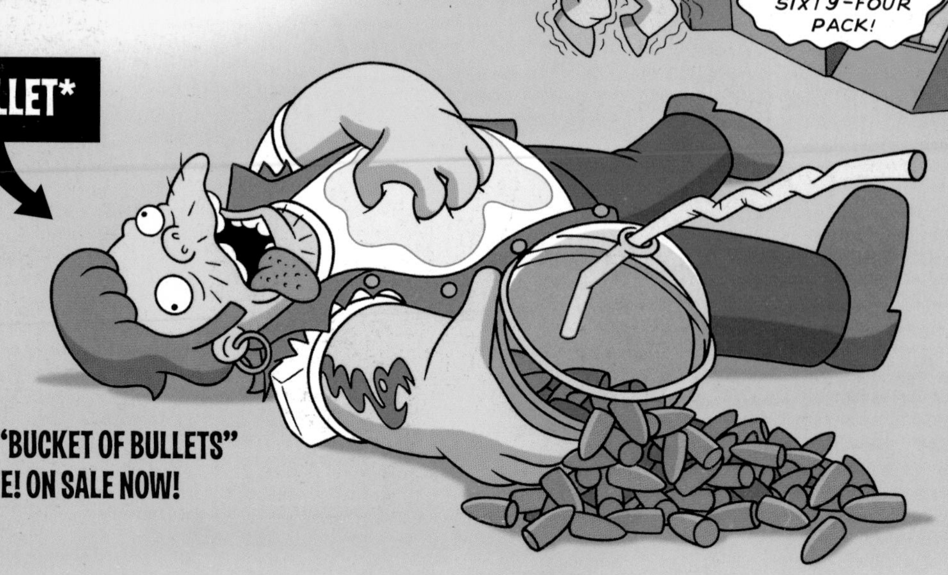

*IN THE NEW "BUCKET OF BULLETS" SQUISHEE! ON SALE NOW!

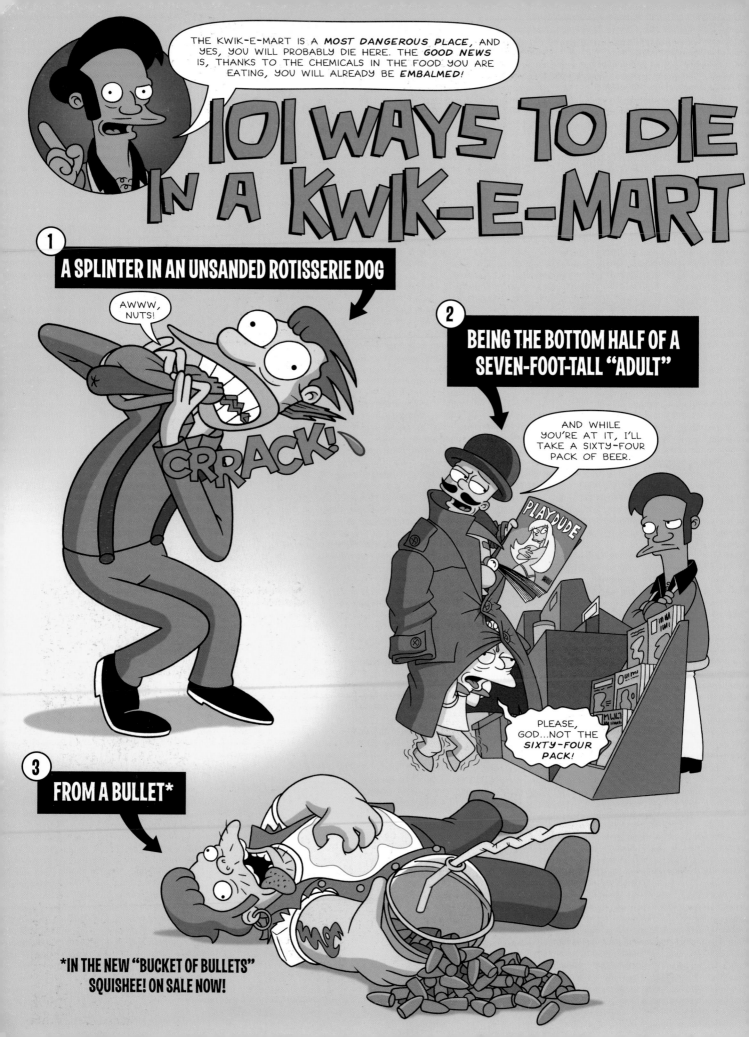

4

TRAMPLED TO DEATH NEAR THE SALES DISPLAY FOR EXPIRED CIRCUS PEANUTS

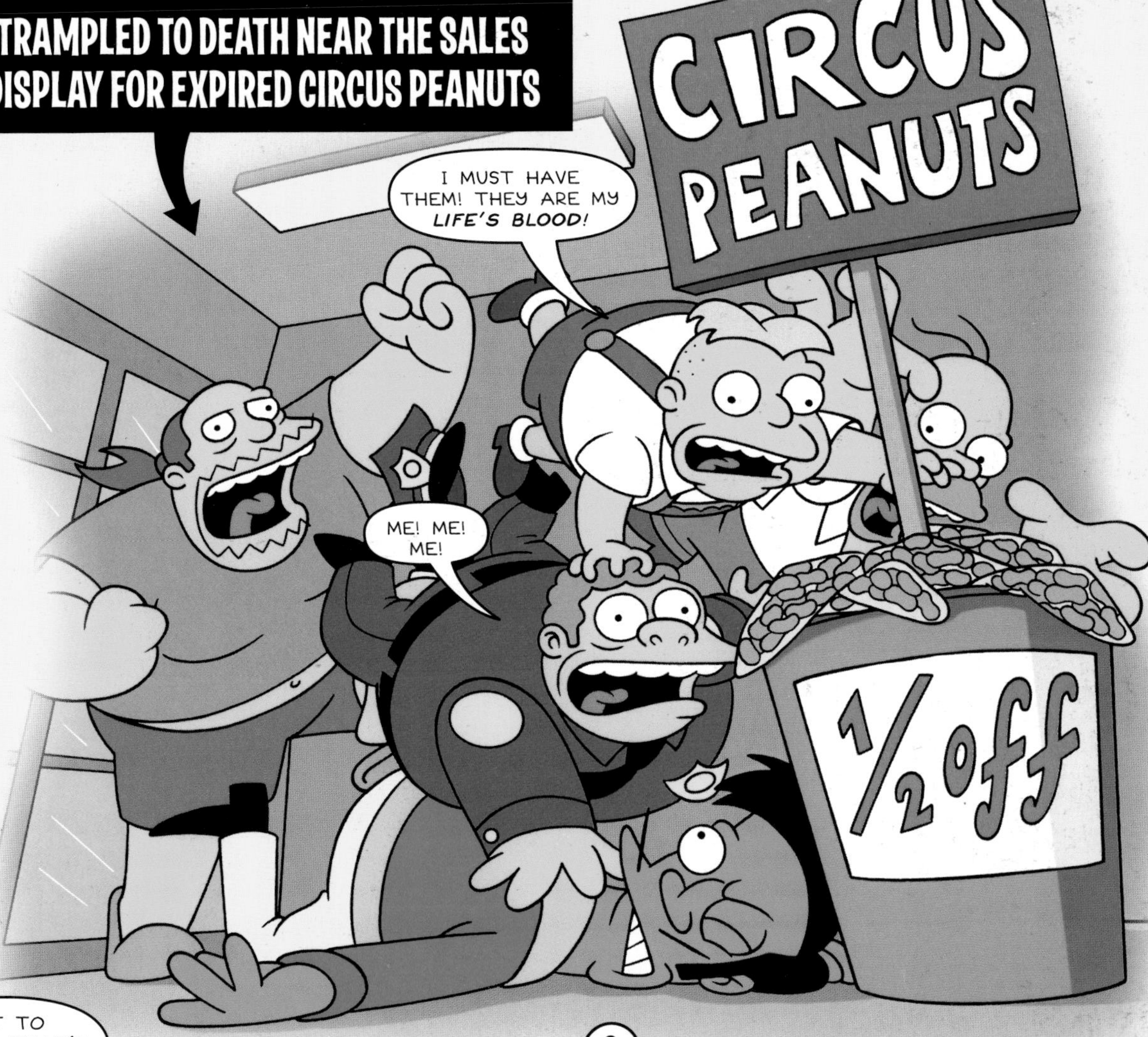

CIRCUS PEANUTS
I MUST HAVE THEM! THEY ARE MY *LIFE'S BLOOD!*
ME! ME! ME!
1/2 off

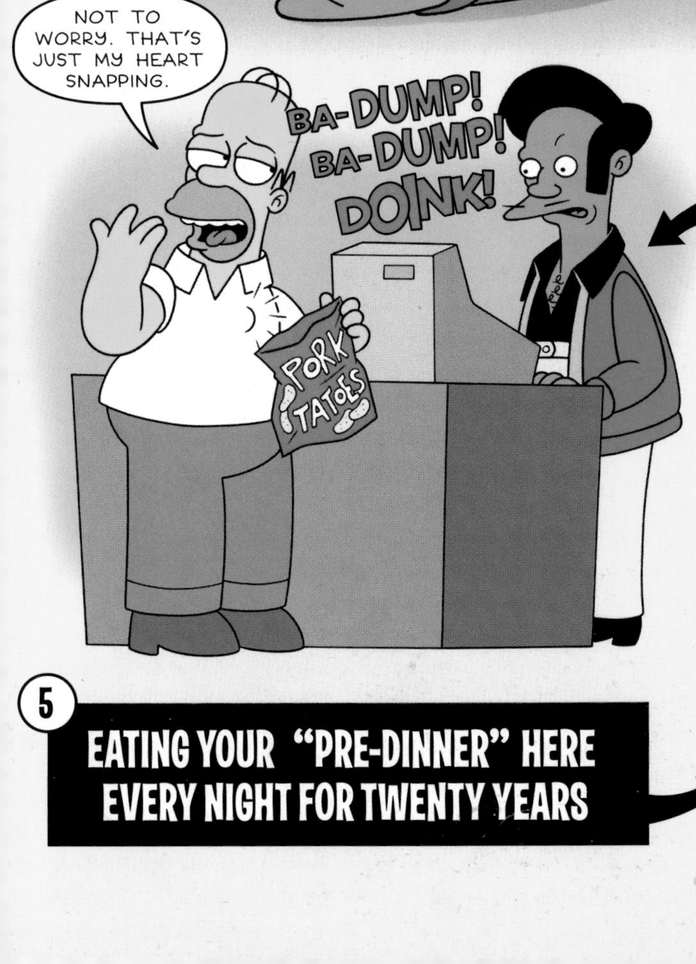

NOT TO WORRY. THAT'S JUST MY HEART SNAPPING.
BA-DUMP! BA-DUMP! DOINK!
PORK TATOES

6

YOUR PACEMAKER GETS TOO CLOSE TO THE MICROWAVE... AND/OR THE NITRATE-LADEN CHILI DOG IN THE MICROWAVE GETS TOO CLOSE TO YOUR MOUTH

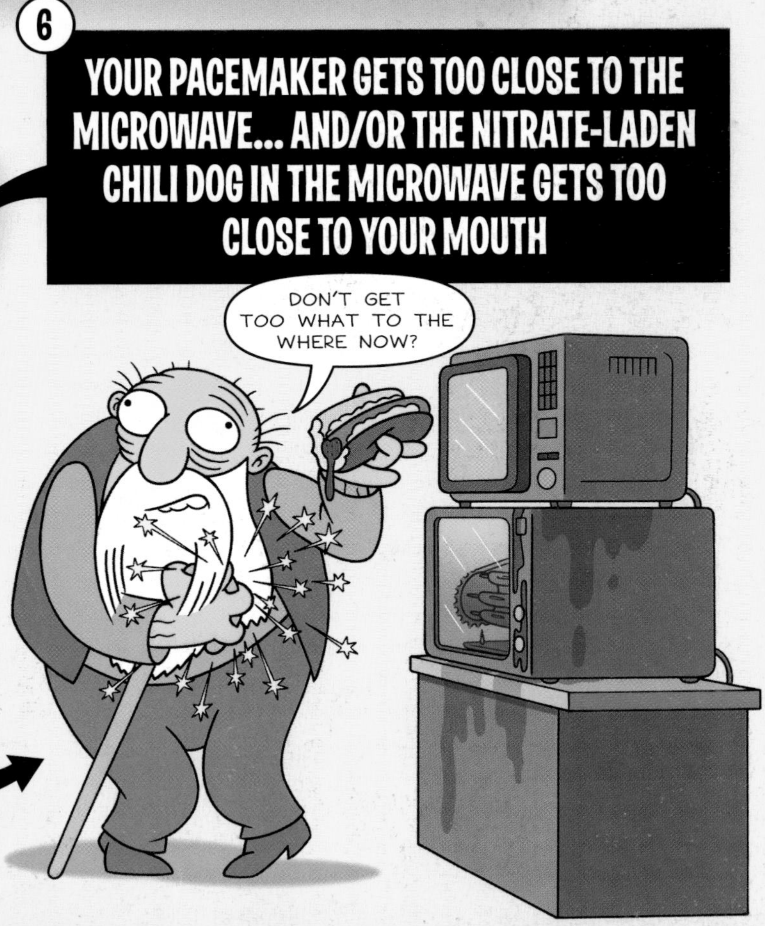

DON'T GET TOO WHAT TO THE WHERE NOW?

5

EATING YOUR "PRE-DINNER" HERE EVERY NIGHT FOR TWENTY YEARS

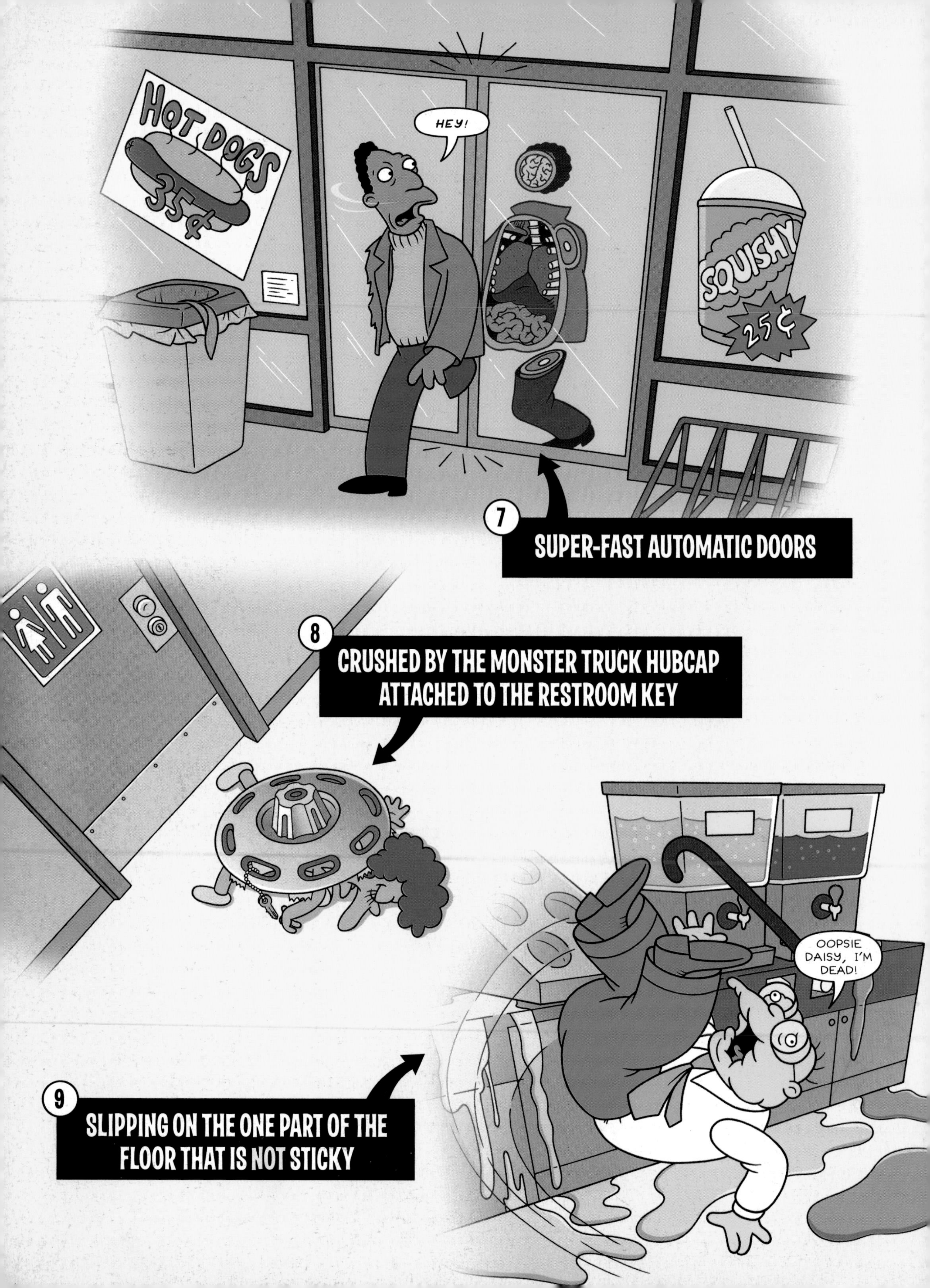
HOT DOGS
35¢
HEY!
SQUISHY
25¢
7
SUPER-FAST AUTOMATIC DOORS
8
CRUSHED BY THE MONSTER TRUCK HUBCAP ATTACHED TO THE RESTROOM KEY
OOPSIE DAISY, I'M DEAD!
9
SLIPPING ON THE ONE PART OF THE FLOOR THAT IS NOT STICKY

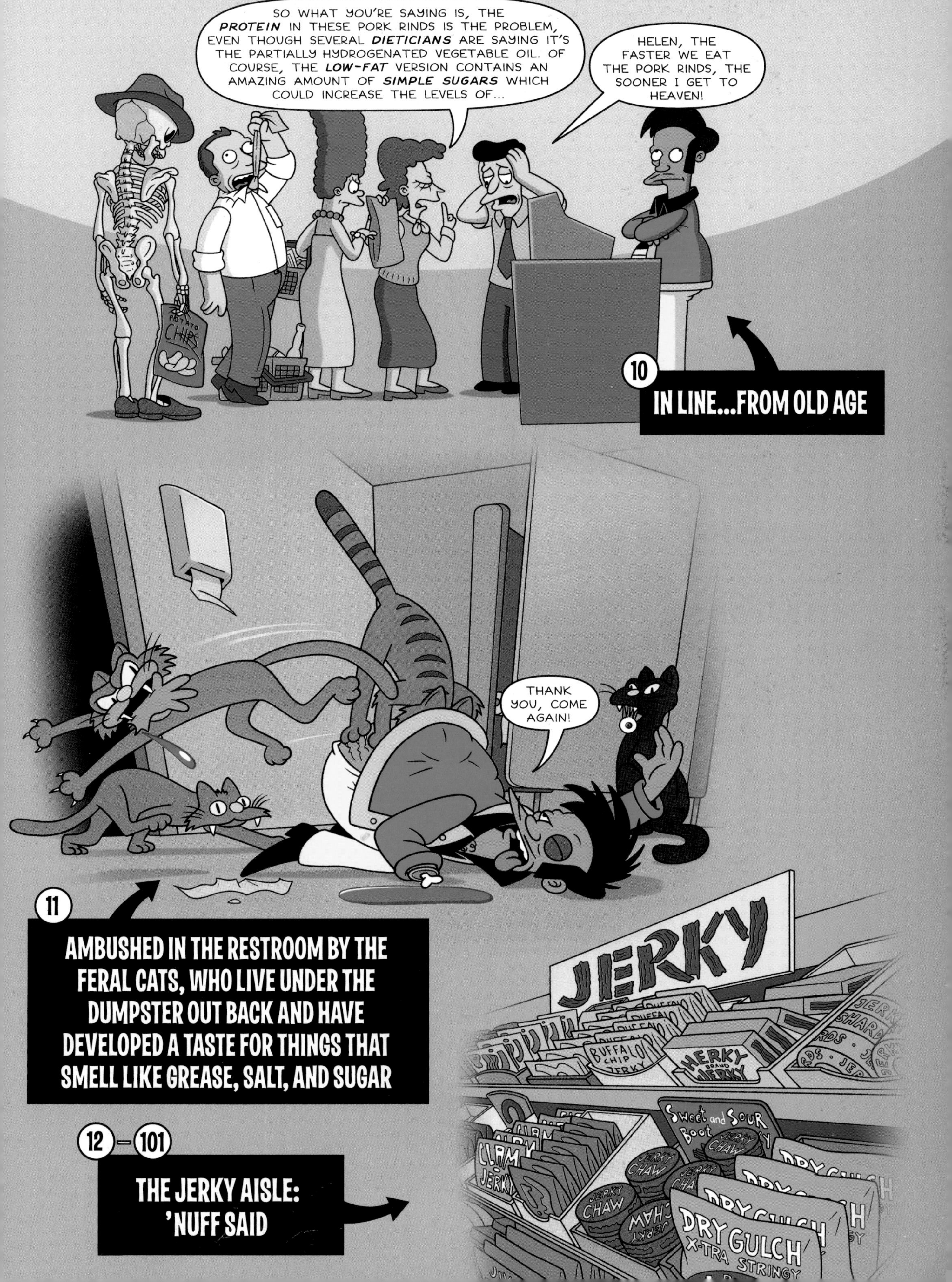

SO WHAT YOU'RE SAYING IS, THE PROTEIN IN THESE PORK RINDS IS THE PROBLEM, EVEN THOUGH SEVERAL DIETICIANS ARE SAYING IT'S THE PARTIALLY HYDROGENATED VEGETABLE OIL. OF COURSE, THE LOW-FAT VERSION CONTAINS AN AMAZING AMOUNT OF SIMPLE SUGARS WHICH COULD INCREASE THE LEVELS OF...
HELEN, THE FASTER WE EAT THE PORK RINDS, THE SOONER I GET TO HEAVEN!
POTATO CHIPS
10
IN LINE...FROM OLD AGE
THANK YOU, COME AGAIN!
11
AMBUSHED IN THE RESTROOM BY THE FERAL CATS, WHO LIVE UNDER THE DUMPSTER OUT BACK AND HAVE DEVELOPED A TASTE FOR THINGS THAT SMELL LIKE GREASE, SALT, AND SUGAR
JERKY
BUFFALO CHIP JERKY
HERKY BRAND JERKY
Sweet and SOUR Boot
JERKY CHAW
CLAM JERKY
DRY GULCH X-TRA STRINGY
12 – 101
THE JERKY AISLE: 'NUFF SAID

COMIC BOOK GUY'S
Best Costumes Ever - Part 3

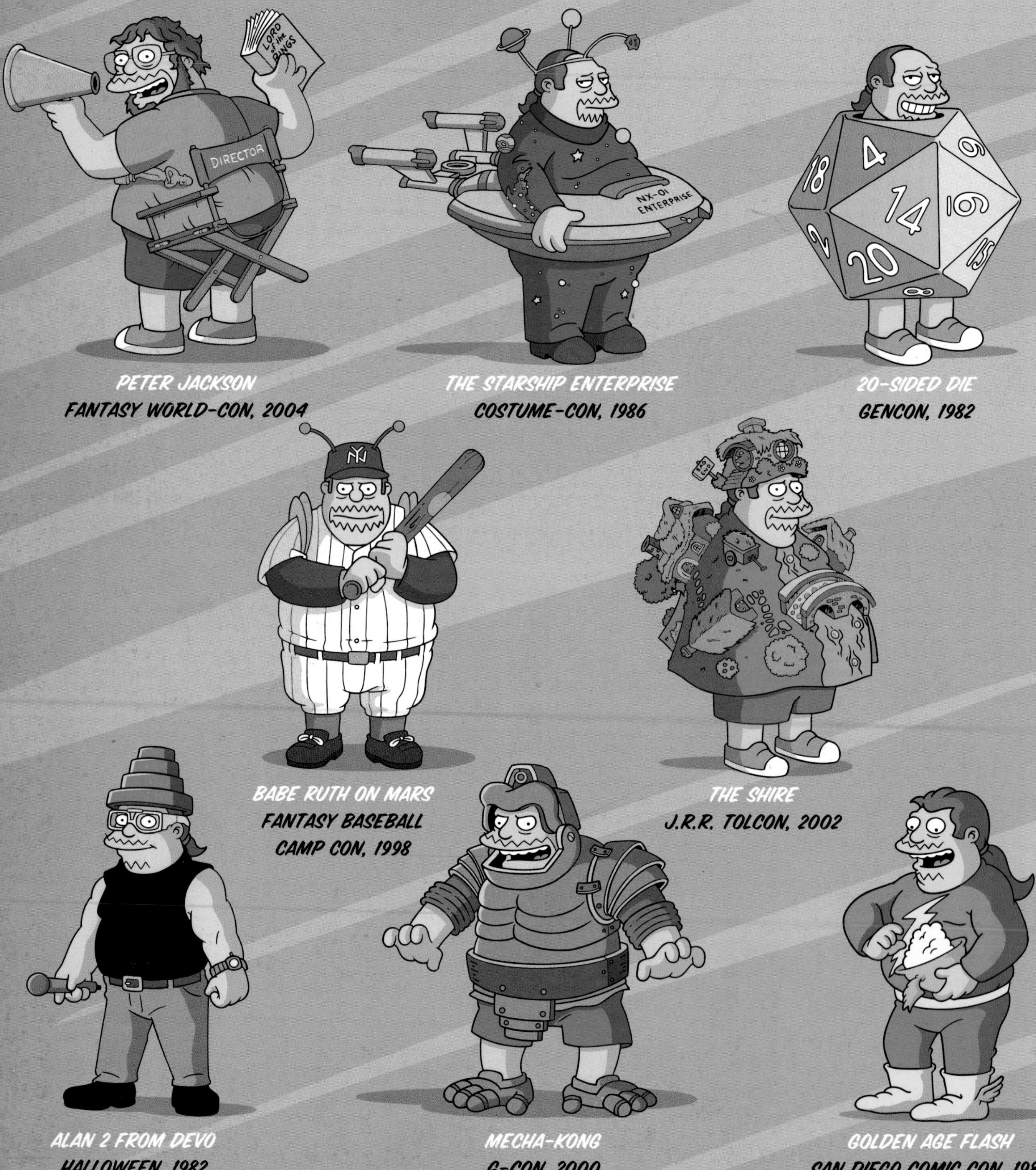
LORD of the RINGS
DIRECTOR
NX-01 ENTERPRISE
NY

PETER JACKSON
FANTASY WORLD-CON, 2004

THE STARSHIP ENTERPRISE
COSTUME-CON, 1986

20-SIDED DIE
GENCON, 1982

BABE RUTH ON MARS
FANTASY BASEBALL
CAMP CON, 1998

THE SHIRE
J.R.R. TOLCON, 2002

ALAN 2 FROM DEVO
HALLOWEEN, 1982

MECHA-KONG
G-CON, 2000

GOLDEN AGE FLASH
SAN DIEGO COMIC CON, 1980

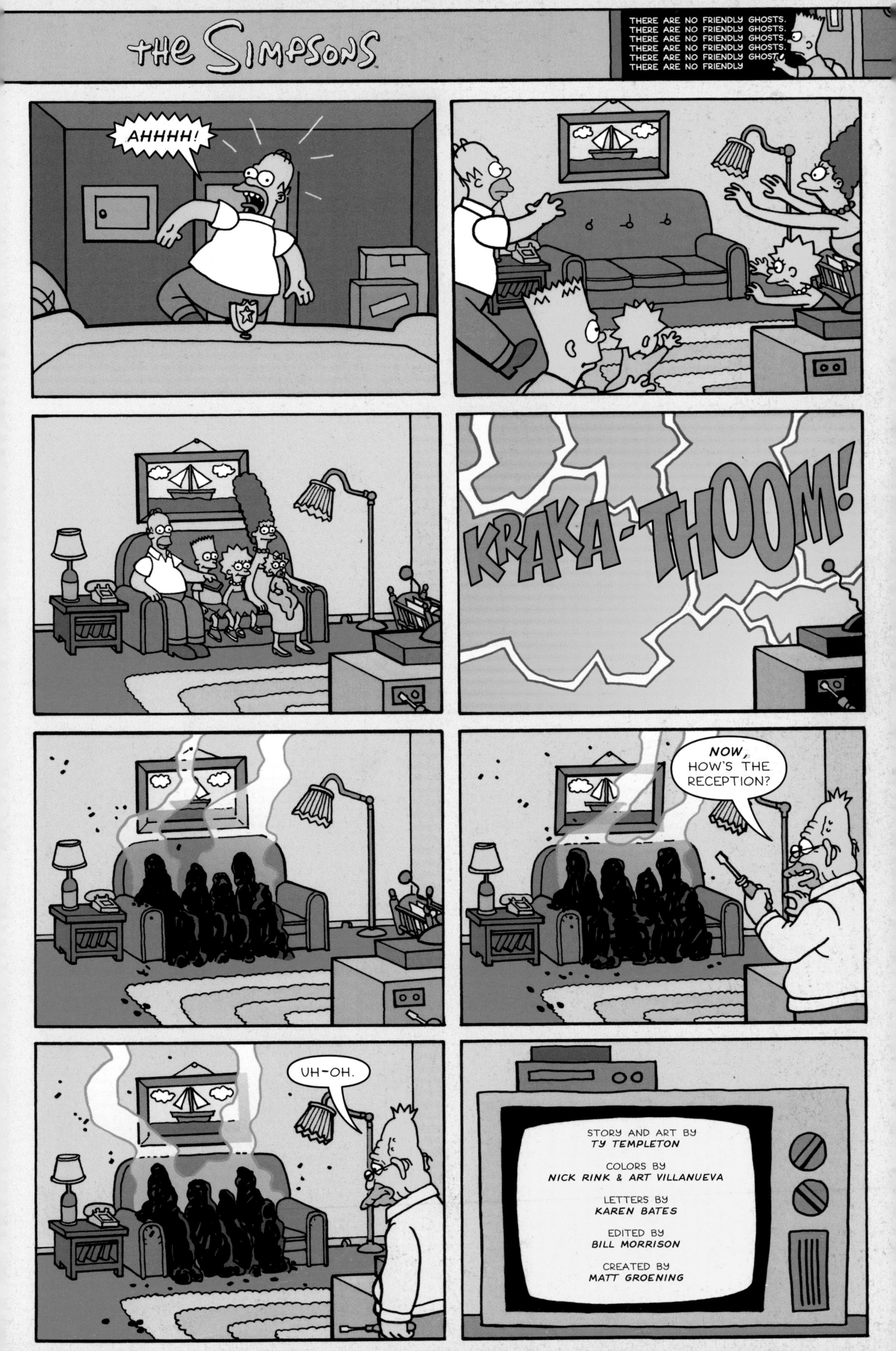
THE SIMPSONS
THERE ARE NO FRIENDLY GHOSTS.
THERE ARE NO FRIENDLY GHOSTS.
THERE ARE NO FRIENDLY GHOSTS.
THERE ARE NO FRIENDLY GHOSTS.
THERE ARE NO FRIENDLY GHOSTS.
THERE ARE NO FRIENDLY
AHHHH!
KRAKA-THOOM!
NOW, HOW'S THE RECEPTION?
UH-OH.
STORY AND ART BY TY TEMPLETON
COLORS BY NICK RINK & ART VILLANUEVA
LETTERS BY KAREN BATES
EDITED BY BILL MORRISON
CREATED BY MATT GROENING

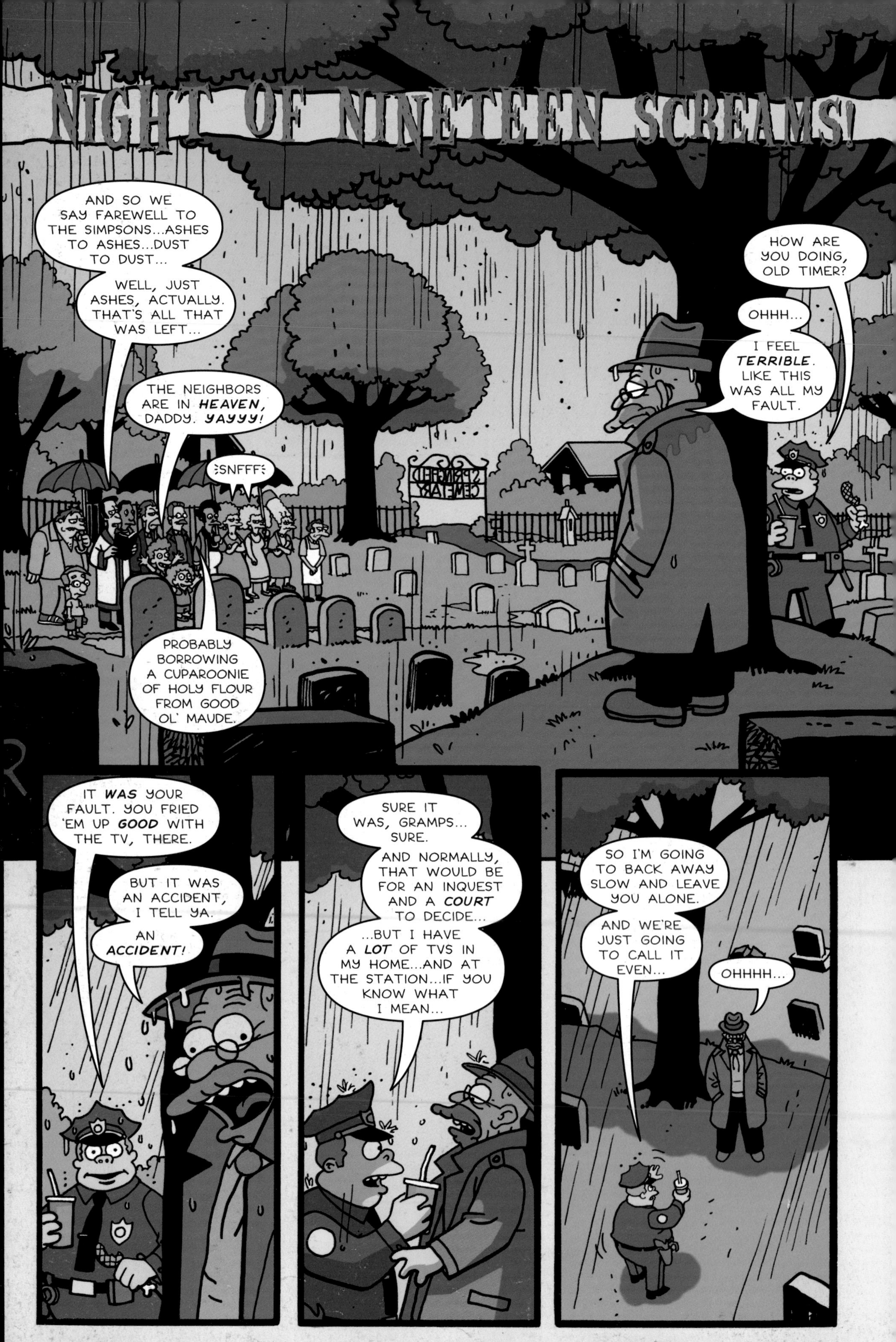
NIGHT OF NINETEEN SCREAMS!
AND SO WE SAY FAREWELL TO THE SIMPSONS...ASHES TO ASHES...DUST TO DUST...
WELL, JUST ASHES, ACTUALLY. THAT'S ALL THAT WAS LEFT...
THE NEIGHBORS ARE IN HEAVEN, DADDY. YAYYY!
SNFFF
PROBABLY BORROWING A CUPAROONIE OF HOLY FLOUR FROM GOOD OL' MAUDE.
SPRINGFIELD CEMETARY
HOW ARE YOU DOING, OLD TIMER?
OHHH...
I FEEL TERRIBLE. LIKE THIS WAS ALL MY FAULT.
IT WAS YOUR FAULT. YOU FRIED 'EM UP GOOD WITH THE TV, THERE.
BUT IT WAS AN ACCIDENT, I TELL YA.
AN ACCIDENT!
SURE IT WAS, GRAMPS... SURE.
AND NORMALLY, THAT WOULD BE FOR AN INQUEST AND A COURT TO DECIDE...
...BUT I HAVE A LOT OF TVS IN MY HOME...AND AT THE STATION...IF YOU KNOW WHAT I MEAN...
SO I'M GOING TO BACK AWAY SLOW AND LEAVE YOU ALONE.
AND WE'RE JUST GOING TO CALL IT EVEN...
OHHHH...

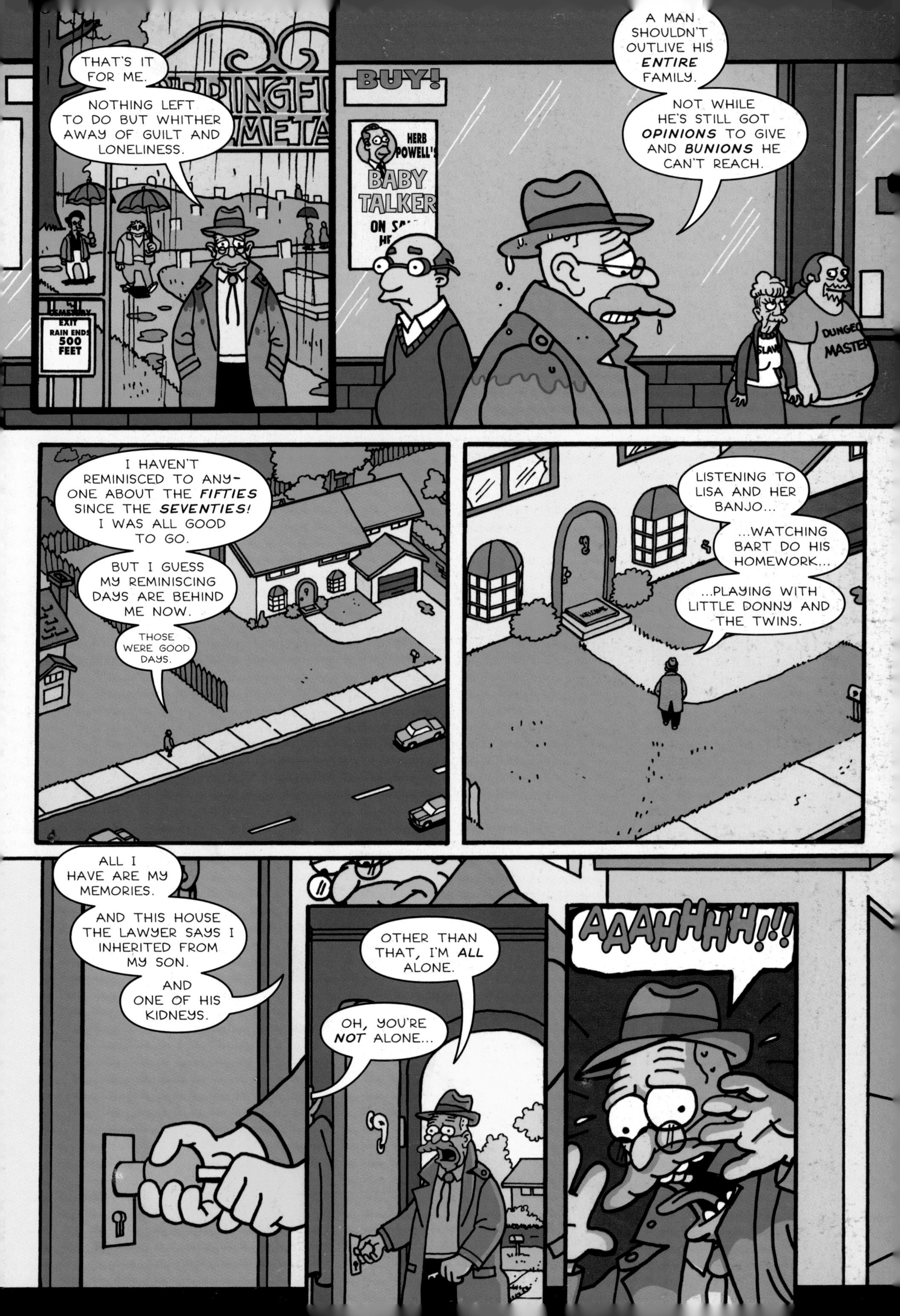
THAT'S IT FOR ME.
NOTHING LEFT TO DO BUT WHITHER AWAY OF GUILT AND LONELINESS.
BUY!
HERB POWELL'S BABY TALKER ON SALE
CEMETERY EXIT RAIN ENDS 500 FEET
A MAN SHOULDN'T OUTLIVE HIS ENTIRE FAMILY.
NOT WHILE HE'S STILL GOT OPINIONS TO GIVE AND BUNIONS HE CAN'T REACH.
DUNGEON MASTER
I HAVEN'T REMINISCED TO ANYONE ABOUT THE FIFTIES SINCE THE SEVENTIES! I WAS ALL GOOD TO GO.
BUT I GUESS MY REMINISCING DAYS ARE BEHIND ME NOW.
THOSE WERE GOOD DAYS.
LISTENING TO LISA AND HER BANJO...
...WATCHING BART DO HIS HOMEWORK...
...PLAYING WITH LITTLE DONNY AND THE TWINS.
WELCOME
ALL I HAVE ARE MY MEMORIES.
AND THIS HOUSE THE LAWYER SAYS I INHERITED FROM MY SON.
AND ONE OF HIS KIDNEYS.
OTHER THAN THAT, I'M ALL ALONE.
OH, YOU'RE NOT ALONE...
AAAHHHH!!!

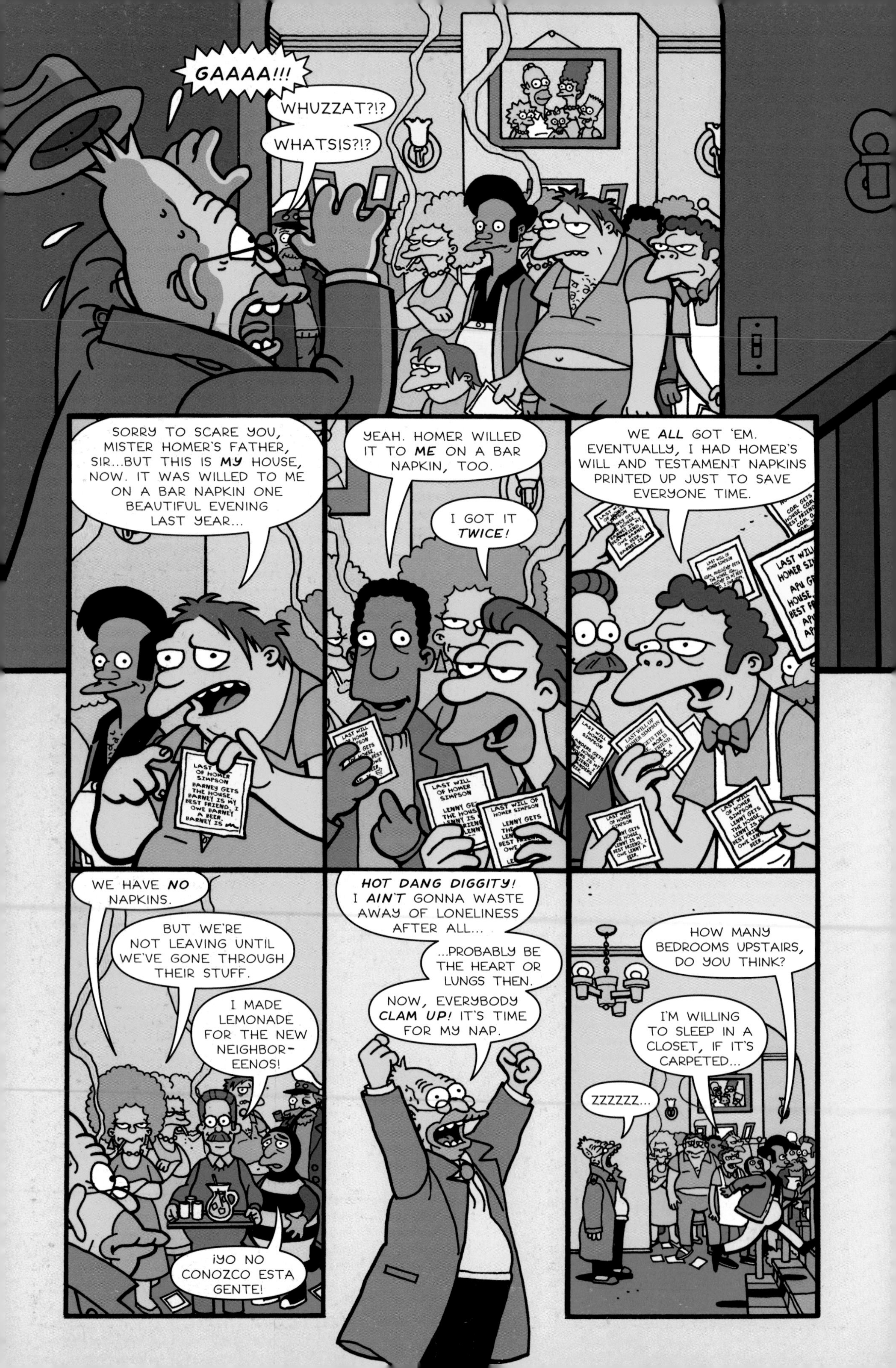
GAAAA!!!
WHUZZAT?!?
WHATSIS?!?
SORRY TO SCARE YOU, MISTER HOMER'S FATHER, SIR...BUT THIS IS MY HOUSE, NOW. IT WAS WILLED TO ME ON A BAR NAPKIN ONE BEAUTIFUL EVENING LAST YEAR...
LAST WILL OF HOMER SIMPSON BARNEY GETS THE HOUSE. BARNEY IS MY BEST FRIEND. I OWE BARNEY A BEER. BARNEY IS
YEAH. HOMER WILLED IT TO ME ON A BAR NAPKIN, TOO.
I GOT IT TWICE!
LAST WILL OF HOMER SIMPSON LENNY GETS THE HOUSE.
WE ALL GOT 'EM. EVENTUALLY, I HAD HOMER'S WILL AND TESTAMENT NAPKINS PRINTED UP JUST TO SAVE EVERYONE TIME.
LAST WILL OF HOMER SIMPSON APU GETS HOUSE. BEST FRIEND.
LAST WILL OF HOMER SIMPSON LENNY GETS THE HOUSE. LENNY IS MY BEST FRIEND. I OWE LENNY A BEER.
WE HAVE NO NAPKINS.
BUT WE'RE NOT LEAVING UNTIL WE'VE GONE THROUGH THEIR STUFF.
I MADE LEMONADE FOR THE NEW NEIGHBOR-EENOS!
¡YO NO CONOZCO ESTA GENTE!
HOT DANG DIGGITY! I AIN'T GONNA WASTE AWAY OF LONELINESS AFTER ALL...
...PROBABLY BE THE HEART OR LUNGS THEN.
NOW, EVERYBODY CLAM UP! IT'S TIME FOR MY NAP.
HOW MANY BEDROOMS UPSTAIRS, DO YOU THINK?
I'M WILLING TO SLEEP IN A CLOSET, IF IT'S CARPETED...
ZZZZZZ...

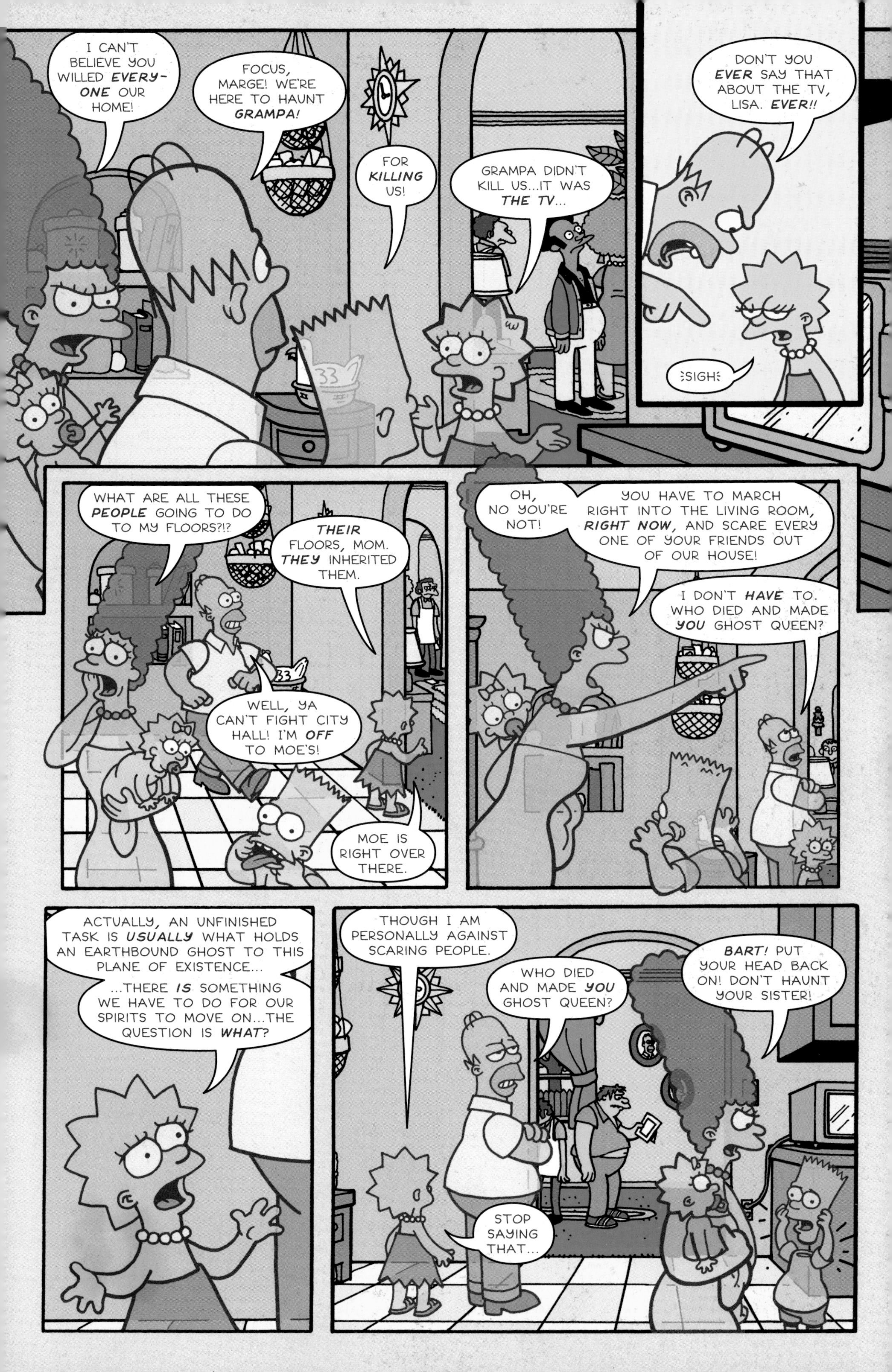
I CAN'T BELIEVE YOU WILLED EVERY-ONE OUR HOME!
FOCUS, MARGE! WE'RE HERE TO HAUNT GRAMPA!
FOR KILLING US!
GRAMPA DIDN'T KILL US...IT WAS THE TV...
DON'T YOU EVER SAY THAT ABOUT THE TV, LISA. EVER!!
:SIGH:
WHAT ARE ALL THESE PEOPLE GOING TO DO TO MY FLOORS?!?
THEIR FLOORS, MOM. THEY INHERITED THEM.
WELL, YA CAN'T FIGHT CITY HALL! I'M OFF TO MOE'S!
MOE IS RIGHT OVER THERE.
OH, NO YOU'RE NOT!
YOU HAVE TO MARCH RIGHT INTO THE LIVING ROOM, RIGHT NOW, AND SCARE EVERY ONE OF YOUR FRIENDS OUT OF OUR HOUSE!
I DON'T HAVE TO. WHO DIED AND MADE YOU GHOST QUEEN?
ACTUALLY, AN UNFINISHED TASK IS USUALLY WHAT HOLDS AN EARTHBOUND GHOST TO THIS PLANE OF EXISTENCE...
...THERE IS SOMETHING WE HAVE TO DO FOR OUR SPIRITS TO MOVE ON...THE QUESTION IS WHAT?
THOUGH I AM PERSONALLY AGAINST SCARING PEOPLE.
WHO DIED AND MADE YOU GHOST QUEEN?
BART! PUT YOUR HEAD BACK ON! DON'T HAUNT YOUR SISTER!
STOP SAYING THAT...

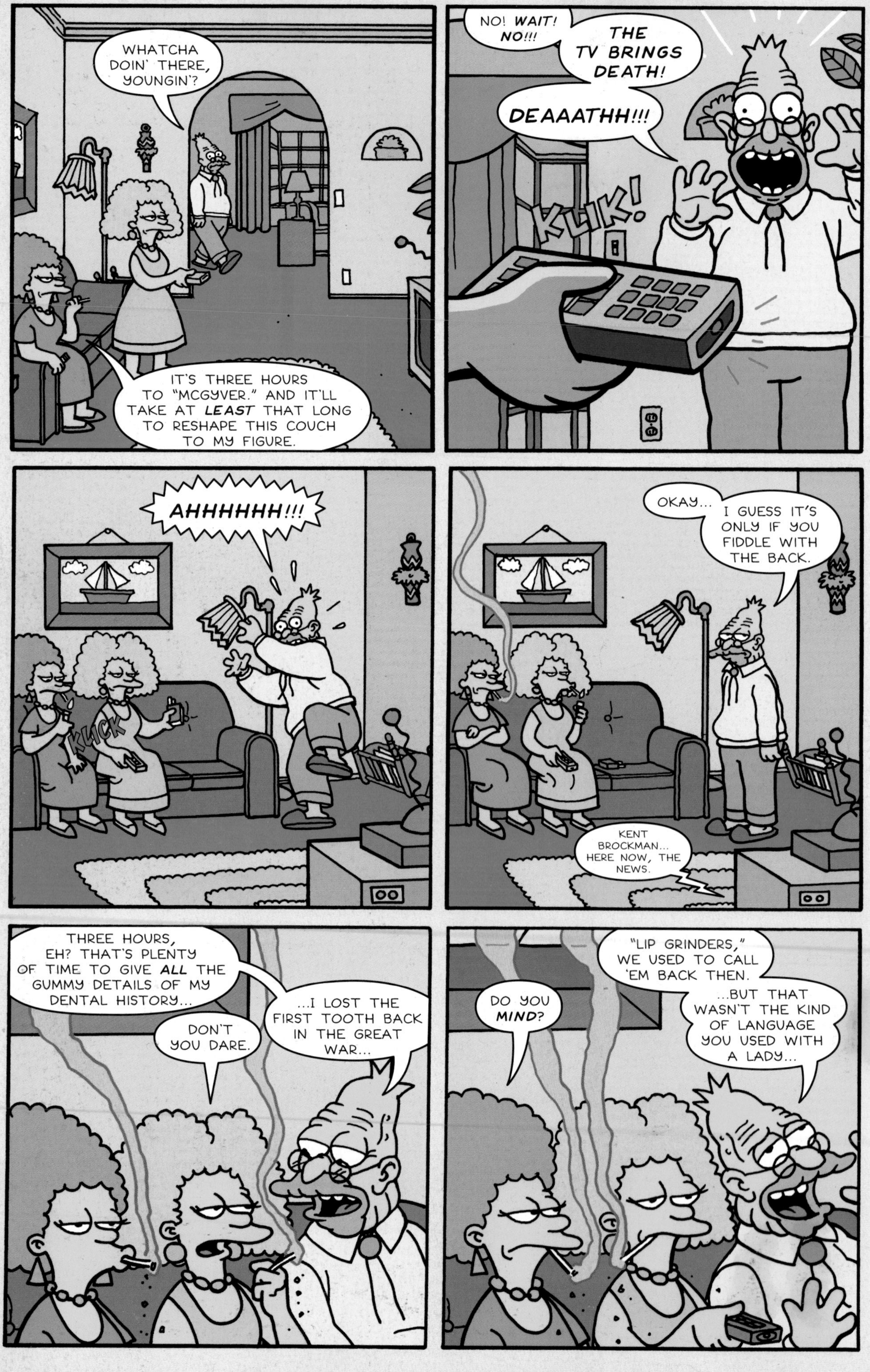
WHATCHA DOIN' THERE, YOUNGIN'?
IT'S THREE HOURS TO "MCGYVER." AND IT'LL TAKE AT LEAST THAT LONG TO RESHAPE THIS COUCH TO MY FIGURE.
NO! WAIT! NO!!!
THE TV BRINGS DEATH!
DEAAATHH!!!
KLIK!
AHHHHHH!!!
KLICK
OKAY...
I GUESS IT'S ONLY IF YOU FIDDLE WITH THE BACK.
KENT BROCKMAN... HERE NOW, THE NEWS.
THREE HOURS, EH? THAT'S PLENTY OF TIME TO GIVE ALL THE GUMMY DETAILS OF MY DENTAL HISTORY...
DON'T YOU DARE.
...I LOST THE FIRST TOOTH BACK IN THE GREAT WAR...
DO YOU MIND?
"LIP GRINDERS," WE USED TO CALL 'EM BACK THEN.
...BUT THAT WASN'T THE KIND OF LANGUAGE YOU USED WITH A LADY...

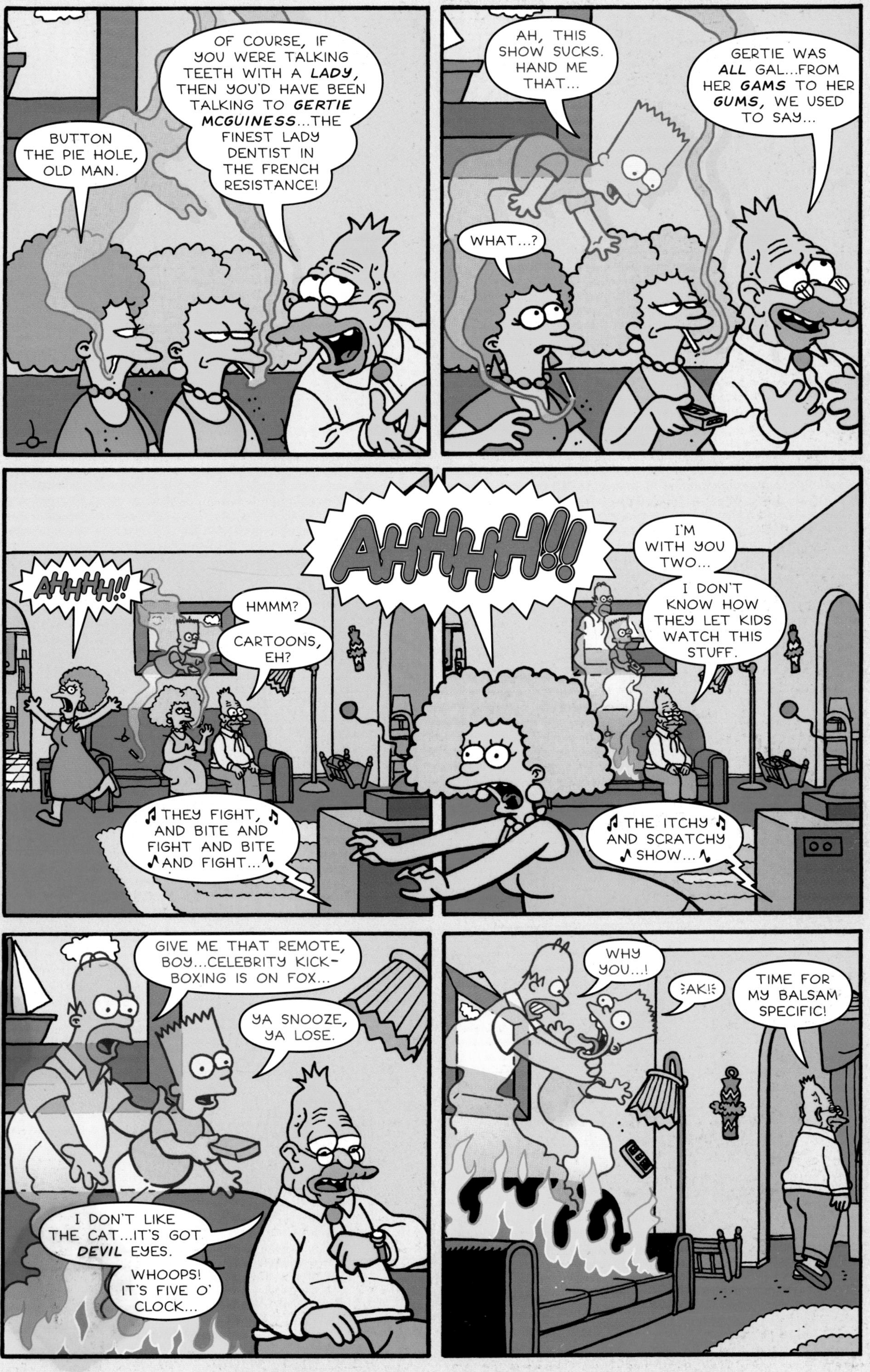

OF COURSE, IF YOU WERE TALKING TEETH WITH A *LADY,* THEN YOU'D HAVE BEEN TALKING TO *GERTIE MCGUINESS*...THE FINEST LADY DENTIST IN THE FRENCH RESISTANCE!
BUTTON THE PIE HOLE, OLD MAN.
AH, THIS SHOW SUCKS. HAND ME THAT...
GERTIE WAS *ALL* GAL...FROM HER *GAMS* TO HER *GUMS,* WE USED TO SAY...
WHAT...?
AHHHH!!
HMMM?
CARTOONS, EH?
THEY FIGHT, AND BITE AND FIGHT AND BITE AND FIGHT...
AHHHHH!!
I'M WITH YOU TWO...
I DON'T KNOW HOW THEY LET KIDS WATCH THIS STUFF.
THE ITCHY AND SCRATCHY SHOW...
GIVE ME THAT REMOTE, BOY...CELEBRITY KICK-BOXING IS ON FOX...
YA SNOOZE, YA LOSE.
I DON'T LIKE THE CAT...IT'S GOT *DEVIL* EYES.
WHOOPS! IT'S FIVE O' CLOCK...
WHY YOU...!
AK!
TIME FOR MY BALSAM SPECIFIC!

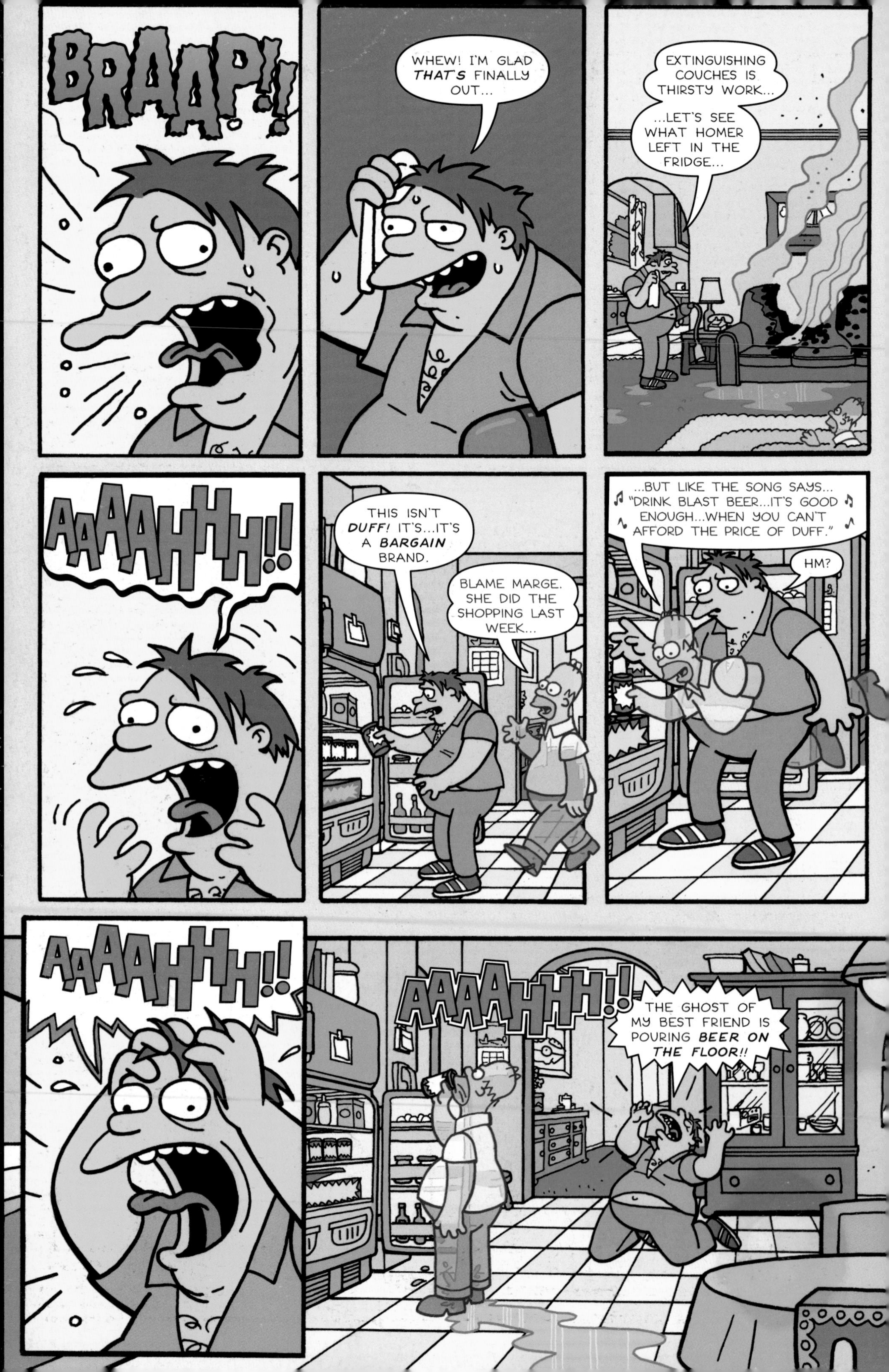

BRAAP!!
WHEW! I'M GLAD THAT'S FINALLY OUT...
EXTINGUISHING COUCHES IS THIRSTY WORK...
...LET'S SEE WHAT HOMER LEFT IN THE FRIDGE...
AAAAHHHH!!
THIS ISN'T DUFF! IT'S...IT'S A BARGAIN BRAND.
BLAME MARGE. SHE DID THE SHOPPING LAST WEEK...
...BUT LIKE THE SONG SAYS... "DRINK BLAST BEER...IT'S GOOD ENOUGH...WHEN YOU CAN'T AFFORD THE PRICE OF DUFF."
HM?
AAAAHHHH!!
AAAAHHH!!
THE GHOST OF MY BEST FRIEND IS POURING BEER ON THE FLOOR!!

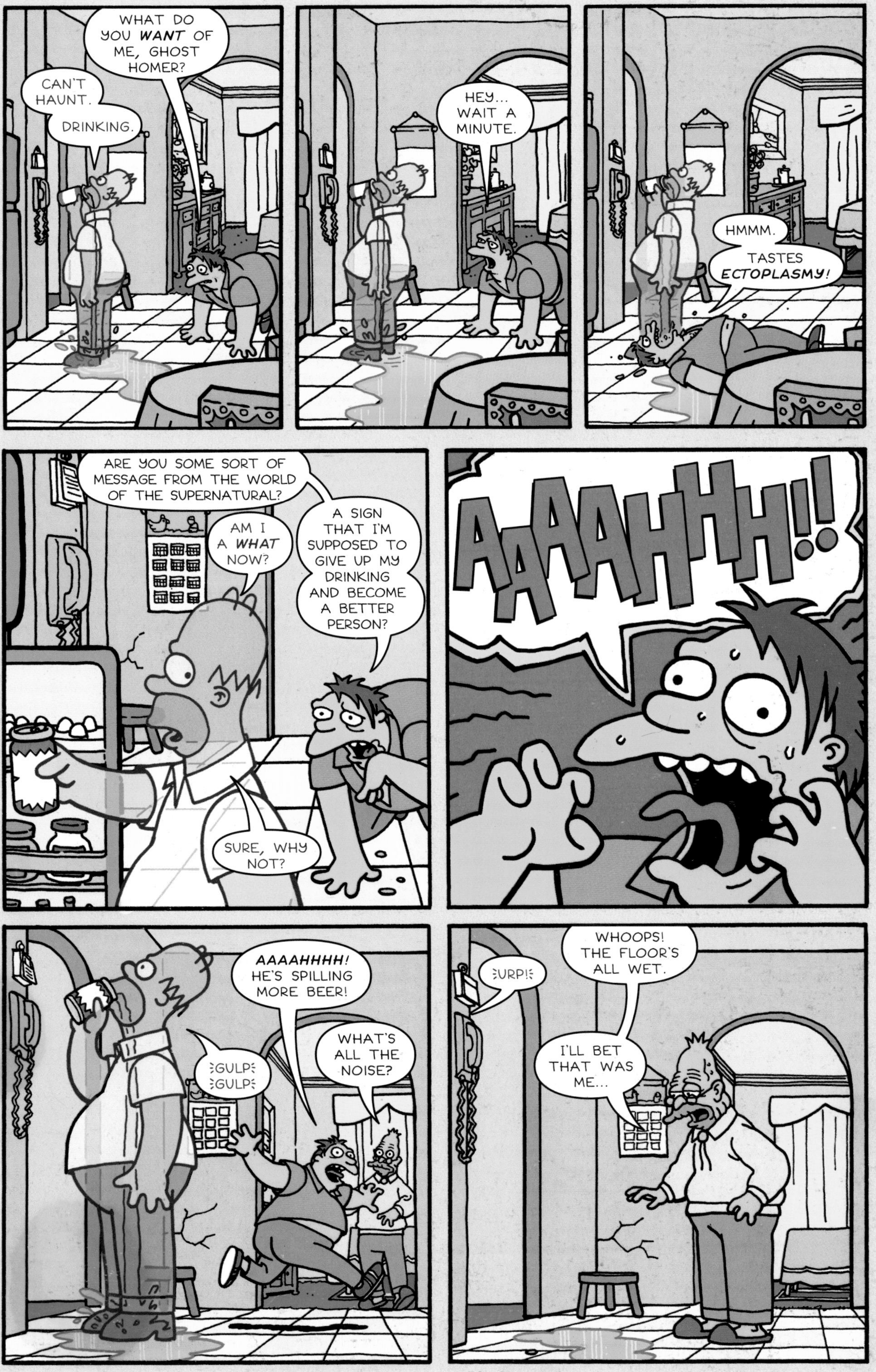

WHAT DO YOU WANT OF ME, GHOST HOMER?
CAN'T HAUNT.
DRINKING.
HEY... WAIT A MINUTE.
HMMM.
TASTES ECTOPLASMY!
ARE YOU SOME SORT OF MESSAGE FROM THE WORLD OF THE SUPERNATURAL?
AM I A WHAT NOW?
A SIGN THAT I'M SUPPOSED TO GIVE UP MY DRINKING AND BECOME A BETTER PERSON?
SURE, WHY NOT?
AAAAHHHH!!
AAAAHHHH! HE'S SPILLING MORE BEER!
GULP GULP
WHAT'S ALL THE NOISE?
URP!
WHOOPS! THE FLOOR'S ALL WET.
I'LL BET THAT WAS ME...

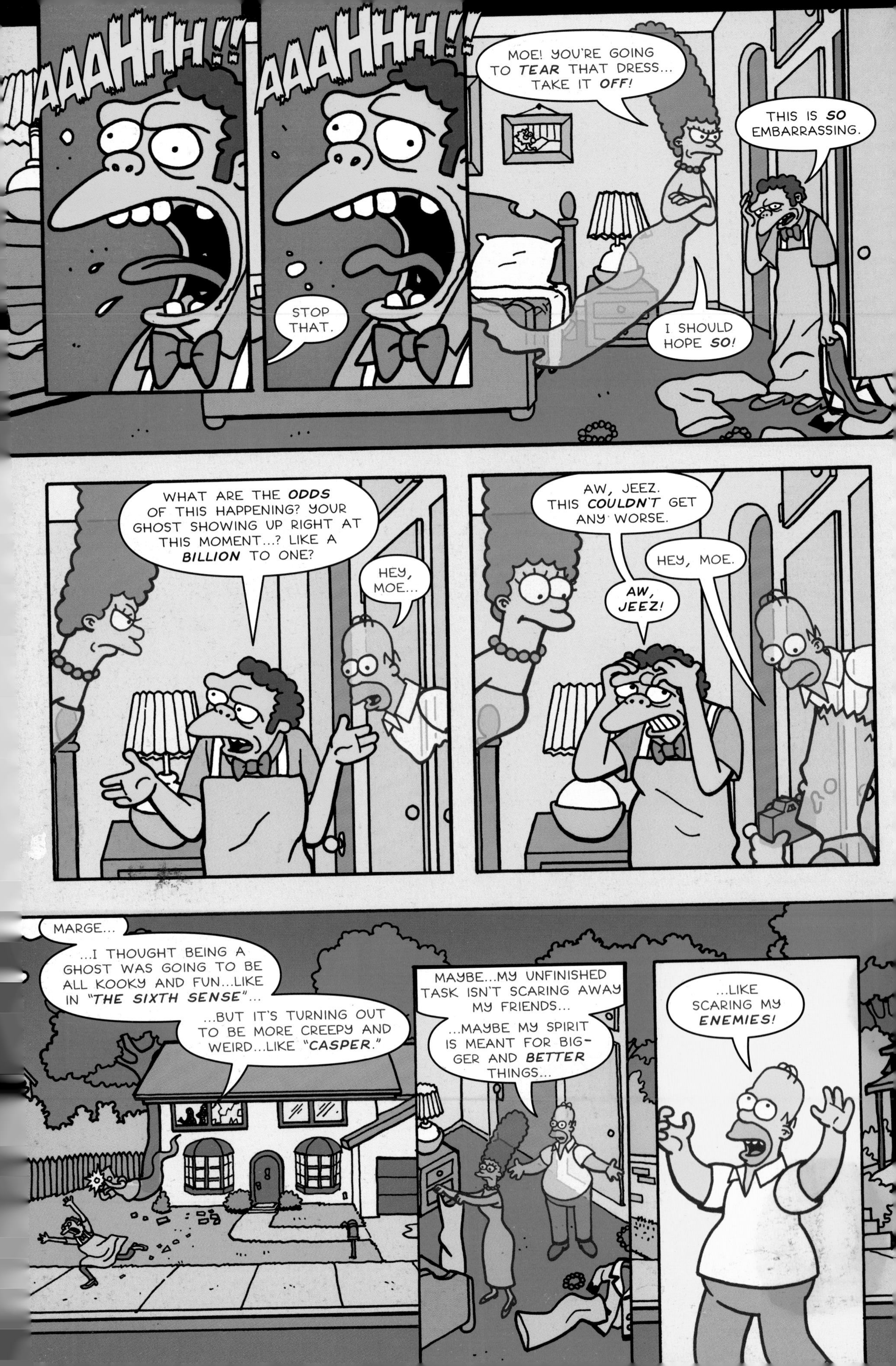
AAAHHH!!
AAAHHH!!
STOP THAT.
MOE! YOU'RE GOING TO TEAR THAT DRESS... TAKE IT OFF!
THIS IS SO EMBARRASSING.
I SHOULD HOPE SO!
WHAT ARE THE ODDS OF THIS HAPPENING? YOUR GHOST SHOWING UP RIGHT AT THIS MOMENT...? LIKE A BILLION TO ONE?
HEY, MOE...
AW, JEEZ. THIS COULDN'T GET ANY WORSE.
HEY, MOE.
AW, JEEZ!
MARGE...
...I THOUGHT BEING A GHOST WAS GOING TO BE ALL KOOKY AND FUN...LIKE IN "THE SIXTH SENSE"...
...BUT IT'S TURNING OUT TO BE MORE CREEPY AND WEIRD...LIKE "CASPER."
MAYBE...MY UNFINISHED TASK ISN'T SCARING AWAY MY FRIENDS...
...MAYBE MY SPIRIT IS MEANT FOR BIGGER AND BETTER THINGS...
...LIKE SCARING MY ENEMIES!

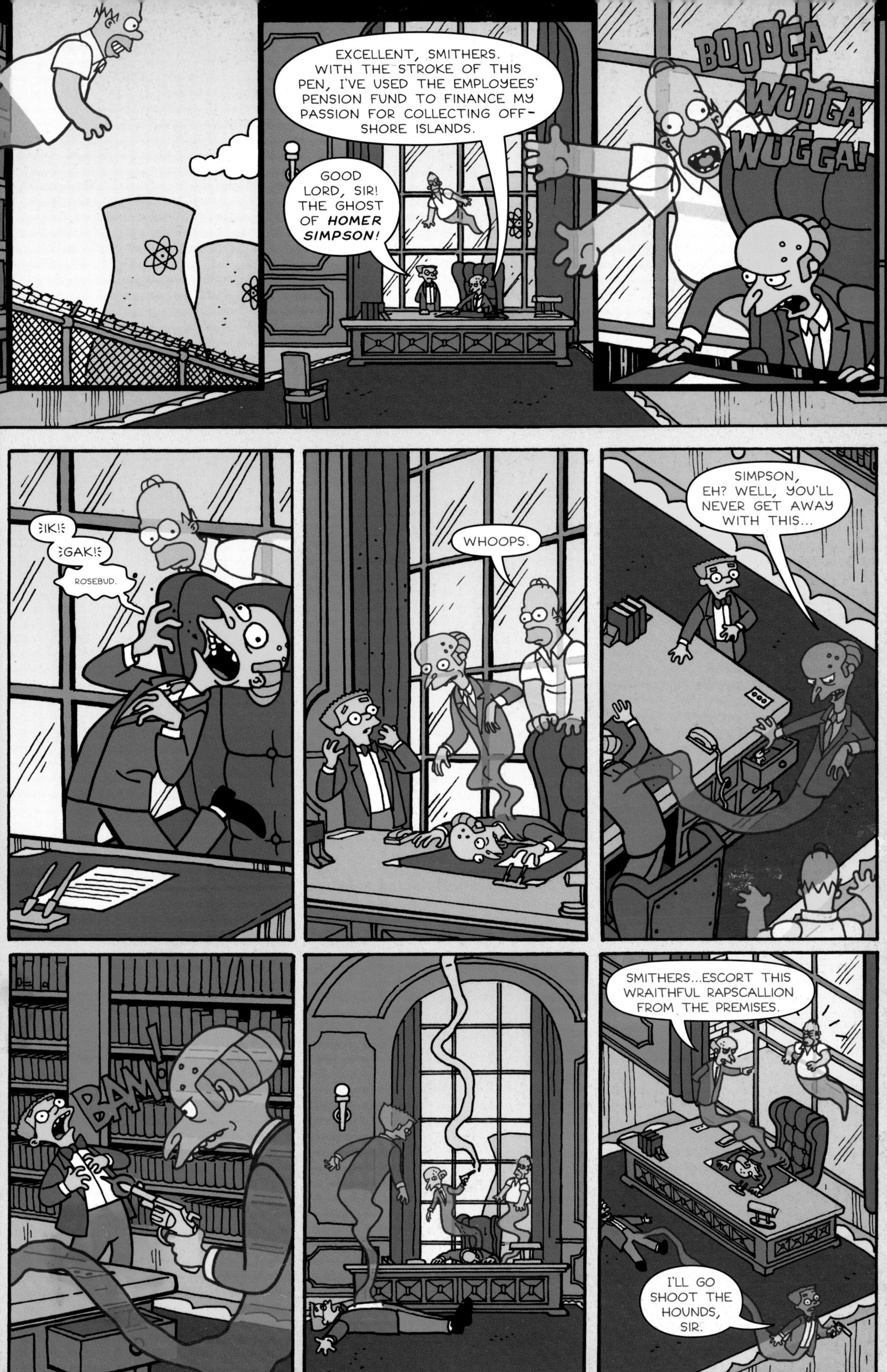
EXCELLENT, SMITHERS. WITH THE STROKE OF THIS PEN, I'VE USED THE EMPLOYEES' PENSION FUND TO FINANCE MY PASSION FOR COLLECTING OFF-SHORE ISLANDS.
GOOD LORD, SIR! THE GHOST OF HOMER SIMPSON!
BOOOGA WOOGA WUGGA!
IK!
GAK!
ROSEBUD.
WHOOPS.
SIMPSON, EH? WELL, YOU'LL NEVER GET AWAY WITH THIS...
BAM!
SMITHERS...ESCORT THIS WRAITHFUL RAPSCALLION FROM THE PREMISES.
I'LL GO SHOOT THE HOUNDS, SIR.

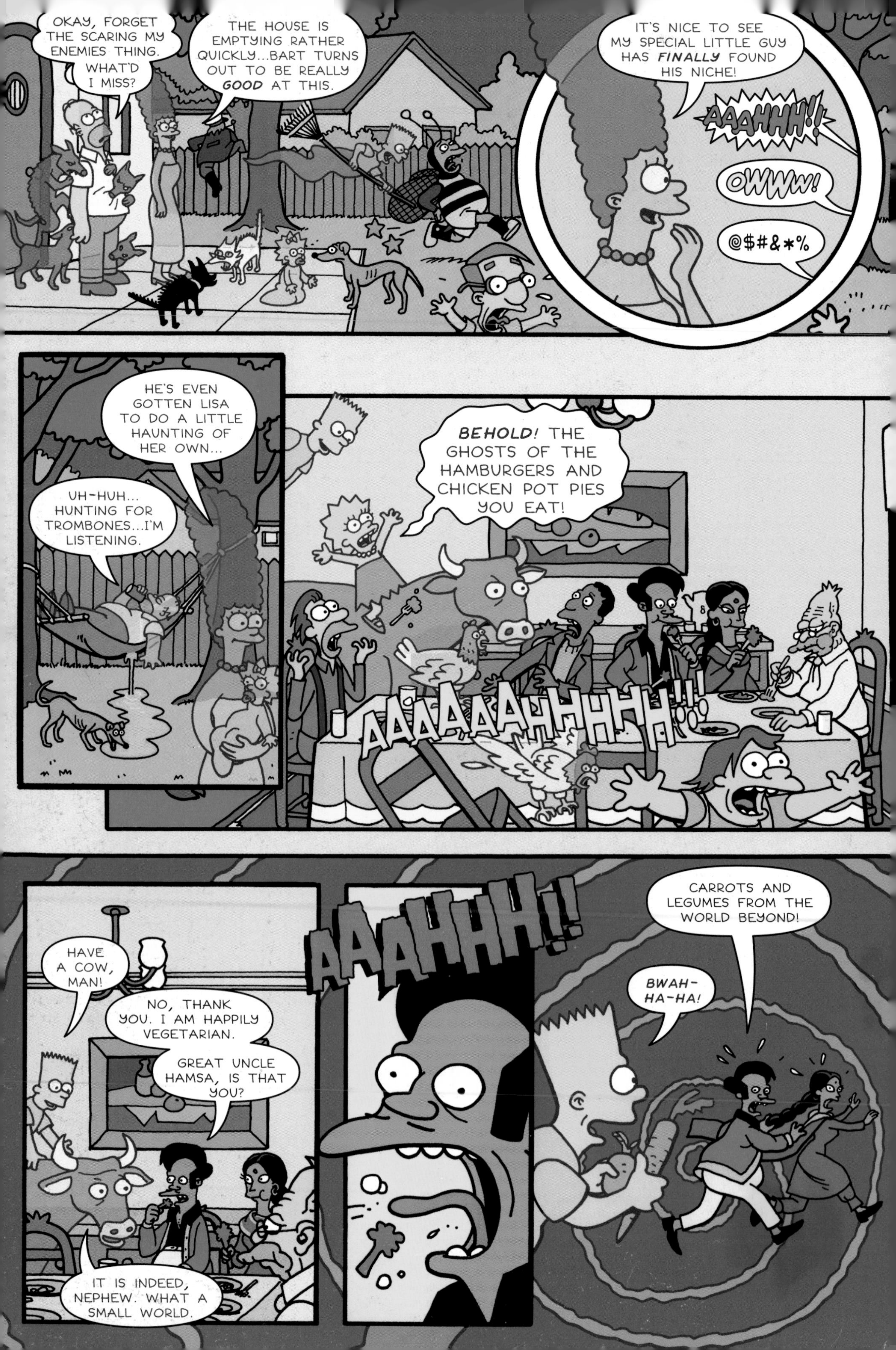
OKAY, FORGET THE SCARING MY ENEMIES THING. WHAT'D I MISS?
THE HOUSE IS EMPTYING RATHER QUICKLY...BART TURNS OUT TO BE REALLY GOOD AT THIS.
IT'S NICE TO SEE MY SPECIAL LITTLE GUY HAS FINALLY FOUND HIS NICHE!
AAAHHH!!
OWWW!
@$#&*%
HE'S EVEN GOTTEN LISA TO DO A LITTLE HAUNTING OF HER OWN...
UH-HUH... HUNTING FOR TROMBONES...I'M LISTENING.
BEHOLD! THE GHOSTS OF THE HAMBURGERS AND CHICKEN POT PIES YOU EAT!
AAAAAAHHHHHH!!!
HAVE A COW, MAN!
NO, THANK YOU. I AM HAPPILY VEGETARIAN.
GREAT UNCLE HAMSA, IS THAT YOU?
IT IS INDEED, NEPHEW. WHAT A SMALL WORLD.
AAAHHH!!
CARROTS AND LEGUMES FROM THE WORLD BEYOND!
BWAH-HA-HA!

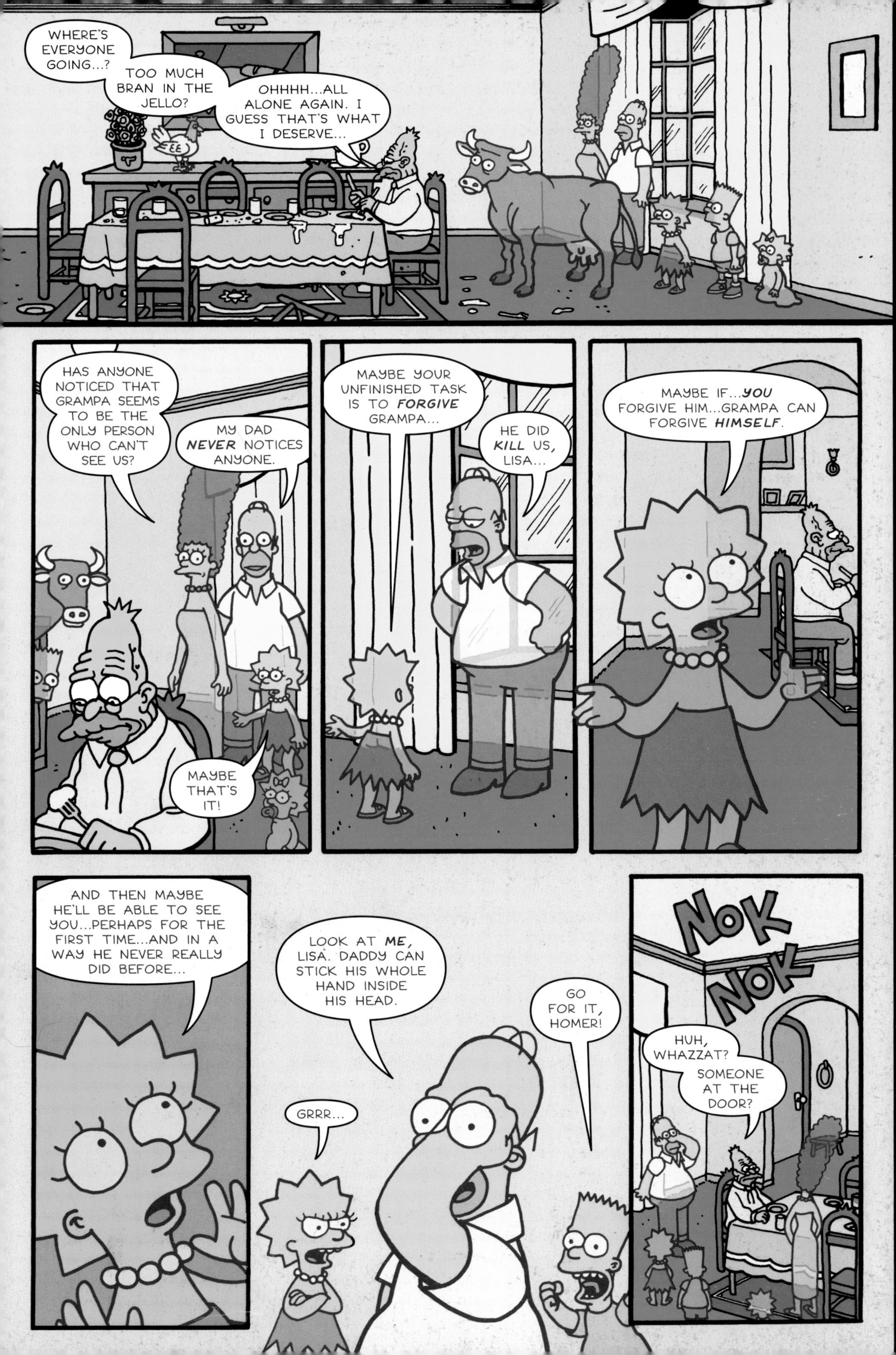
WHERE'S EVERYONE GOING...?
TOO MUCH BRAN IN THE JELLO?
OHHHH...ALL ALONE AGAIN. I GUESS THAT'S WHAT I DESERVE...
HAS ANYONE NOTICED THAT GRAMPA SEEMS TO BE THE ONLY PERSON WHO CAN'T SEE US?
MY DAD **NEVER** NOTICES ANYONE.
MAYBE THAT'S IT!
MAYBE YOUR UNFINISHED TASK IS TO **FORGIVE** GRAMPA...
HE DID **KILL** US, LISA...
MAYBE IF...**YOU** FORGIVE HIM...GRAMPA CAN FORGIVE **HIMSELF**.
AND THEN MAYBE HE'LL BE ABLE TO SEE YOU...PERHAPS FOR THE FIRST TIME...AND IN A WAY HE NEVER REALLY DID BEFORE...
LOOK AT **ME**, LISA. DADDY CAN STICK HIS WHOLE HAND INSIDE HIS HEAD.
GRRR...
GO FOR IT, HOMER!
NOK
NOK
HUH, WHAZZAT?
SOMEONE AT THE DOOR?

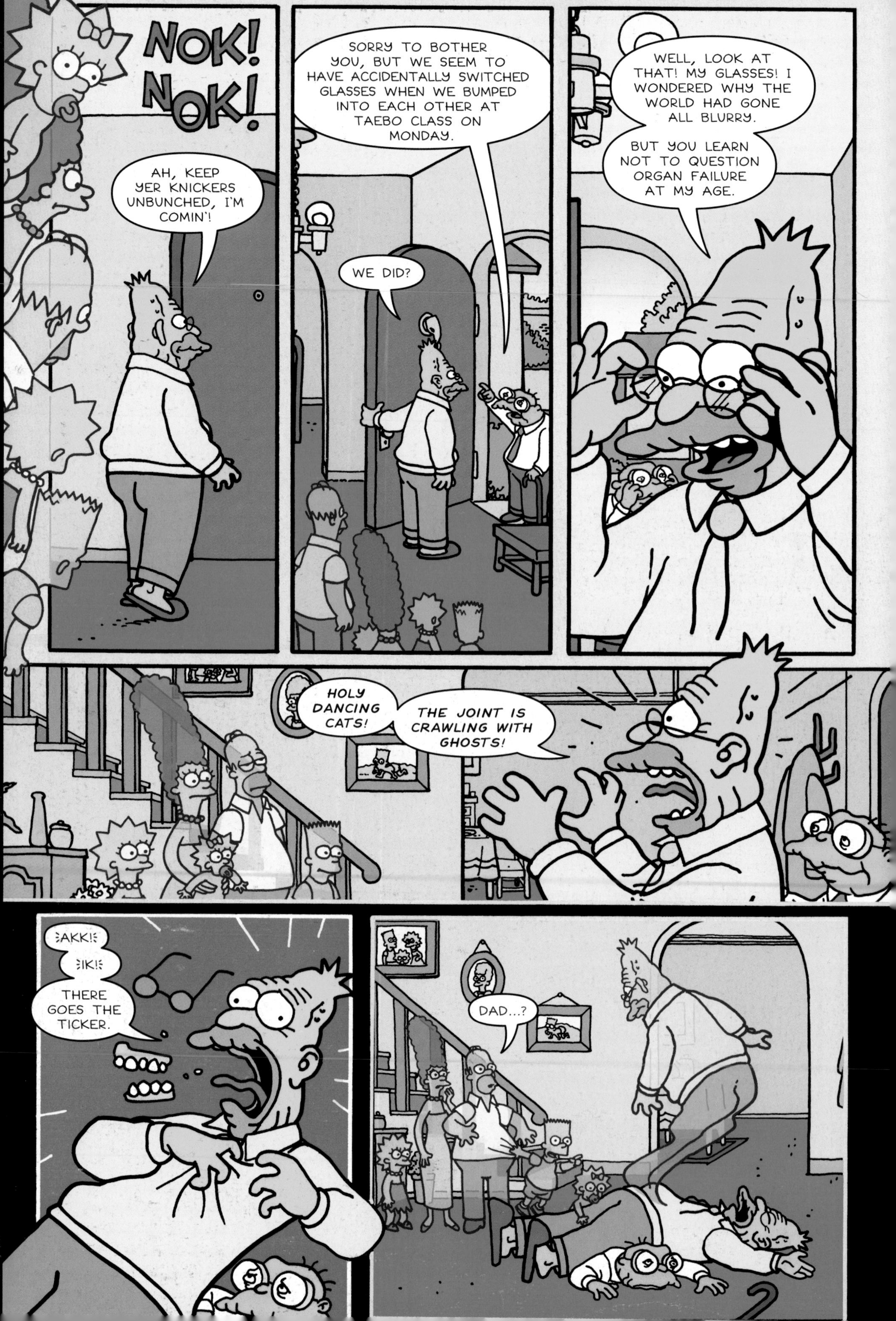
NOK! NOK!
AH, KEEP YER KNICKERS UNBUNCHED, I'M COMIN'!
SORRY TO BOTHER YOU, BUT WE SEEM TO HAVE ACCIDENTALLY SWITCHED GLASSES WHEN WE BUMPED INTO EACH OTHER AT TAEBO CLASS ON MONDAY.
WE DID?
WELL, LOOK AT THAT! MY GLASSES! I WONDERED WHY THE WORLD HAD GONE ALL BLURRY.
BUT YOU LEARN NOT TO QUESTION ORGAN FAILURE AT MY AGE.
HOLY DANCING CATS!
THE JOINT IS CRAWLING WITH GHOSTS!
AKK!
IK!
THERE GOES THE TICKER.
DAD...?

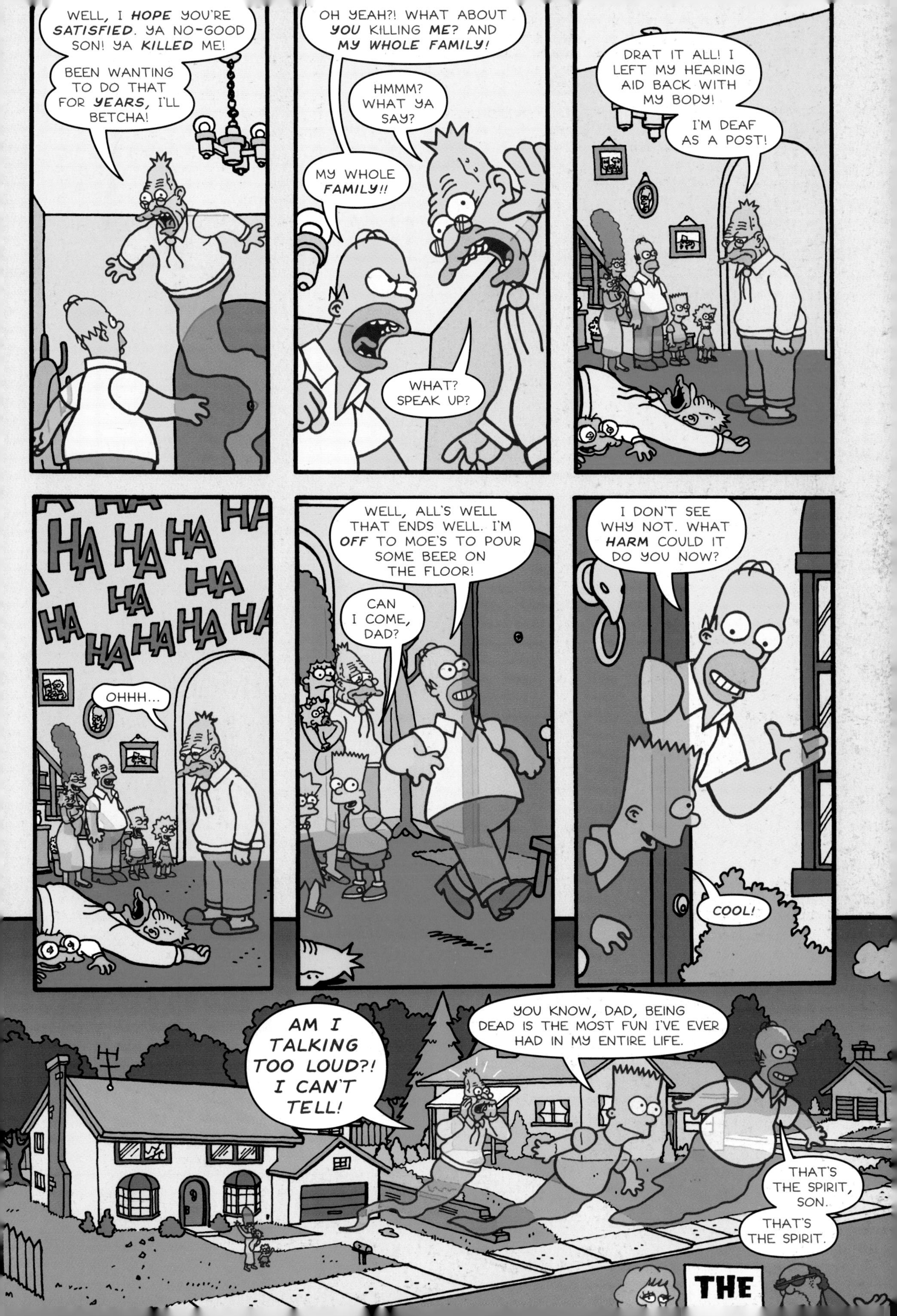

WELL, I HOPE YOU'RE SATISFIED. YA NO-GOOD SON! YA KILLED ME!
BEEN WANTING TO DO THAT FOR YEARS, I'LL BETCHA!
OH YEAH?! WHAT ABOUT YOU KILLING ME? AND MY WHOLE FAMILY!
HMMM? WHAT YA SAY?
MY WHOLE FAMILY!!
WHAT? SPEAK UP?
DRAT IT ALL! I LEFT MY HEARING AID BACK WITH MY BODY!
I'M DEAF AS A POST!
HA HA HA HA HA HA HA HA HA HA HA HA HA HA HA
OHHH...
WELL, ALL'S WELL THAT ENDS WELL. I'M OFF TO MOE'S TO POUR SOME BEER ON THE FLOOR!
CAN I COME, DAD?
I DON'T SEE WHY NOT. WHAT HARM COULD IT DO YOU NOW?
COOL!
AM I TALKING TOO LOUD?! I CAN'T TELL!
YOU KNOW, DAD, BEING DEAD IS THE MOST FUN I'VE EVER HAD IN MY ENTIRE LIFE.
THAT'S THE SPIRIT, SON.
THAT'S THE SPIRIT.
THE

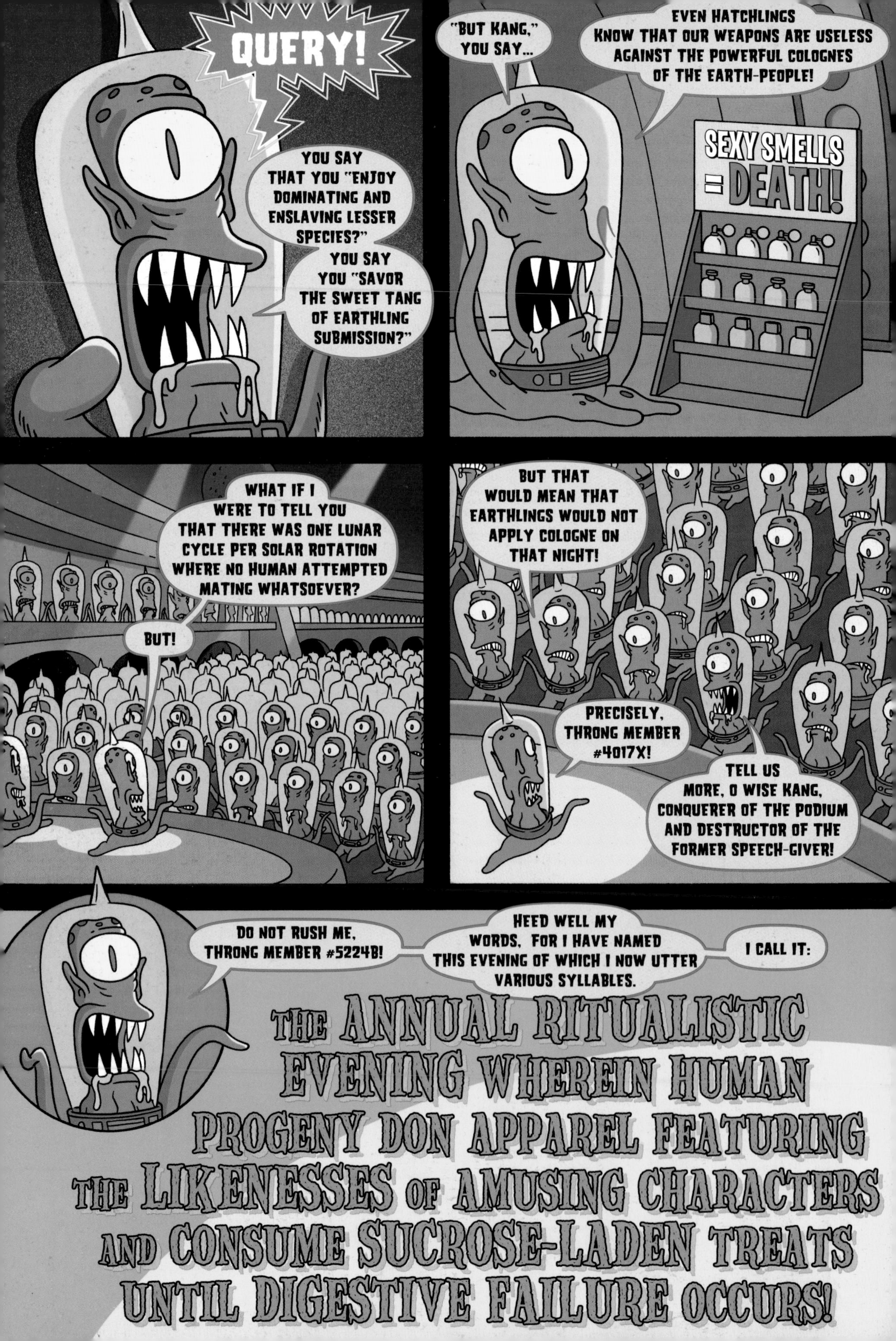
QUERY!
YOU SAY THAT YOU "ENJOY DOMINATING AND ENSLAVING LESSER SPECIES?"
YOU SAY YOU "SAVOR THE SWEET TANG OF EARTHLING SUBMISSION?"
"BUT KANG," YOU SAY...
EVEN HATCHLINGS KNOW THAT OUR WEAPONS ARE USELESS AGAINST THE POWERFUL COLOGNES OF THE EARTH-PEOPLE!
SEXY SMELLS = DEATH!
WHAT IF I WERE TO TELL YOU THAT THERE WAS ONE LUNAR CYCLE PER SOLAR ROTATION WHERE NO HUMAN ATTEMPTED MATING WHATSOEVER?
BUT!
BUT THAT WOULD MEAN THAT EARTHLINGS WOULD NOT APPLY COLOGNE ON THAT NIGHT!
PRECISELY, THRONG MEMBER #4017X!
TELL US MORE, O WISE KANG, CONQUERER OF THE PODIUM AND DESTRUCTOR OF THE FORMER SPEECH-GIVER!
DO NOT RUSH ME, THRONG MEMBER #5224B!
HEED WELL MY WORDS, FOR I HAVE NAMED THIS EVENING OF WHICH I NOW UTTER VARIOUS SYLLABLES.
I CALL IT:
THE ANNUAL RITUALISTIC EVENING WHEREIN HUMAN PROGENY DON APPAREL FEATURING THE LIKENESSES OF AMUSING CHARACTERS AND CONSUME SUCROSE-LADEN TREATS UNTIL DIGESTIVE FAILURE OCCURS!

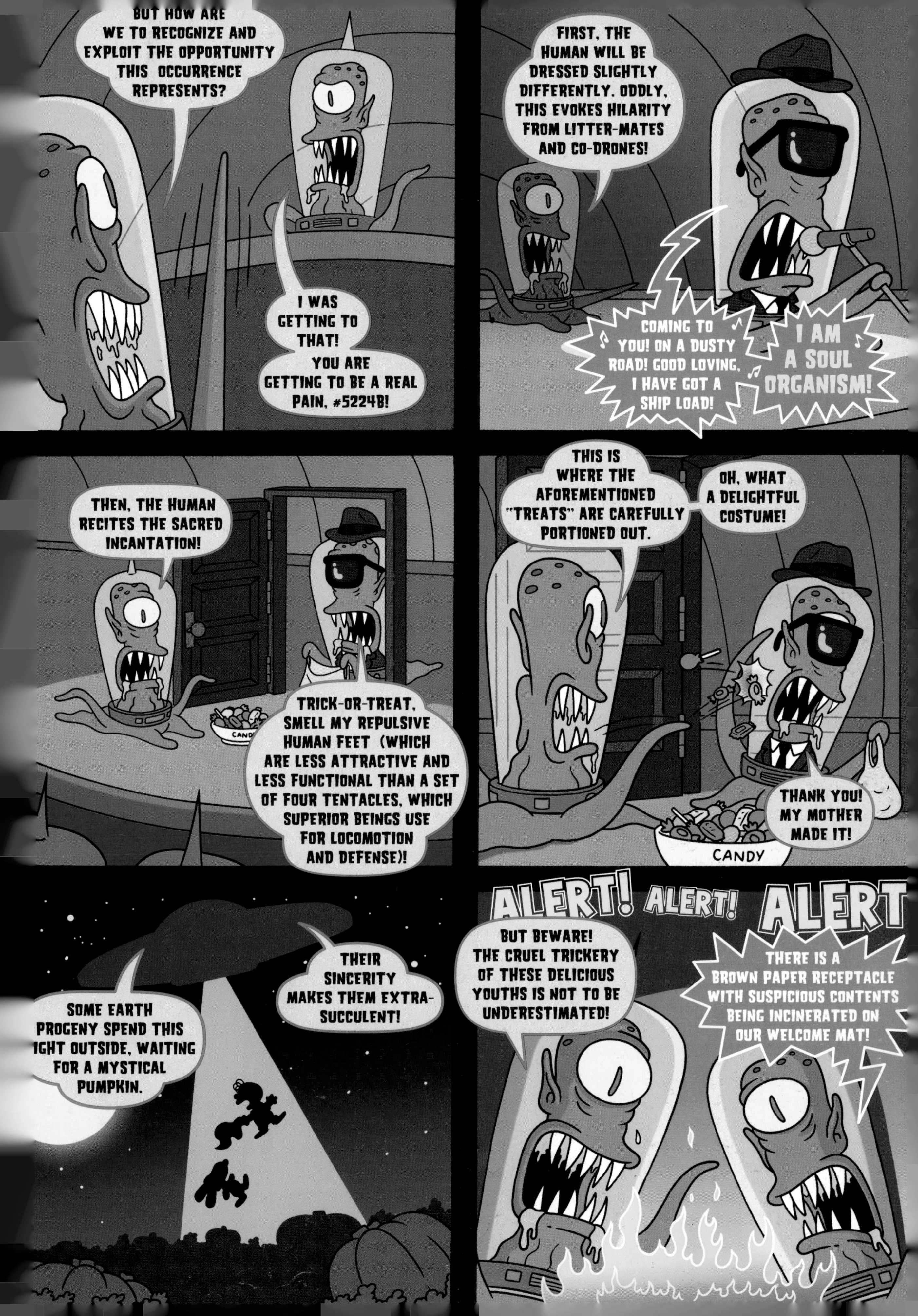
BUT HOW ARE WE TO RECOGNIZE AND EXPLOIT THE OPPORTUNITY THIS OCCURRENCE REPRESENTS?
I WAS GETTING TO THAT!
YOU ARE GETTING TO BE A REAL PAIN, #5224B!
FIRST, THE HUMAN WILL BE DRESSED SLIGHTLY DIFFERENTLY. ODDLY, THIS EVOKES HILARITY FROM LITTER-MATES AND CO-DRONES!
COMING TO YOU! ON A DUSTY ROAD! GOOD LOVING, I HAVE GOT A SHIP LOAD!
I AM A SOUL ORGANISM!
THEN, THE HUMAN RECITES THE SACRED INCANTATION!
TRICK-OR-TREAT, SMELL MY REPULSIVE HUMAN FEET (WHICH ARE LESS ATTRACTIVE AND LESS FUNCTIONAL THAN A SET OF FOUR TENTACLES, WHICH SUPERIOR BEINGS USE FOR LOCOMOTION AND DEFENSE)!
THIS IS WHERE THE AFOREMENTIONED "TREATS" ARE CAREFULLY PORTIONED OUT.
OH, WHAT A DELIGHTFUL COSTUME!
THANK YOU! MY MOTHER MADE IT!
CANDY
SOME EARTH PROGENY SPEND THIS IGHT OUTSIDE, WAITING FOR A MYSTICAL PUMPKIN.
THEIR SINCERITY MAKES THEM EXTRA-SUCCULENT!
ALERT! ALERT! ALERT
BUT BEWARE! THE CRUEL TRICKERY OF THESE DELICIOUS YOUTHS IS NOT TO BE UNDERESTIMATED!
THERE IS A BROWN PAPER RECEPTACLE WITH SUSPICIOUS CONTENTS BEING INCINERATED ON OUR WELCOME MAT!

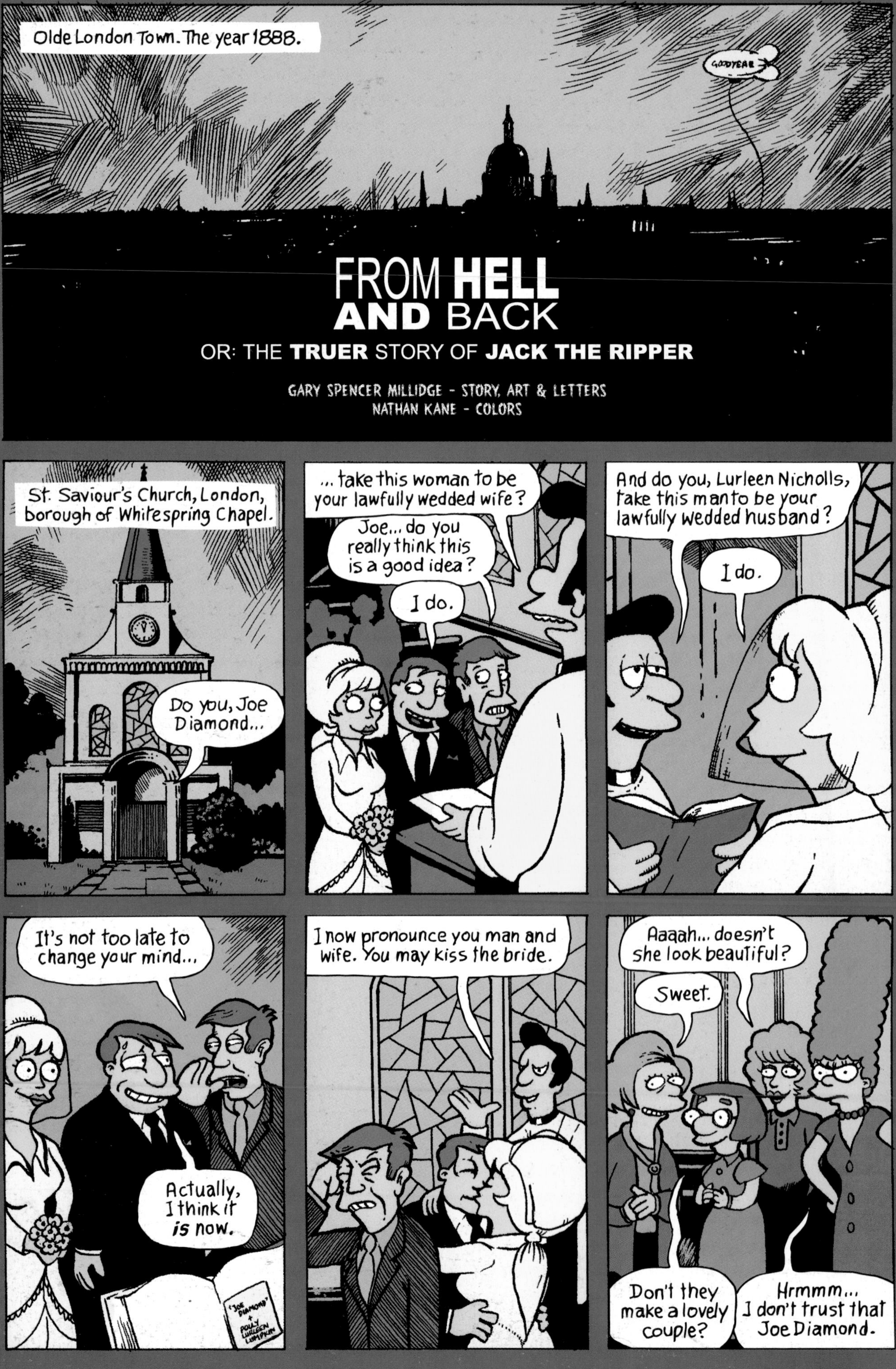
Olde London Town. The year 1888.
FROM HELL AND BACK
OR: THE TRUER STORY OF JACK THE RIPPER
GARY SPENCER MILLIDGE - STORY, ART & LETTERS
NATHAN KANE - COLORS
St. Saviour's Church, London, borough of Whitespring Chapel.
Do you, Joe Diamond...
...take this woman to be your lawfully wedded wife?
Joe... do you really think this is a good idea?
I do.
And do you, Lurleen Nicholls, take this man to be your lawfully wedded husband?
I do.
It's not too late to change your mind...
Actually, I think it *is* now.
I now pronounce you man and wife. You may kiss the bride.
Aaaah... doesn't she look beautiful?
Sweet.
Don't they make a lovely couple?
Hrmmm... I don't trust that Joe Diamond.

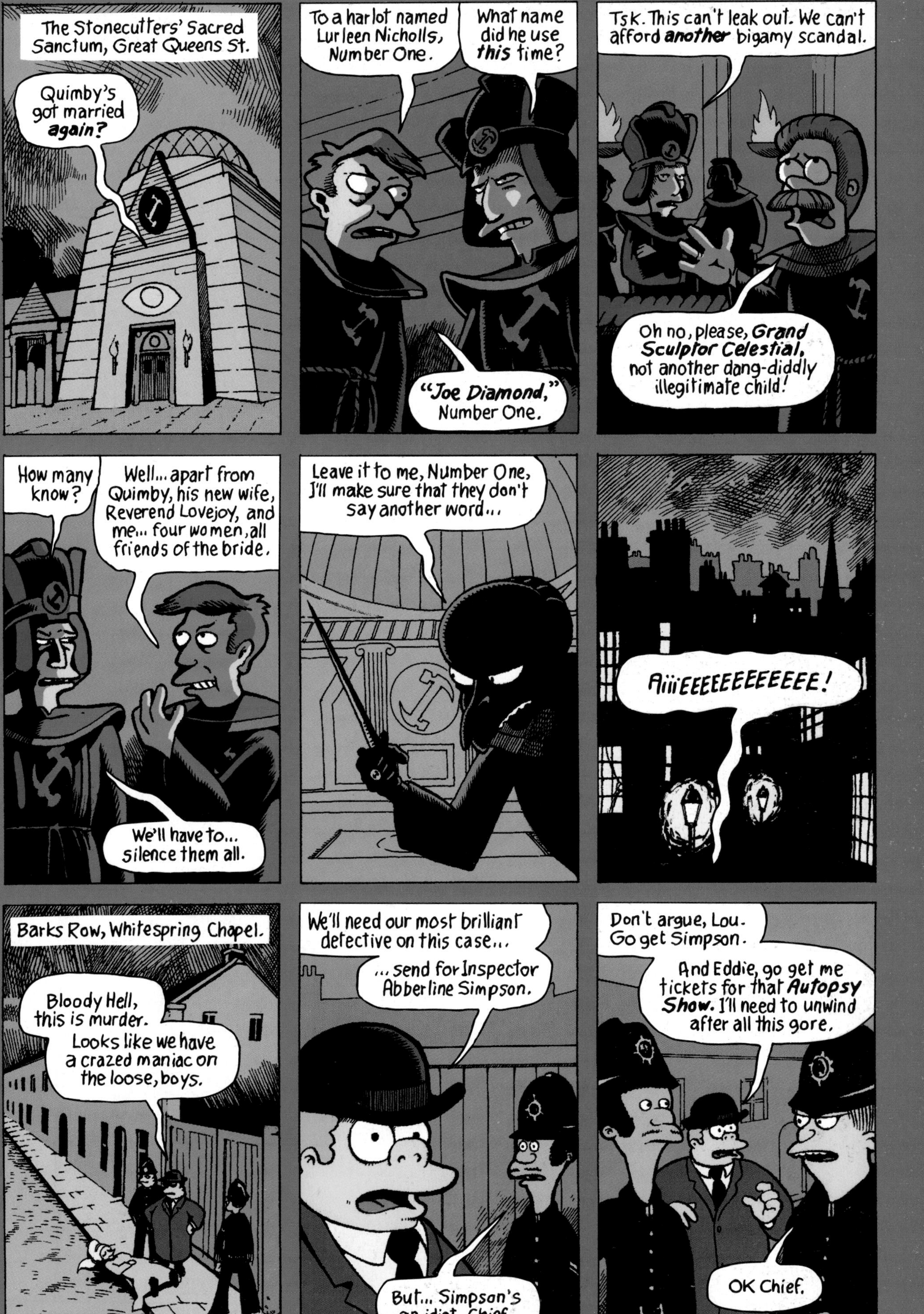
The Stonecutters' Sacred Sanctum, Great Queens St.
Quimby's got married **again?**
To a harlot named Lurleen Nicholls, Number One.
What name did he use **this** time?
"Joe Diamond," Number One.
Tsk. This can't leak out. We can't afford **another** bigamy scandal.
Oh no, please, **Grand Sculptor Celestial,** not another dang-diddly illegitimate child!
How many know?
Well... apart from Quimby, his new wife, Reverend Lovejoy, and me... four women, all friends of the bride.
We'll have to... silence them all.
Leave it to me, Number One, I'll make sure that they don't say another word...
AiiiEEEEEEEEEEE!
Barks Row, Whitespring Chapel.
Bloody Hell, this is murder.
Looks like we have a crazed maniac on the loose, boys.
We'll need our most brilliant detective on this case...
... send for Inspector Abberline Simpson.
But... Simpson's an idiot, Chief.
Don't argue, Lou. Go get Simpson.
And Eddie, go get me tickets for that **Autopsy Show.** I'll need to unwind after all this gore.
OK Chief.

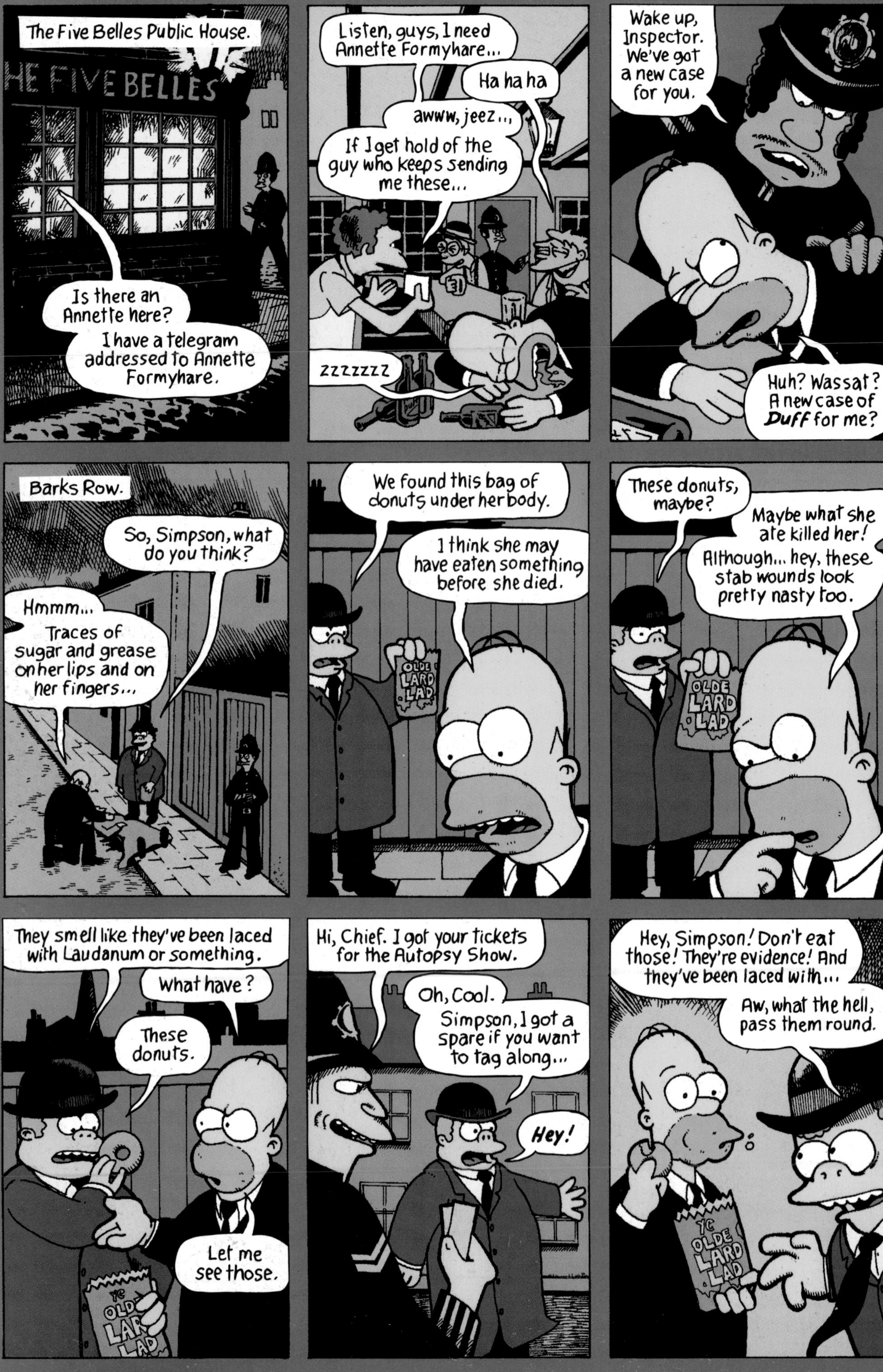

The Five Belles Public House.
THE FIVE BELLES
Is there an Annette here?
I have a telegram addressed to Annette Formyhare.
Listen, guys, I need Annette Formyhare...
Ha ha ha
awww, jeez...
If I get hold of the guy who keeps sending me these...
ZZZZZZZ
Wake up, Inspector. We've got a new case for you.
Huh? Wassat? A new case of DUFF for me?
Barks Row.
So, Simpson, what do you think?
Hmmm...
Traces of sugar and grease on her lips and on her fingers...
We found this bag of donuts under her body.
I think she may have eaten something before she died.
OLDE LARD LAD
These donuts, maybe?
Maybe what she ate killed her!
Although... hey, these stab wounds look pretty nasty too.
OLDE LARD LAD
They smell like they've been laced with Laudanum or something.
What have?
These donuts.
Let me see those.
YE OLDE LARD LAD
Hi, Chief. I got your tickets for the Autopsy Show.
Oh, Cool.
Simpson, I got a spare if you want to tag along...
Hey!
Hey, Simpson! Don't eat those! They're evidence! And they've been laced with...
Aw, what the hell, pass them round.
YE OLDE LARD LAD

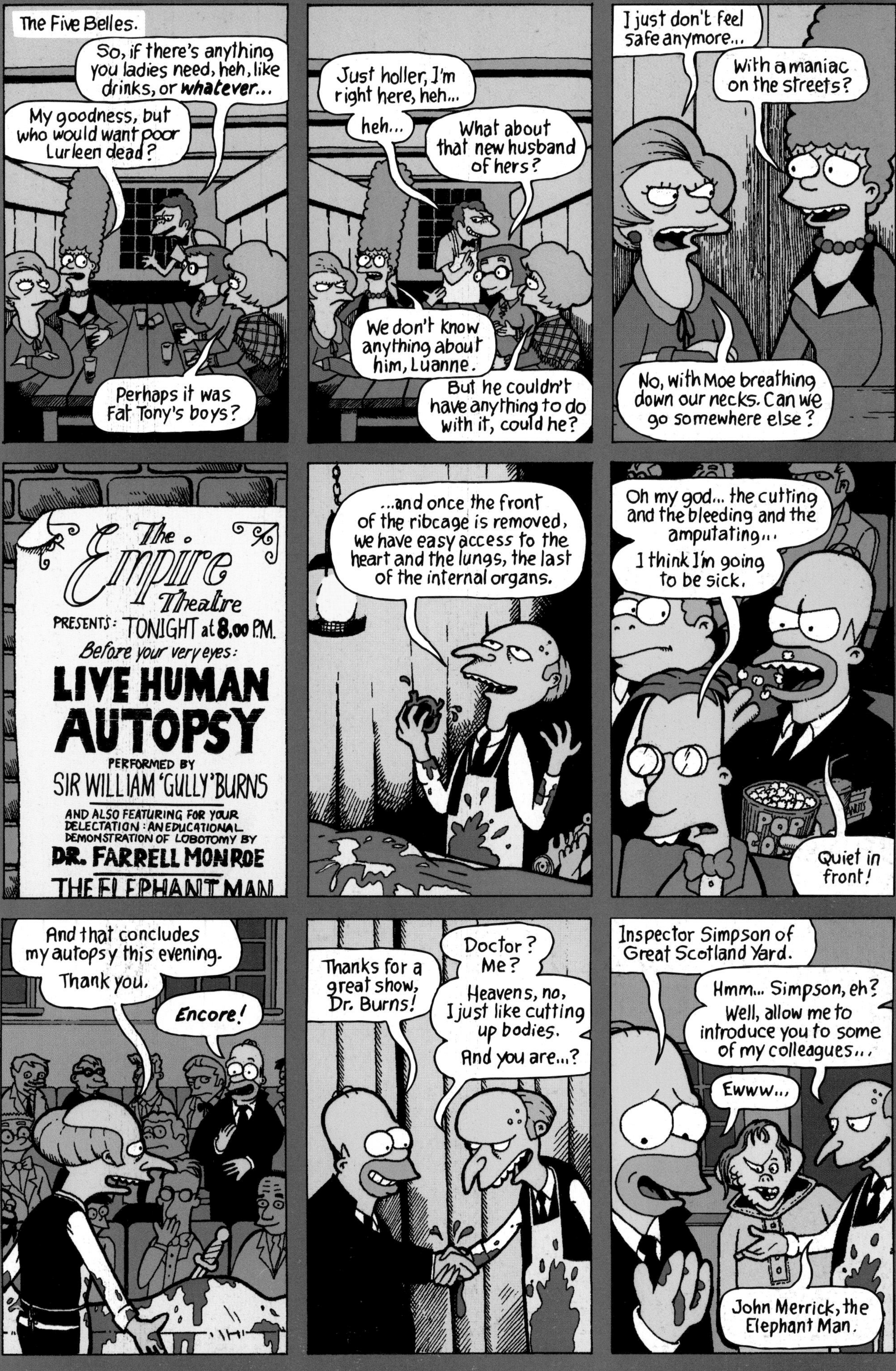
The Five Belles.
So, if there's anything you ladies need, heh, like drinks, or whatever...
My goodness, but who would want poor Lurleen dead?
Perhaps it was Fat Tony's boys?
Just holler, I'm right here, heh...
heh...
What about that new husband of hers?
We don't know anything about him, Luanne.
But he couldn't have anything to do with it, could he?
I just don't feel safe anymore...
With a maniac on the streets?
No, with Moe breathing down our necks. Can we go somewhere else?
The Empire Theatre
PRESENTS: TONIGHT at 8.00 P.M.
Before your very eyes:
LIVE HUMAN AUTOPSY
PERFORMED BY
SIR WILLIAM 'GULLY' BURNS
AND ALSO FEATURING FOR YOUR DELECTATION: AN EDUCATIONAL DEMONSTRATION OF LOBOTOMY BY
DR. FARRELL MONROE
THE ELEPHANT MAN
...and once the front of the ribcage is removed, we have easy access to the heart and the lungs, the last of the internal organs.
Oh my god... the cutting and the bleeding and the amputating...
I think I'm going to be sick.
Quiet in front!
And that concludes my autopsy this evening.
Thank you.
Encore!
Thanks for a great show, Dr. Burns!
Doctor? Me?
Heavens, no, I just like cutting up bodies.
And you are...?
Inspector Simpson of Great Scotland Yard.
Hmm... Simpson, eh? Well, allow me to introduce you to some of my colleagues...
Ewww...
John Merrick, the Elephant Man.

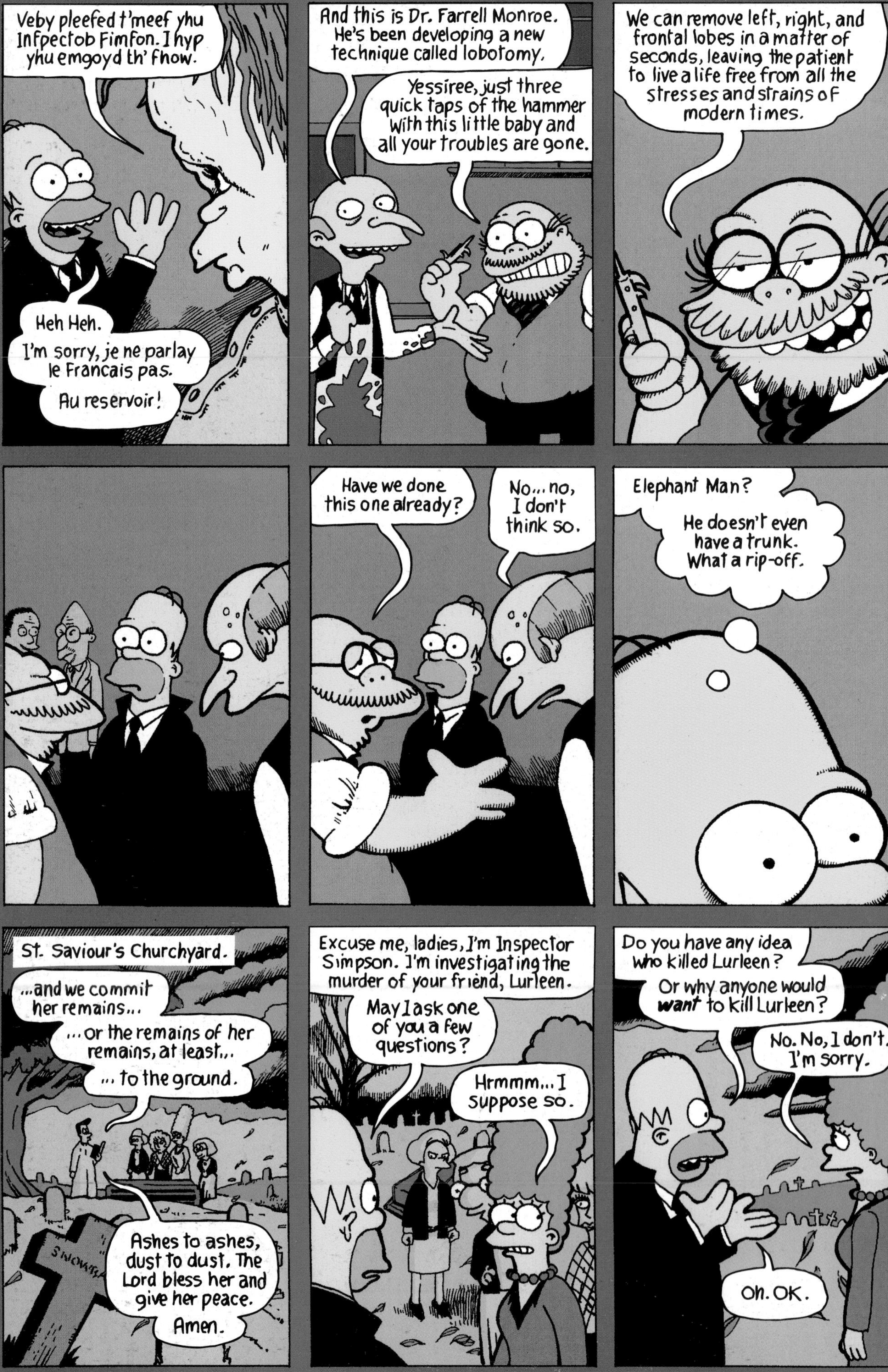

Veby pleefed t'meef yhu Infpectob Fimfon. I hyp yhu emgoyd th' fhow.
Heh Heh.
I'm sorry, je ne parlay le Francais pas.
Au reservoir!
And this is Dr. Farrell Monroe. He's been developing a new technique called lobotomy.
Yessiree, just three quick taps of the hammer with this little baby and all your troubles are gone.
We can remove left, right, and frontal lobes in a matter of seconds, leaving the patient to live a life free from all the stresses and strains of modern times.
Have we done this one already?
No... no, I don't think so.
Elephant Man?
He doesn't even have a trunk. What a rip-off.
St. Saviour's Churchyard.
...and we commit her remains...
...or the remains of her remains, at least...
...to the ground.
Ashes to ashes, dust to dust. The Lord bless her and give her peace.
Amen.
Excuse me, ladies, I'm Inspector Simpson. I'm investigating the murder of your friend, Lurleen.
May I ask one of you a few questions?
Hrmmm... I suppose so.
Do you have any idea who killed Lurleen?
Or why anyone would *want* to kill Lurleen?
No. No, I don't. I'm sorry.
Oh. OK.

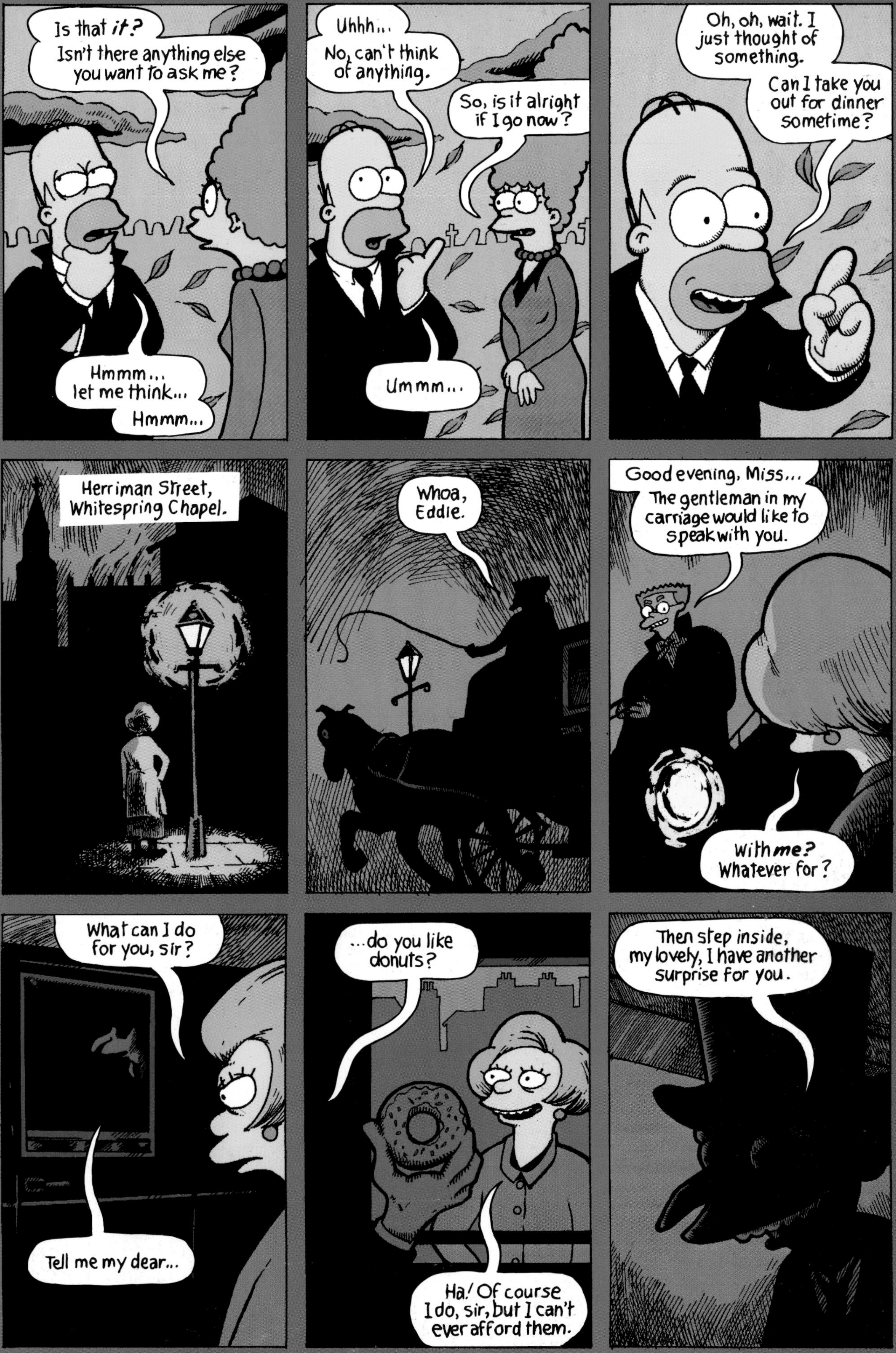
Is that *it?*
Isn't there anything else you want to ask me?
Hmmm... let me think...
Hmmm...
Uhhh...
No, can't think of anything.
So, is it alright if I go now?
Ummm...
Oh, oh, wait. I just thought of something.
Can I take you out for dinner sometime?
Herriman Street, Whitespring Chapel.
Whoa, Eddie.
Good evening, Miss...
The gentleman in my carriage would like to speak with you.
With *me?* Whatever for?
What can I do for you, sir?
Tell me my dear...
...do you like donuts?
Ha! Of course I do, sir, but I can't ever afford them.
Then step inside, my lovely, I have another surprise for you.

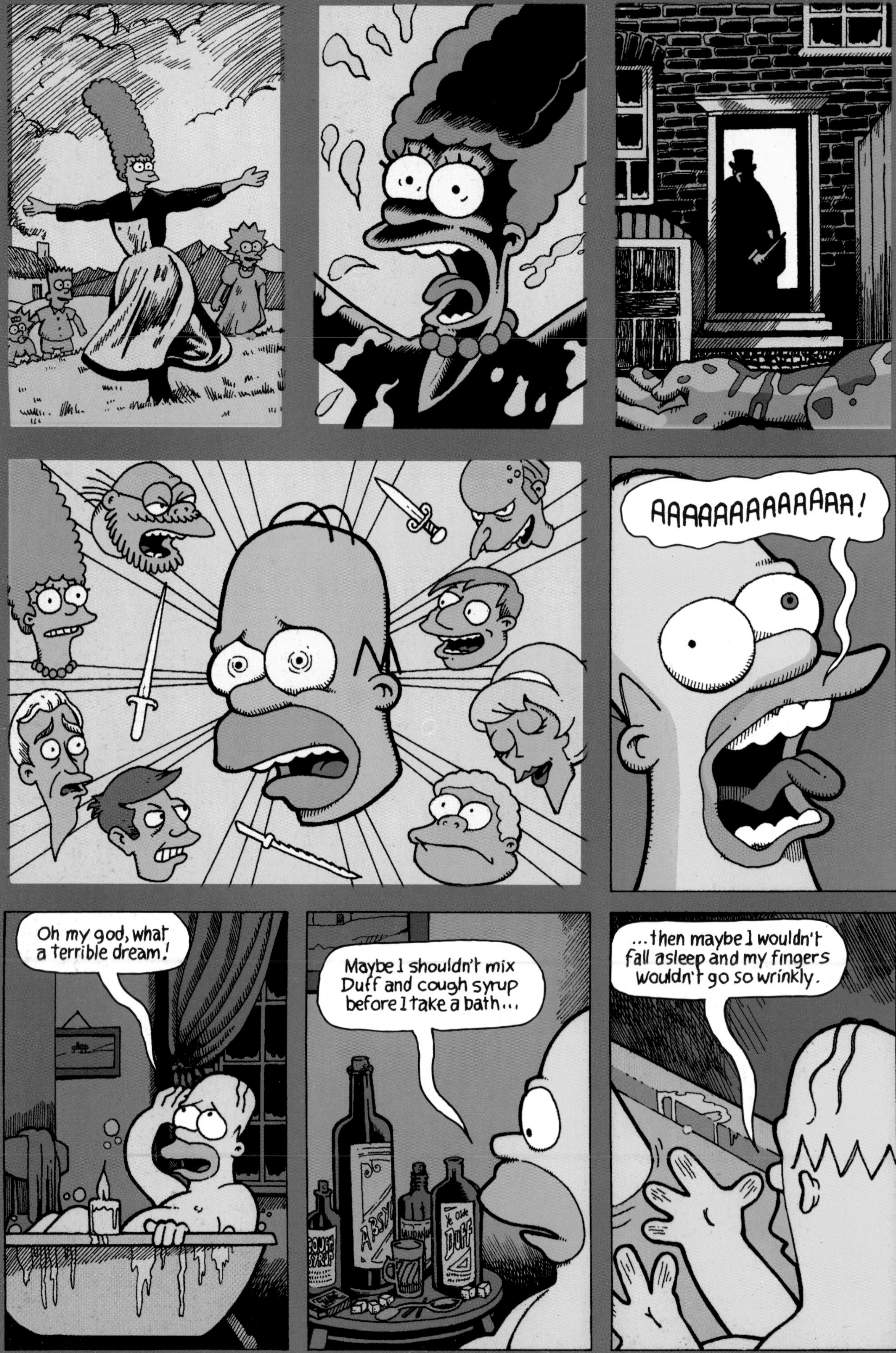
AAAAAAAAAAAAA!
Oh my god, what a terrible dream!
Maybe I shouldn't mix Duff and cough syrup before I take a bath...
...then maybe I wouldn't fall asleep and my fingers wouldn't go so wrinkly.

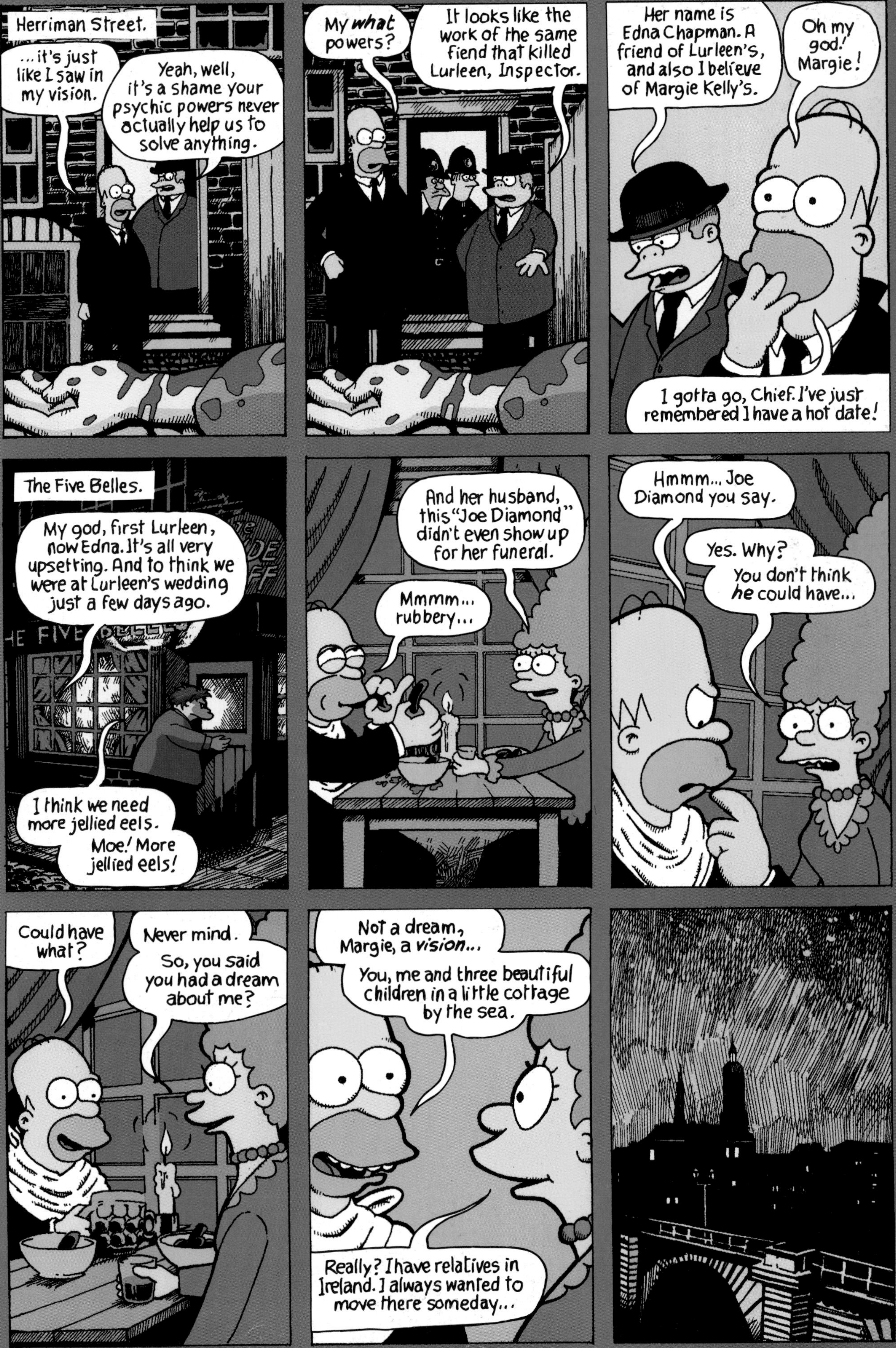

Herriman Street.
...it's just like I saw in my vision.
Yeah, well, it's a shame your psychic powers never actually help us to solve anything.
My *what* powers?
It looks like the work of the same fiend that killed Lurleen, Inspector.
Her name is Edna Chapman. A friend of Lurleen's, and also I believe of Margie Kelly's.
Oh my god! Margie!
I gotta go, Chief. I've just remembered I have a hot date!
The Five Belles.
My god, first Lurleen, now Edna. It's all very upsetting. And to think we were at Lurleen's wedding just a few days ago.
I think we need more jellied eels.
Moe! More jellied eels!
Mmmm... rubbery...
And her husband, this "Joe Diamond" didn't even show up for her funeral.
Hmmm... Joe Diamond you say.
Yes. Why?
You don't think *he* could have...
Could have what?
Never mind.
So, you said you had a dream about me?
Not a dream, Margie, a *vision*...
You, me and three beautiful children in a little cottage by the sea.
Really? I have relatives in Ireland. I always wanted to move there someday...

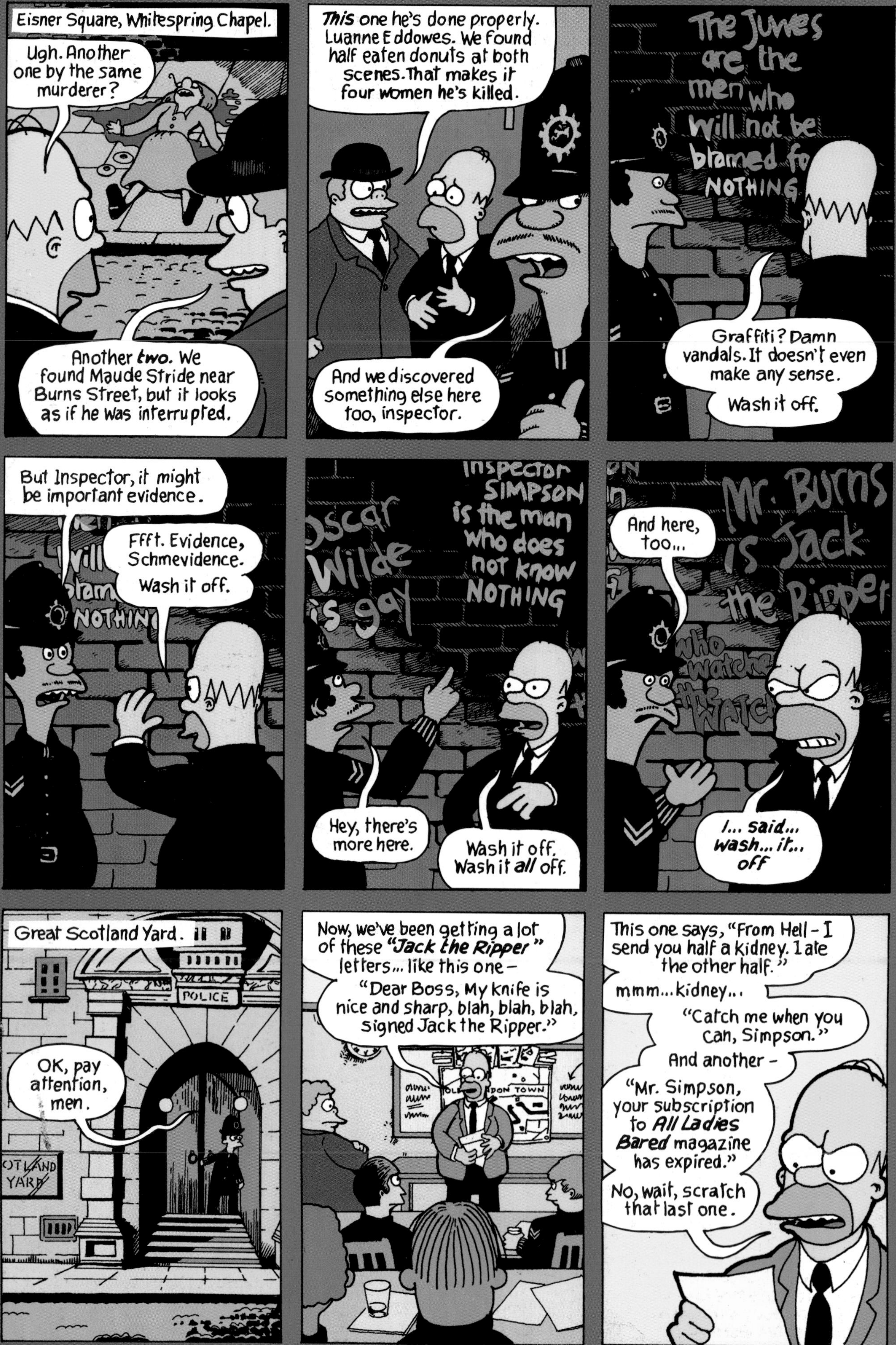
Eisner Square, Whitespring Chapel.
Ugh. Another one by the same murderer?
Another *two.* We found Maude Stride near Burns Street, but it looks as if he was interrupted.
This one he's done properly. Luanne Eddowes. We found half eaten donuts at both scenes. That makes it four women he's killed.
And we discovered something else here too, inspector.
The Juwes are the men who Will not be blamed for NOTHING
Graffiti? Damn vandals. It doesn't even make any sense.
Wash it off.
But Inspector, it might be important evidence.
Ffft. Evidence, Schmevidence.
Wash it off.
Inspector SIMPSON is the man who does not know NOTHING
Oscar Wilde is gay
Hey, there's more here.
Wash it off. Wash it *all* off.
Mr. Burns is Jack the Ripper
And here, too...
I... said... wash... it... off
Great Scotland Yard.
POLICE
OK, pay attention, men.
Now, we've been getting a lot of these *"Jack the Ripper"* letters... like this one –
"Dear Boss, My knife is nice and sharp, blah, blah, blah, signed Jack the Ripper."
This one says, "From Hell – I send you half a kidney. I ate the other half."
mmm... kidney...
"Catch me when you can, Simpson."
And another –
"Mr. Simpson, your subscription to *All Ladies Bared* magazine has expired."
No, wait, scratch that last one.

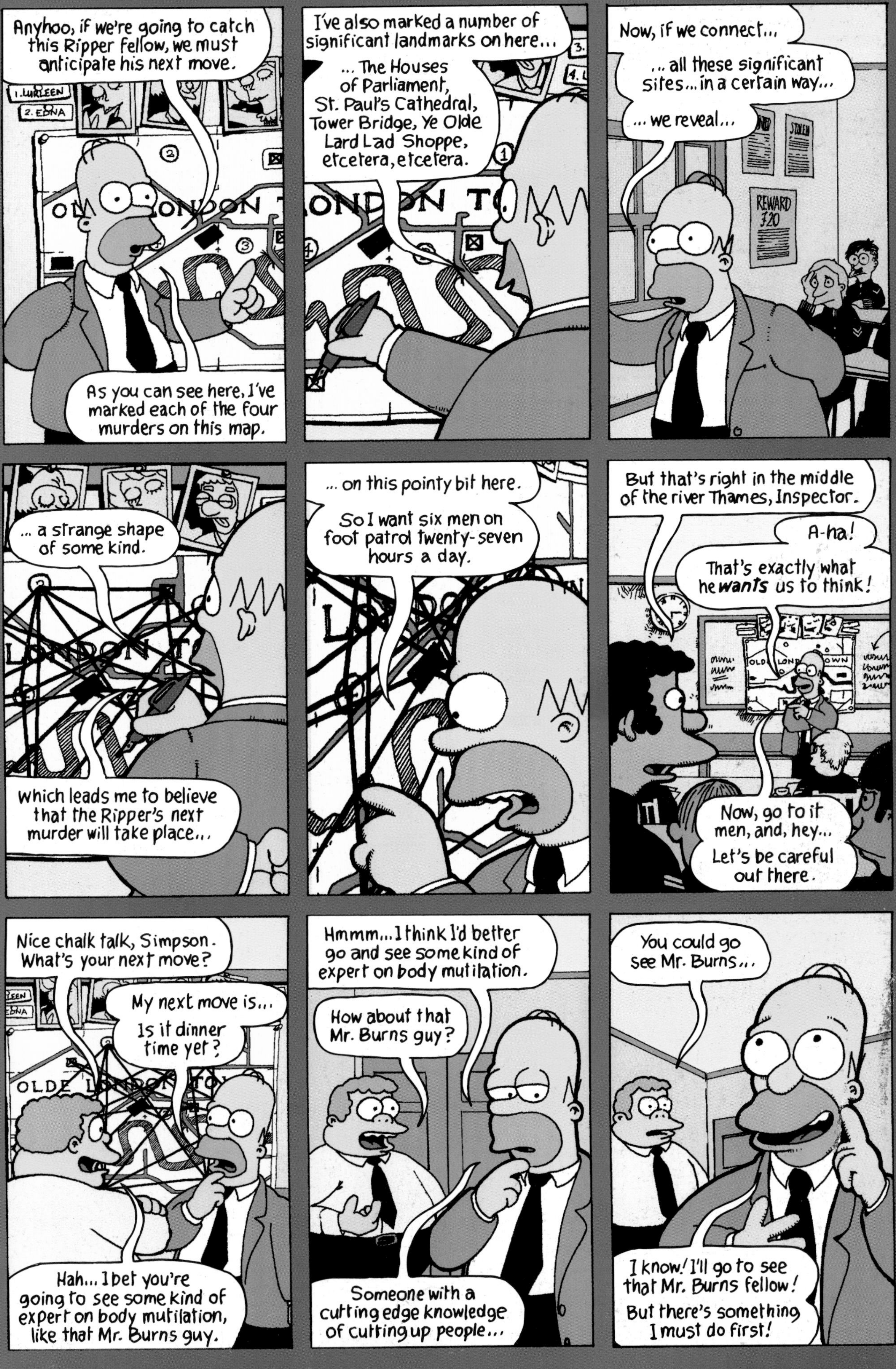
Anyhoo, if we're going to catch this Ripper fellow, we must anticipate his next move.
1. LURLEEN
2. EDNA
As you can see here, I've marked each of the four murders on this map.
I've also marked a number of significant landmarks on here...
... The Houses of Parliament, St. Paul's Cathedral, Tower Bridge, Ye Olde Lard Lad Shoppe, etcetera, etcetera.
Now, if we connect...
... all these significant sites... in a certain way...
... we reveal...
STOLEN
REWARD £20
... a strange shape of some kind.
Which leads me to believe that the Ripper's next murder will take place...
... on this pointy bit here.
So I want six men on foot patrol twenty-seven hours a day.
But that's right in the middle of the river Thames, Inspector.
A-ha!
That's exactly what he ***wants*** us to think!
Now, go to it men, and, hey...
Let's be careful out there.
Nice chalk talk, Simpson. What's your next move?
My next move is...
Is it dinner time yet?
OLDE
Hah... I bet you're going to see some kind of expert on body mutilation, like that Mr. Burns guy.
Hmmm... I think I'd better go and see some kind of expert on body mutilation.
How about that Mr. Burns guy?
Someone with a cutting edge knowledge of cutting up people...
You could go see Mr. Burns...
I know! I'll go to see that Mr. Burns fellow!
But there's something I must do first!

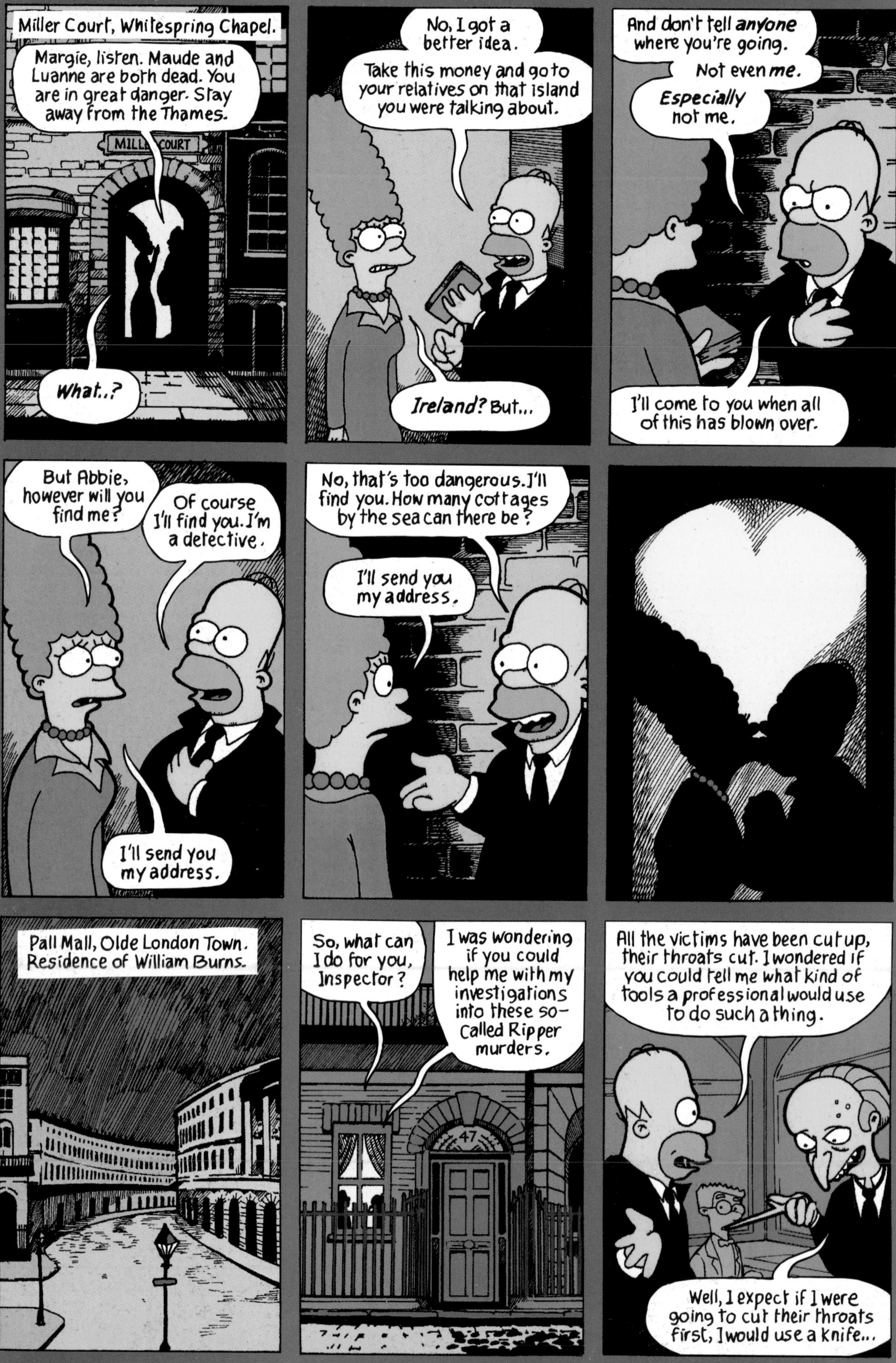
Miller Court, Whitespring Chapel.
Margie, listen. Maude and Luanne are both dead. You are in great danger. Stay away from the Thames.
What..?
No, I got a better idea.
Take this money and go to your relatives on that island you were talking about.
Ireland? But...
And don't tell anyone where you're going.
Not even me.
Especially not me.
I'll come to you when all of this has blown over.
But Abbie, however will you find me?
Of course I'll find you. I'm a detective.
I'll send you my address.
No, that's too dangerous. I'll find you. How many cottages by the sea can there be?
I'll send you my address.
Pall Mall, Olde London Town. Residence of William Burns.
So, what can I do for you, Inspector?
I was wondering if you could help me with my investigations into these so-called Ripper murders.
47
All the victims have been cut up, their throats cut. I wondered if you could tell me what kind of tools a professional would use to do such a thing.
Well, I expect if I were going to cut their throats first, I would use a knife...

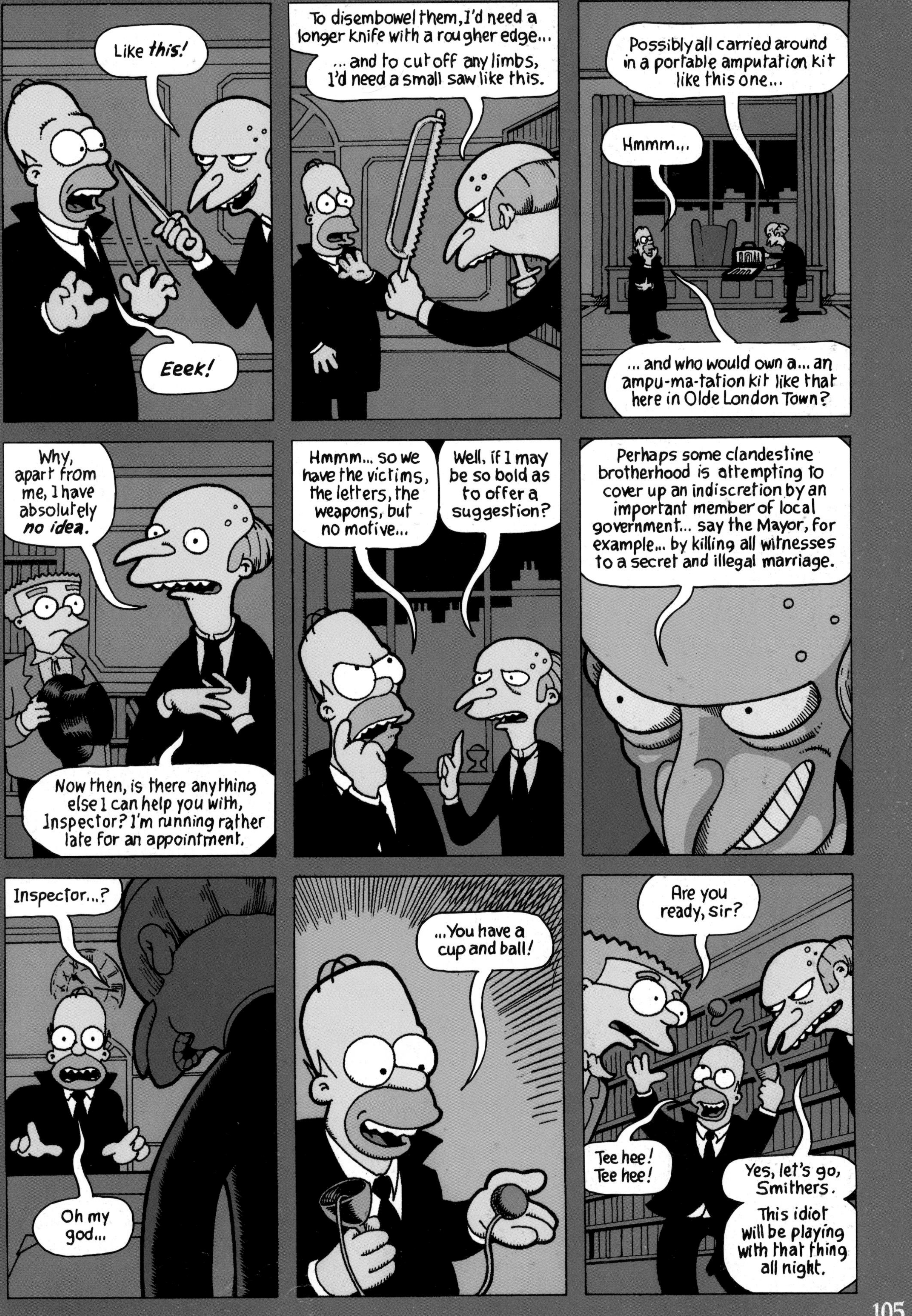

Like *this!*
Eeek!
To disembowel them, I'd need a longer knife with a rougher edge...
... and to cut off any limbs, I'd need a small saw like this.
Possibly all carried around in a portable amputation kit like this one...
Hmmm...
... and who would own a... an ampu-ma-tation kit like that here in Olde London Town?
Why, apart from me, I have absolutely *no idea.*
Now then, is there anything else I can help you with, Inspector? I'm running rather late for an appointment.
Hmmm... so we have the victims, the letters, the weapons, but no motive...
Well, if I may be so bold as to offer a suggestion?
Perhaps some clandestine brotherhood is attempting to cover up an indiscretion by an important member of local government... say the Mayor, for example... by killing all witnesses to a secret and illegal marriage.
Inspector...?
Oh my god...
...You have a cup and ball!
Are you ready, sir?
Tee hee! Tee hee!
Yes, let's go, Smithers.
This idiot will be playing with that thing all night.

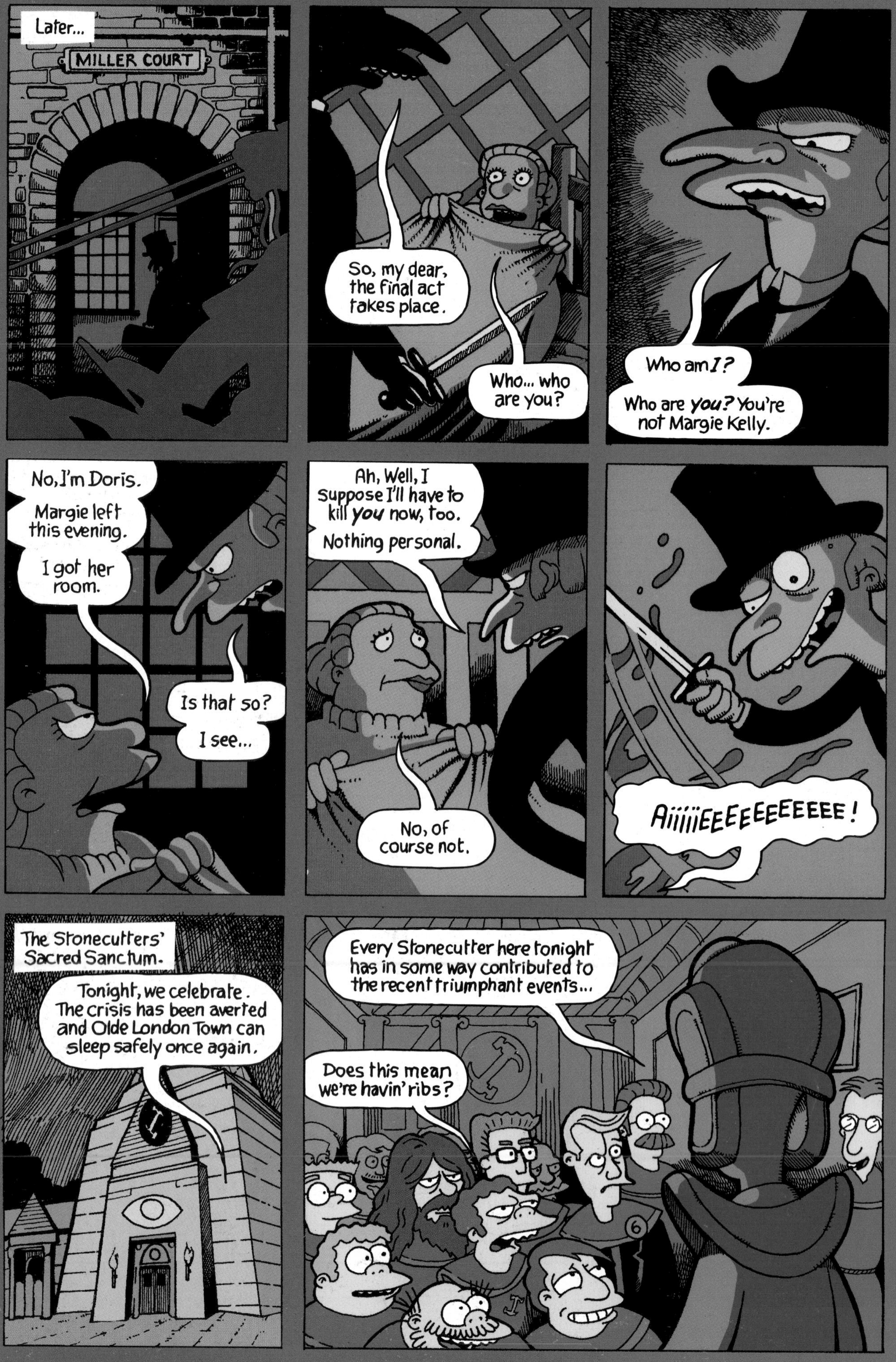

Later...
MILLER COURT
So, my dear, the final act takes place.
Who... who are you?
Who am *I*?
Who are *you?* You're not Margie Kelly.
No, I'm Doris.
Margie left this evening.
I got her room.
Is that so?
I see...
Ah, Well, I suppose I'll have to kill *you* now, too.
Nothing personal.
No, of course not.
AiiiiiEEEEEEEEEEE!
The Stonecutters' Sacred Sanctum.
Tonight, we celebrate. The crisis has been averted and Olde London Town can sleep safely once again.
Every Stonecutter here tonight has in some way contributed to the recent triumphant events...
Does this mean we're havin' ribs?

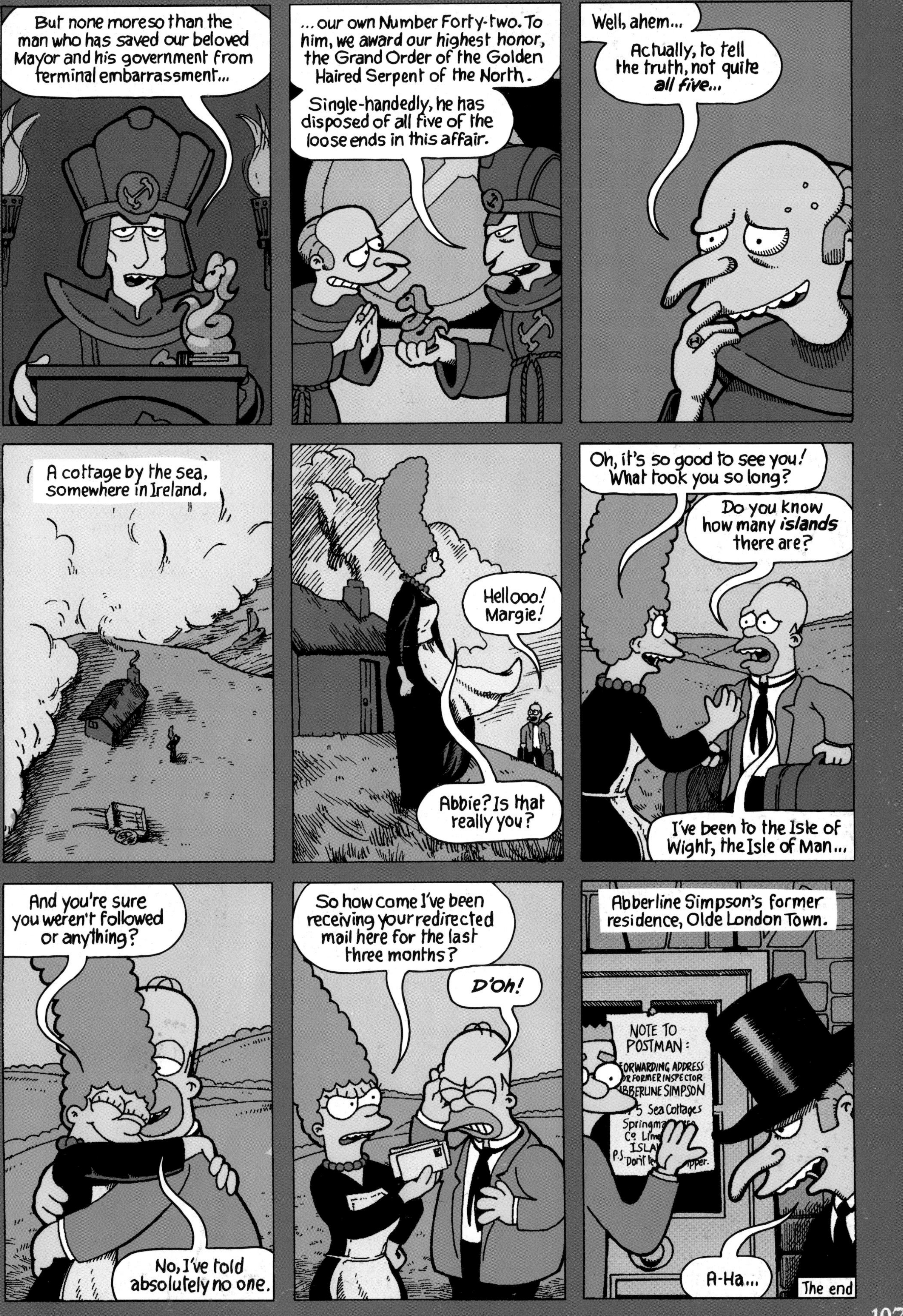
But none moreso than the man who has saved our beloved Mayor and his government from terminal embarrassment...
...our own Number Forty-two. To him, we award our highest honor, the Grand Order of the Golden Haired Serpent of the North.
Single-handedly, he has disposed of all five of the loose ends in this affair.
Well, ahem...
Actually, to tell the truth, not quite *all five*...
A cottage by the sea, somewhere in Ireland.
Hellooo! Margie!
Abbie? Is that really you?
Oh, it's so good to see you! What took you so long?
Do you know how many *islands* there are?
I've been to the Isle of Wight, the Isle of Man...
And you're sure you weren't followed or anything?
No, I've told absolutely no one.
So how come I've been receiving your redirected mail here for the last three months?
D'Oh!
Abberline Simpson's former residence, Olde London Town.
NOTE TO POSTMAN:
FORWARDING ADDRESS
A-Ha...
The end

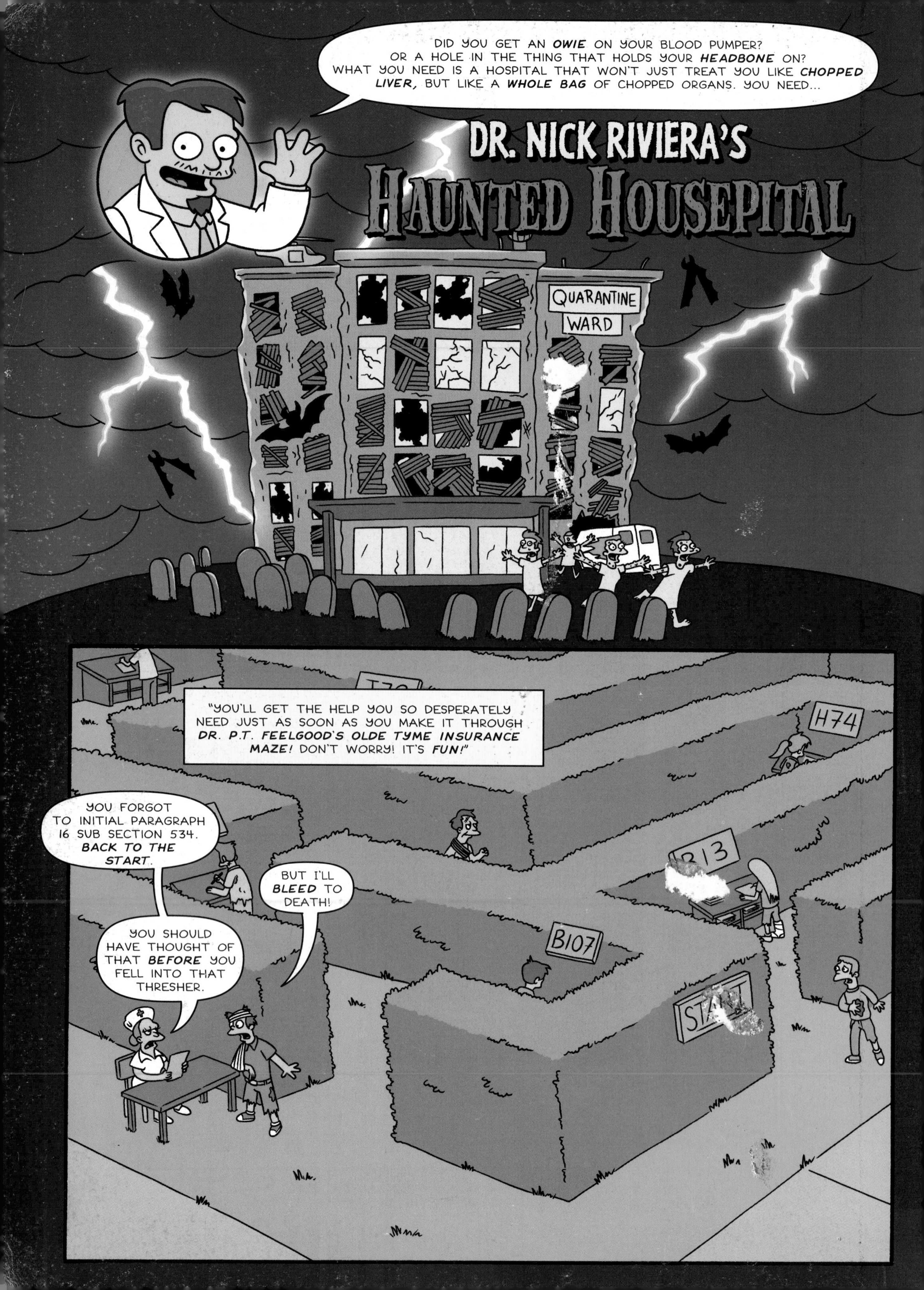
DID YOU GET AN OWIE ON YOUR BLOOD PUMPER? OR A HOLE IN THE THING THAT HOLDS YOUR HEADBONE ON? WHAT YOU NEED IS A HOSPITAL THAT WON'T JUST TREAT YOU LIKE CHOPPED LIVER, BUT LIKE A WHOLE BAG OF CHOPPED ORGANS. YOU NEED...
DR. NICK RIVIERA'S
HAUNTED HOUSEPITAL
QUARANTINE WARD
"YOU'LL GET THE HELP YOU SO DESPERATELY NEED JUST AS SOON AS YOU MAKE IT THROUGH DR. P.T. FEELGOOD'S OLDE TYME INSURANCE MAZE! DON'T WORRY! IT'S FUN!"
H74
YOU FORGOT TO INITIAL PARAGRAPH 16 SUB SECTION 534. BACK TO THE START.
BUT I'LL BLEED TO DEATH!
YOU SHOULD HAVE THOUGHT OF THAT BEFORE YOU FELL INTO THAT THRESHER.
B107
START

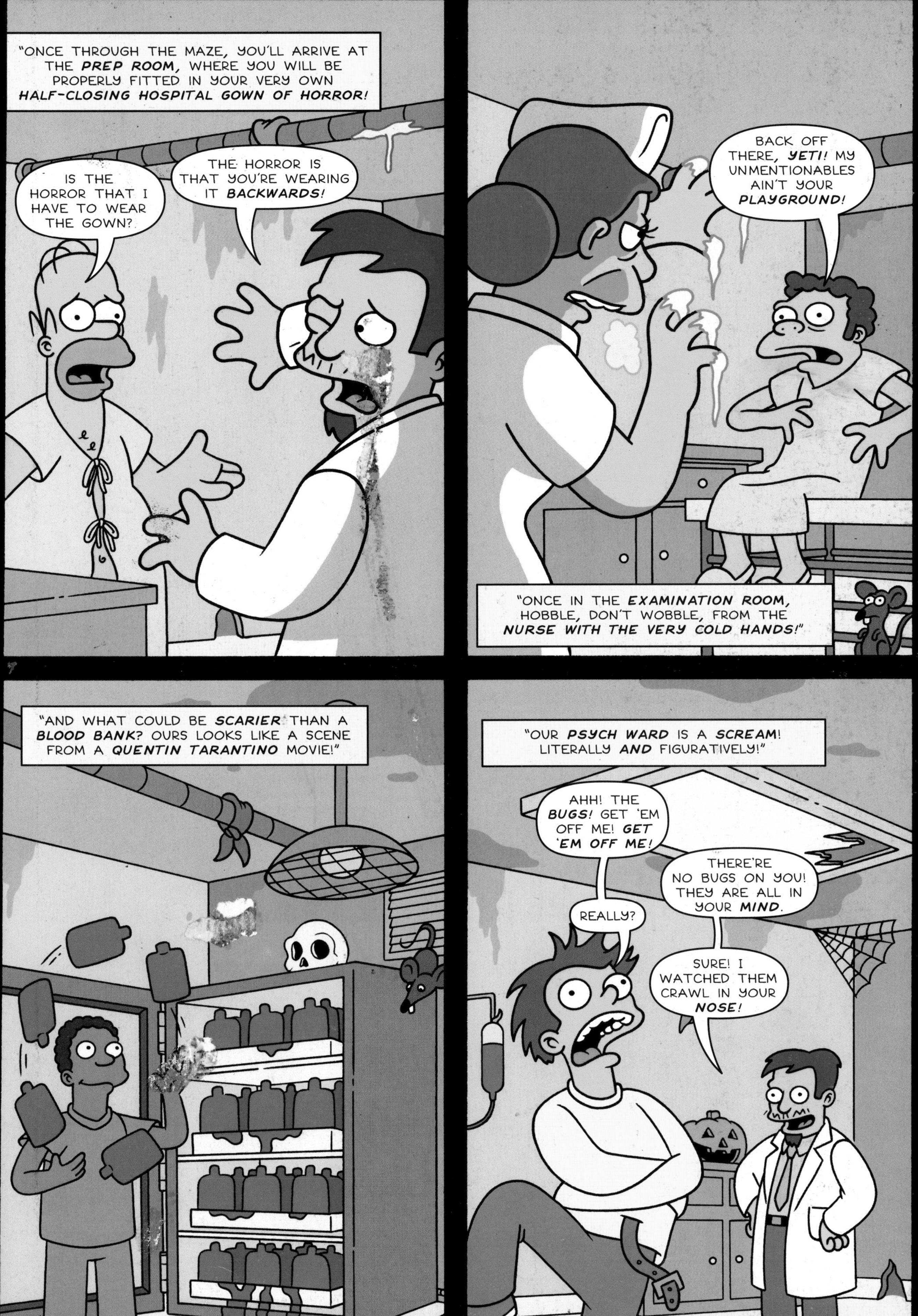
"ONCE THROUGH THE MAZE, YOU'LL ARRIVE AT THE PREP ROOM, WHERE YOU WILL BE PROPERLY FITTED IN YOUR VERY OWN HALF-CLOSING HOSPITAL GOWN OF HORROR!
IS THE HORROR THAT I HAVE TO WEAR THE GOWN?
THE HORROR IS THAT YOU'RE WEARING IT BACKWARDS!
BACK OFF THERE, YETI! MY UNMENTIONABLES AIN'T YOUR PLAYGROUND!
"ONCE IN THE EXAMINATION ROOM, HOBBLE, DON'T WOBBLE, FROM THE NURSE WITH THE VERY COLD HANDS!"
"AND WHAT COULD BE SCARIER THAN A BLOOD BANK? OURS LOOKS LIKE A SCENE FROM A QUENTIN TARANTINO MOVIE!"
"OUR PSYCH WARD IS A SCREAM! LITERALLY AND FIGURATIVELY!"
AHH! THE BUGS! GET 'EM OFF ME! GET 'EM OFF ME!
THERE'RE NO BUGS ON YOU! THEY ARE ALL IN YOUR MIND.
REALLY?
SURE! I WATCHED THEM CRAWL IN YOUR NOSE!

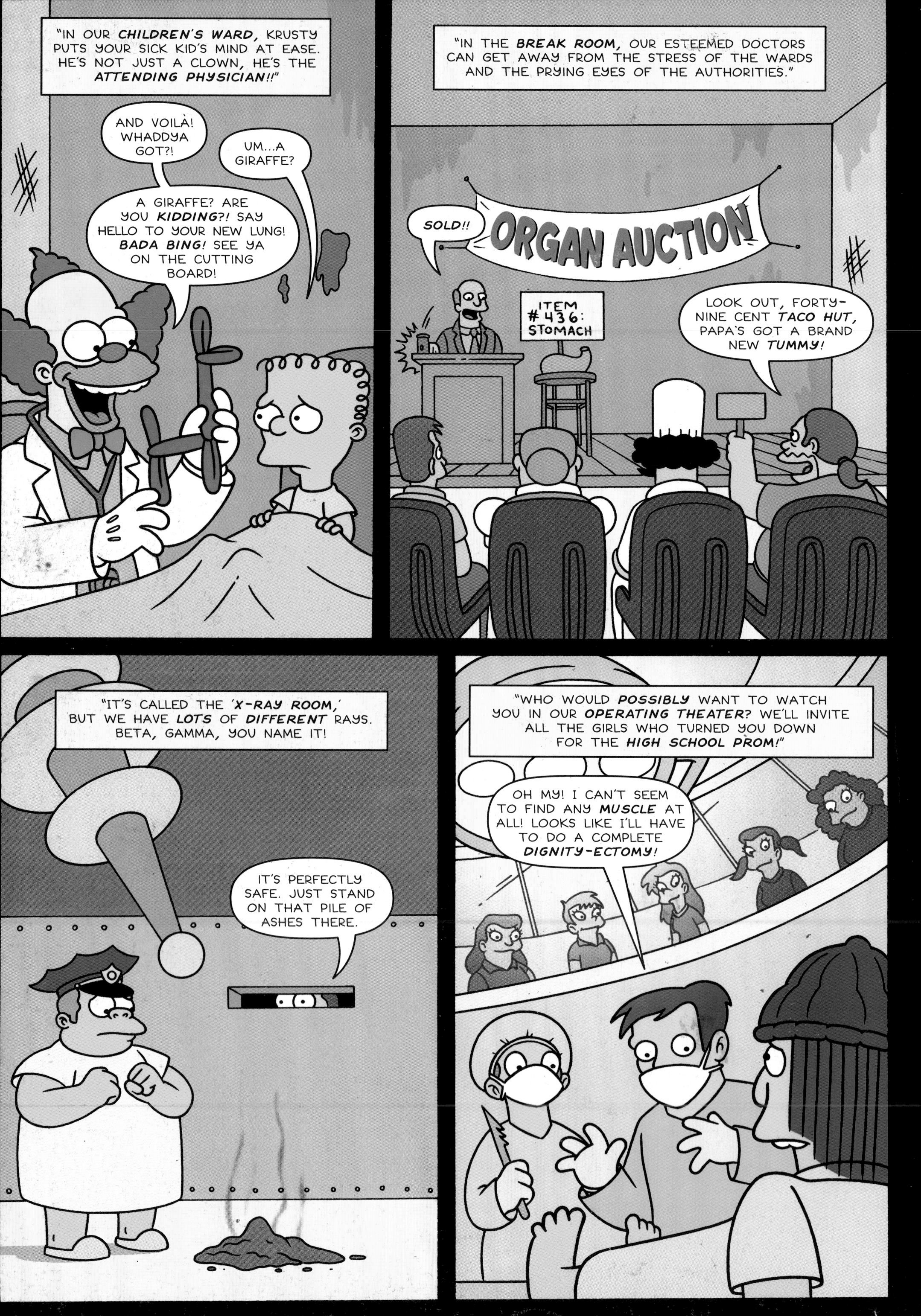
"IN OUR CHILDREN'S WARD, KRUSTY PUTS YOUR SICK KID'S MIND AT EASE. HE'S NOT JUST A CLOWN, HE'S THE ATTENDING PHYSICIAN!!"
AND VOILÀ! WHADDYA GOT?!
UM...A GIRAFFE?
A GIRAFFE? ARE YOU KIDDING?! SAY HELLO TO YOUR NEW LUNG! BADA BING! SEE YA ON THE CUTTING BOARD!
"IN THE BREAK ROOM, OUR ESTEEMED DOCTORS CAN GET AWAY FROM THE STRESS OF THE WARDS AND THE PRYING EYES OF THE AUTHORITIES."
ORGAN AUCTION
SOLD!!
ITEM #436: STOMACH
LOOK OUT, FORTY-NINE CENT TACO HUT, PAPA'S GOT A BRAND NEW TUMMY!
"IT'S CALLED THE 'X-RAY ROOM,' BUT WE HAVE LOTS OF DIFFERENT RAYS. BETA, GAMMA, YOU NAME IT!
IT'S PERFECTLY SAFE. JUST STAND ON THAT PILE OF ASHES THERE.
"WHO WOULD POSSIBLY WANT TO WATCH YOU IN OUR OPERATING THEATER? WE'LL INVITE ALL THE GIRLS WHO TURNED YOU DOWN FOR THE HIGH SCHOOL PROM!"
OH MY! I CAN'T SEEM TO FIND ANY MUSCLE AT ALL! LOOKS LIKE I'LL HAVE TO DO A COMPLETE DIGNITY-ECTOMY!

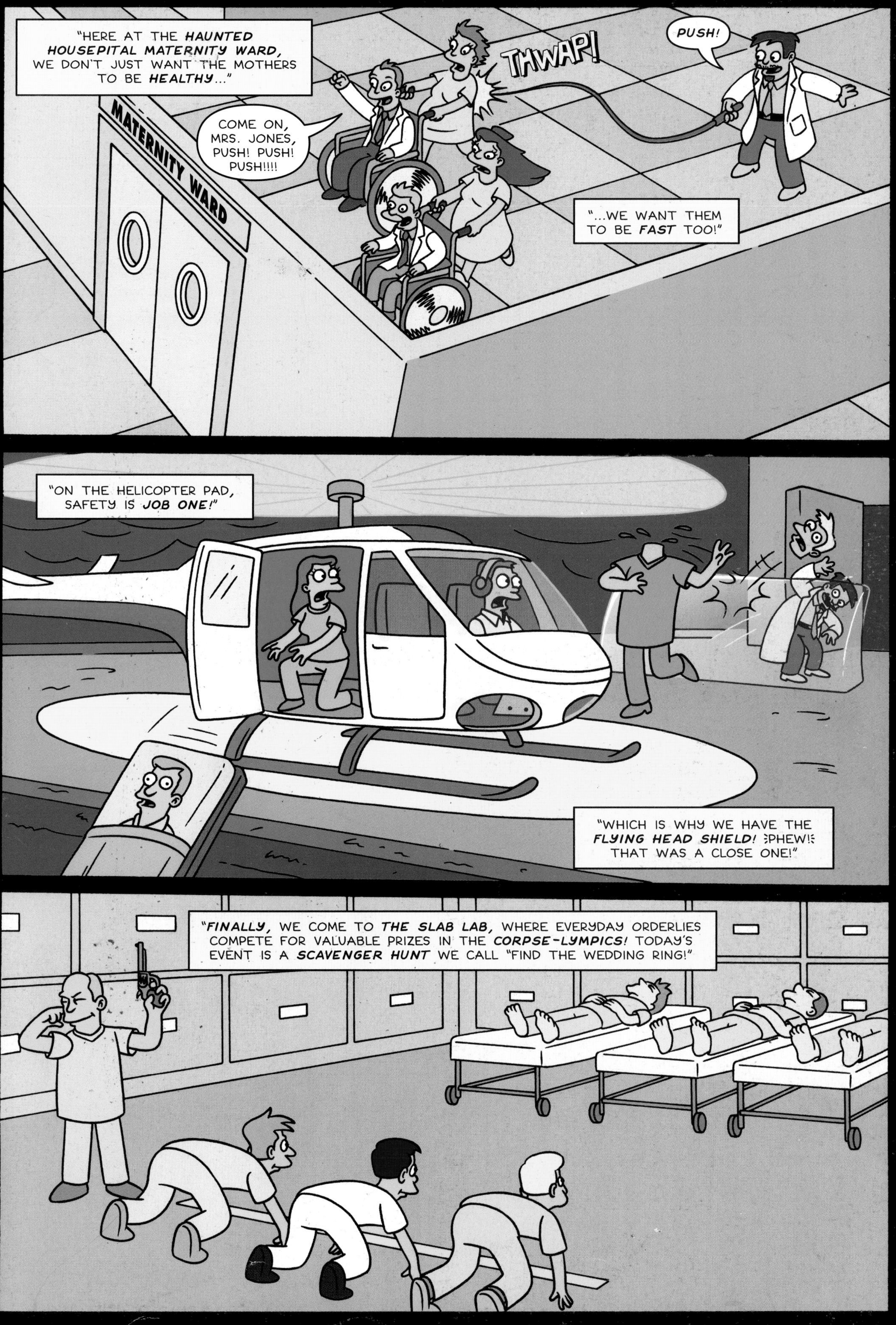
"HERE AT THE HAUNTED HOUSEPITAL MATERNITY WARD, WE DON'T JUST WANT THE MOTHERS TO BE HEALTHY..."
MATERNITY WARD
COME ON, MRS. JONES, PUSH! PUSH! PUSH!!!!
THWAP!
PUSH!
"...WE WANT THEM TO BE FAST TOO!"
"ON THE HELICOPTER PAD, SAFETY IS JOB ONE!"
"WHICH IS WHY WE HAVE THE FLYING HEAD SHIELD! PHEW! THAT WAS A CLOSE ONE!"
"FINALLY, WE COME TO THE SLAB LAB, WHERE EVERYDAY ORDERLIES COMPETE FOR VALUABLE PRIZES IN THE CORPSE-LYMPICS! TODAY'S EVENT IS A SCAVENGER HUNT WE CALL "FIND THE WEDDING RING!"

COMIC BOOK GUY'S
Best Costumes Ever - Part 4

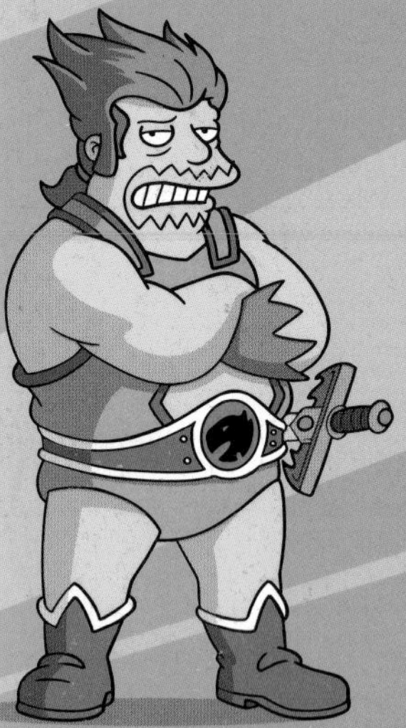

LION-O
HALLOWEEN, 1986

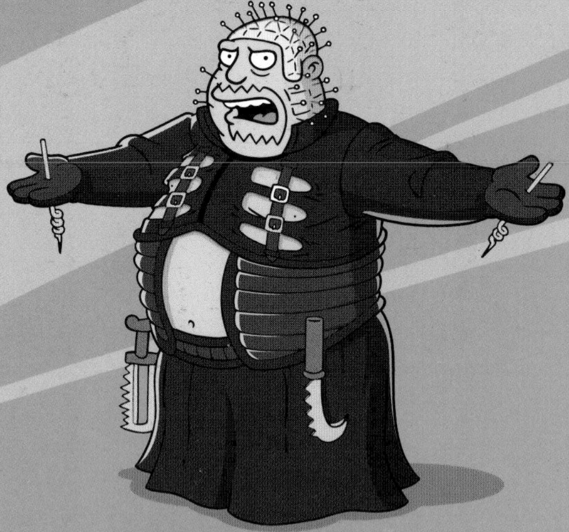

PINHEAD
CHILLER CON, 1994

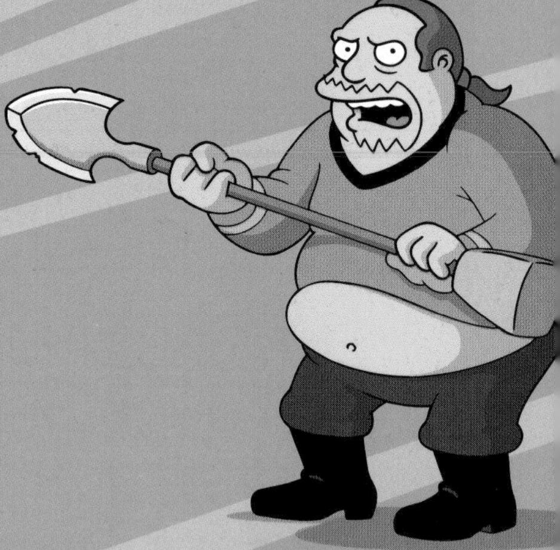

CAPTAIN JAMES T. KIRK
DALLAS FANTASY FAIR, 1989

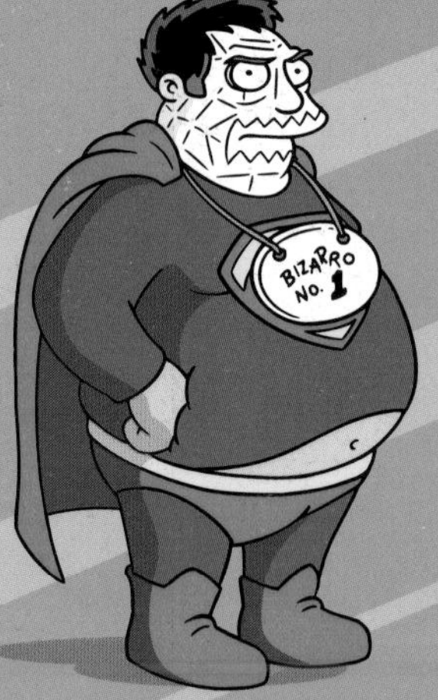
BIZARRO NO. 1

BIZARRO WORLD CBG
CLOSE ENCOUNTERS OF THE COMIC BOOK KIND COMIC BOOK CONVENTION, 2000

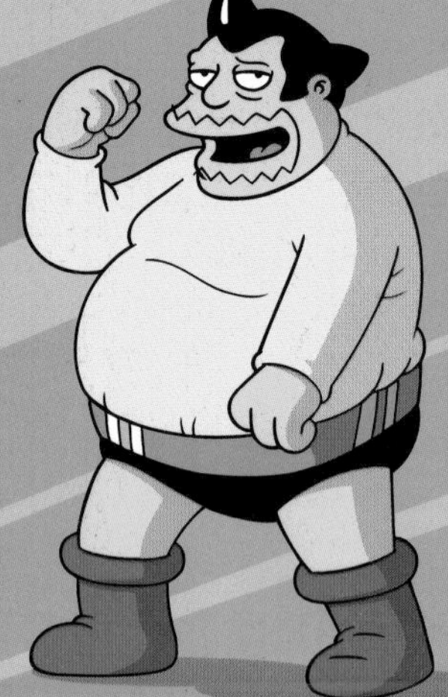

ASTRO BOY
OTAKU CON, 1998

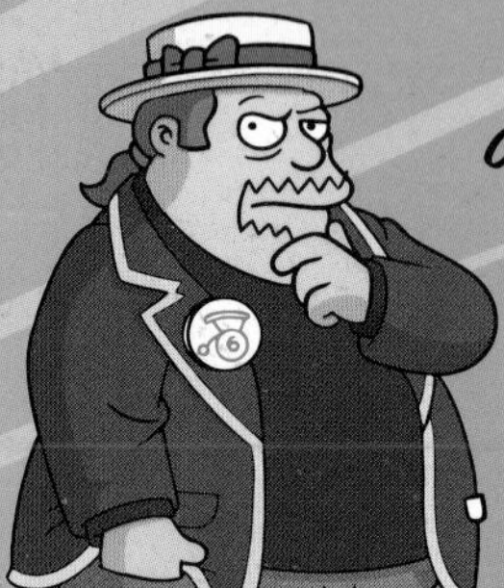

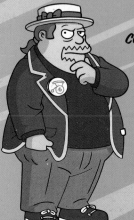

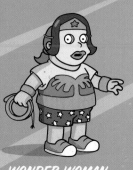

#6
SIX OF ONE CON, 1997

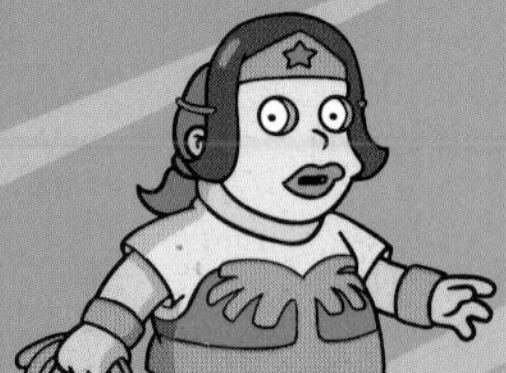

WONDER WOMAN
WORST HALLOWEEN EVER, 1970

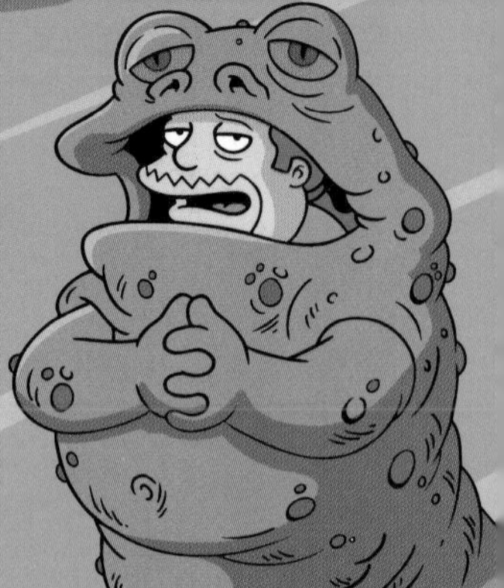

JABBA THE HUT
LUCAS-CON, 1994

THE CASK OF AMONTILLA-D'OH

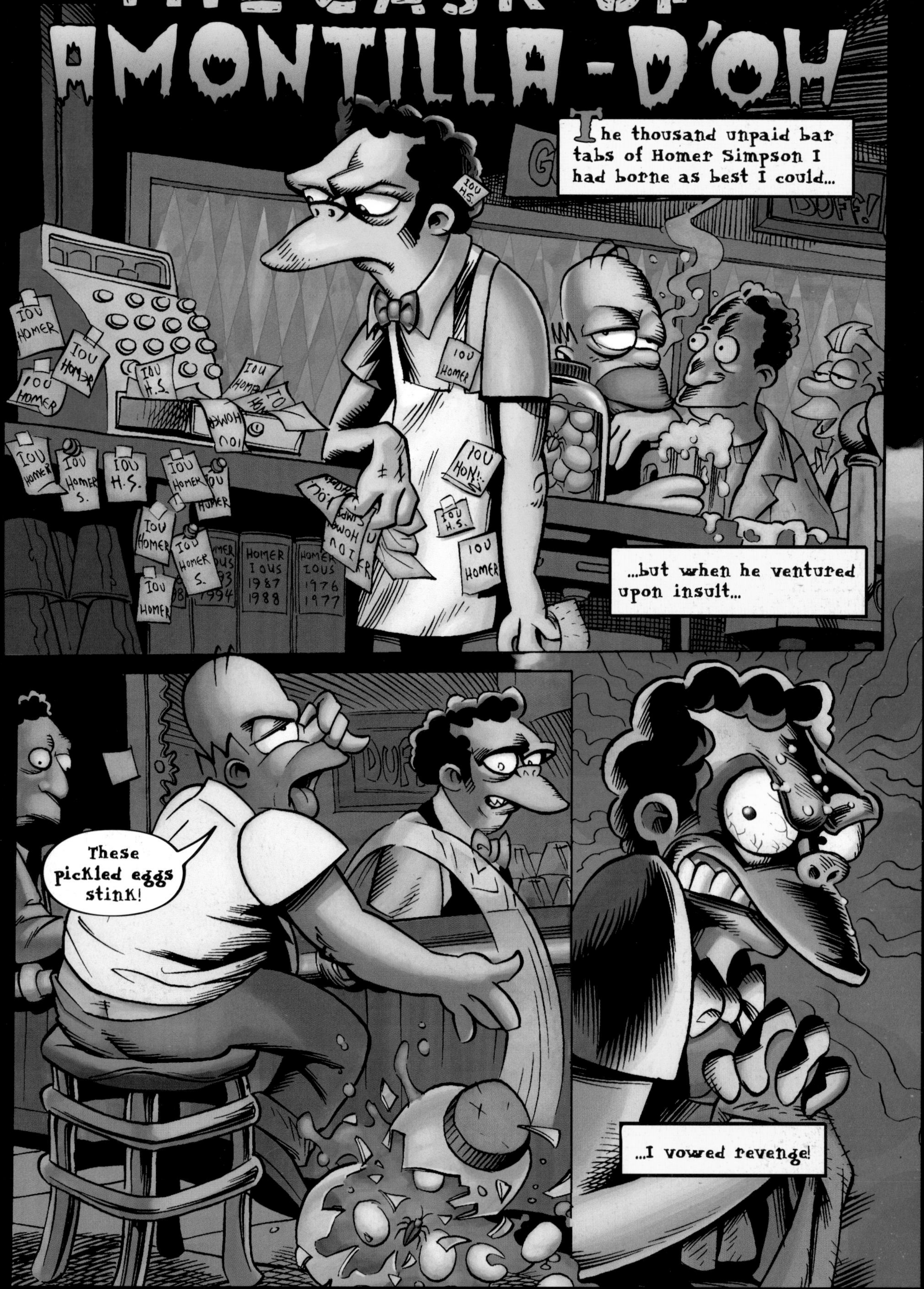
The thousand unpaid bar tabs of Homer Simpson I had borne as best I could...
...but when he ventured upon insult...
These pickled eggs stink!
...I vowed revenge!

PAUL DINI STORY **DAN BRERETON** PENCILS **TED NAIFEH** INKS **NATHAN KANE** COLORS **KAREN BATES** LETTERS

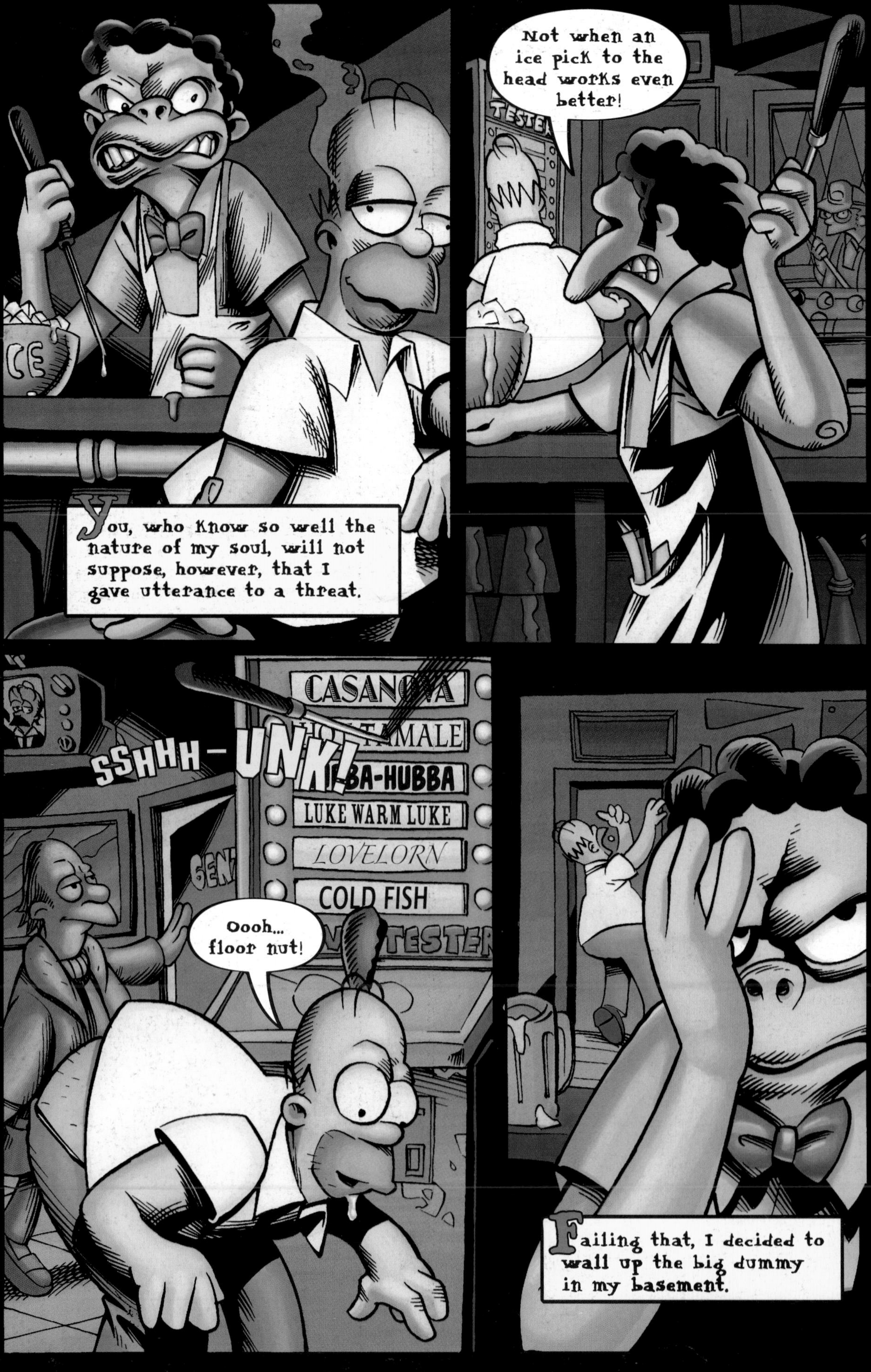
You, who know so well the nature of my soul, will not suppose, however, that I gave utterance to a threat.
Not when an ice pick to the head works even better!
CASANOVA
LUKE WARM LUKE
LOVELORN
COLD FISH
SSHHH-UNK!
Oooh... floor nut!
Failing that, I decided to wall up the big dummy in my basement.

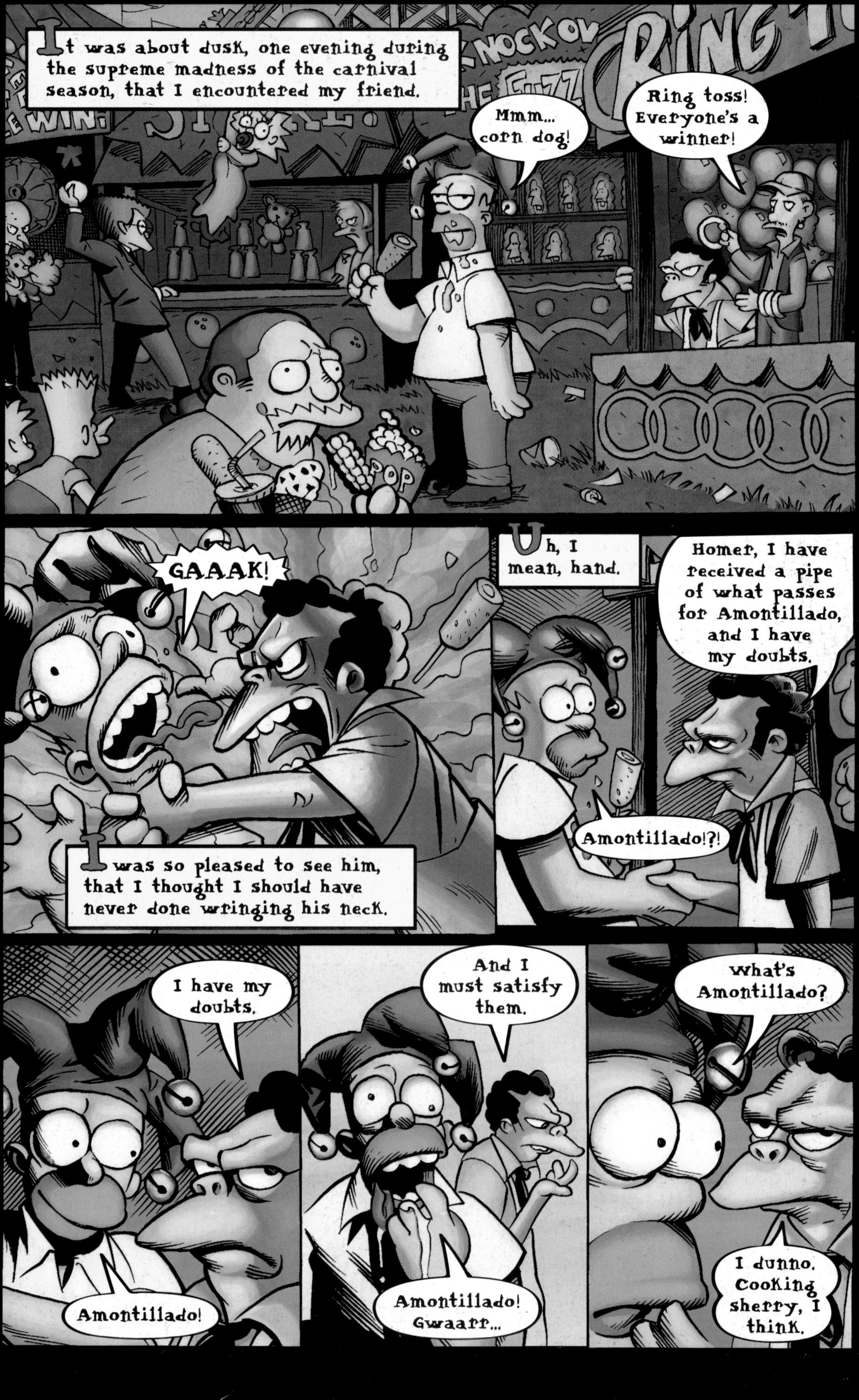
It was about dusk, one evening during the supreme madness of the carnival season, that I encountered my friend.
Mmm... corn dog!
Ring toss! Everyone's a winner!
GAAAK!
I was so pleased to see him, that I thought I should have never done wringing his neck.
Uh, I mean, hand.
Homer, I have received a pipe of what passes for Amontillado, and I have my doubts.
Amontillado!?!
I have my doubts.
Amontillado!
And I must satisfy them.
Amontillado! Gwaarr...
What's Amontillado?
I dunno. Cooking sherry, I think.

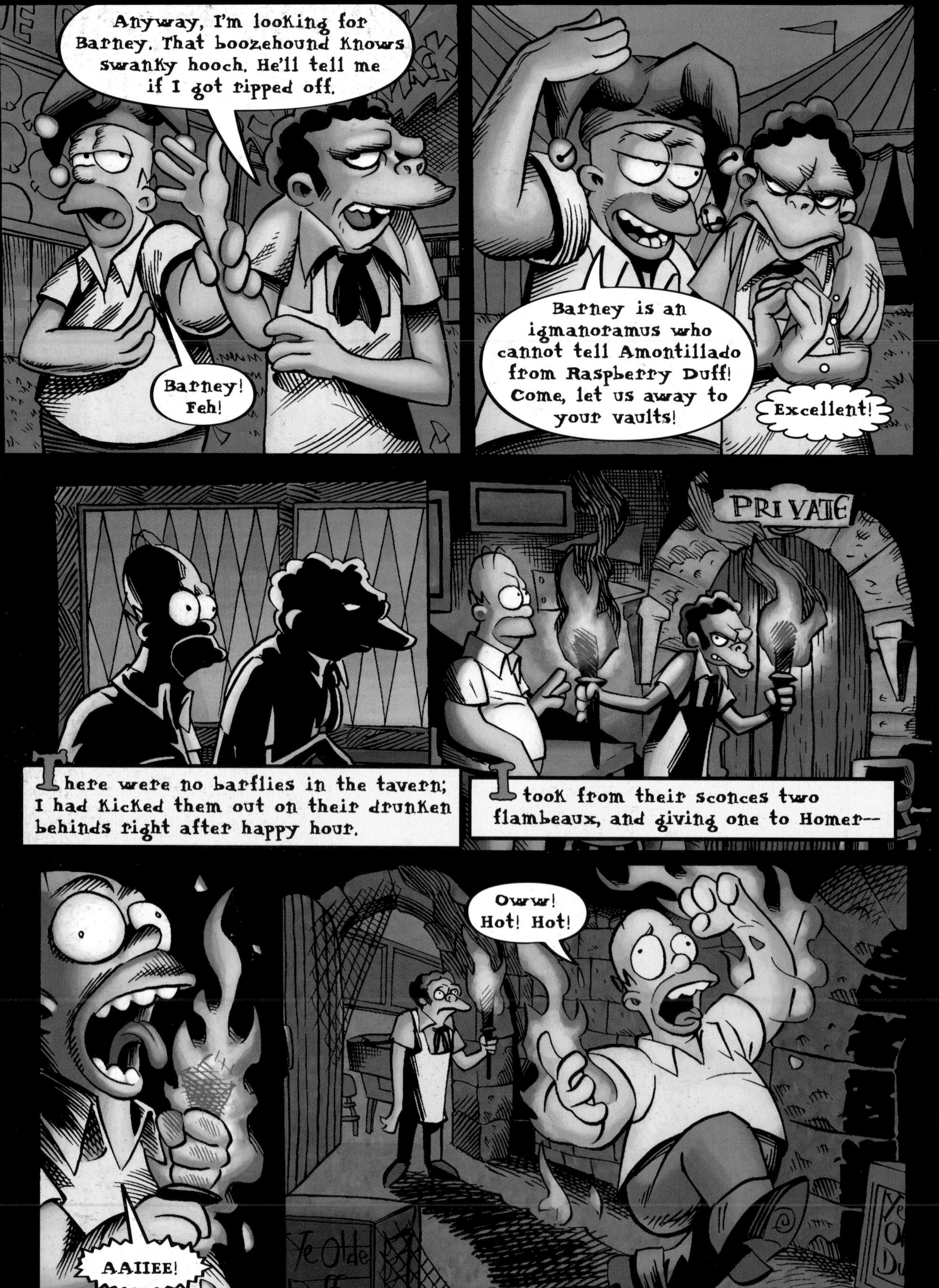
Anyway, I'm looking for Barney. That boozehound knows swanky hooch. He'll tell me if I got ripped off.
Barney! Feh!
Barney is an igmanoramus who cannot tell Amontillado from Raspberry Duff! Come, let us away to your vaults!
Excellent!
There were no barflies in the tavern; I had kicked them out on their drunken behinds right after happy hour.
PRIVATE
I took from their sconces two flambeaux, and giving one to Homer--
AAIIEE!
Oww! Hot! Hot!
Ye Olde Duffe

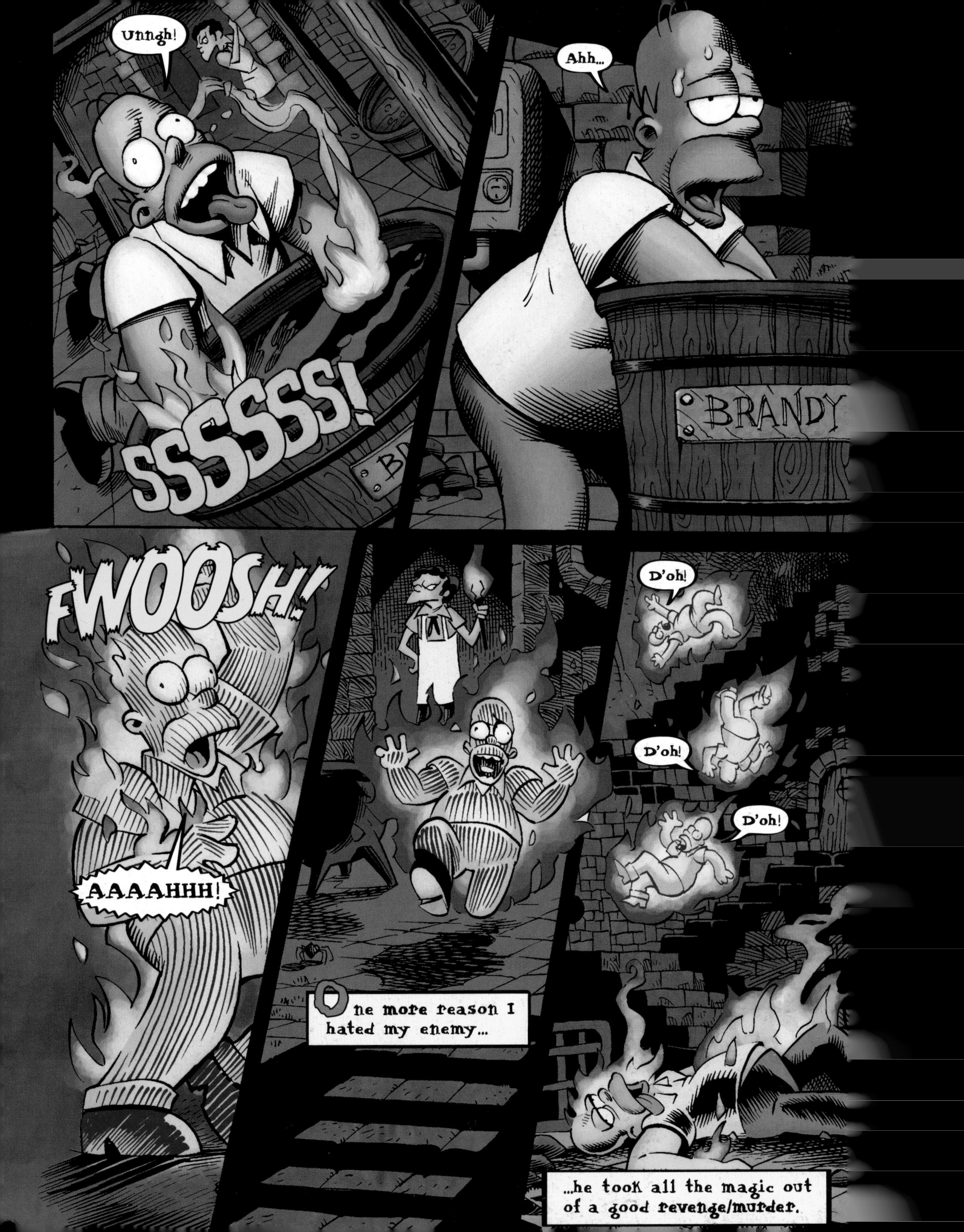

Unngh!
SSSSSS!
Ahh...
BRANDY
FWOOSH!
AAAAHHH!
D'oh!
D'oh!
D'oh!
One more reason I hated my enemy...
...he took all the magic out of a good revenge/murder.

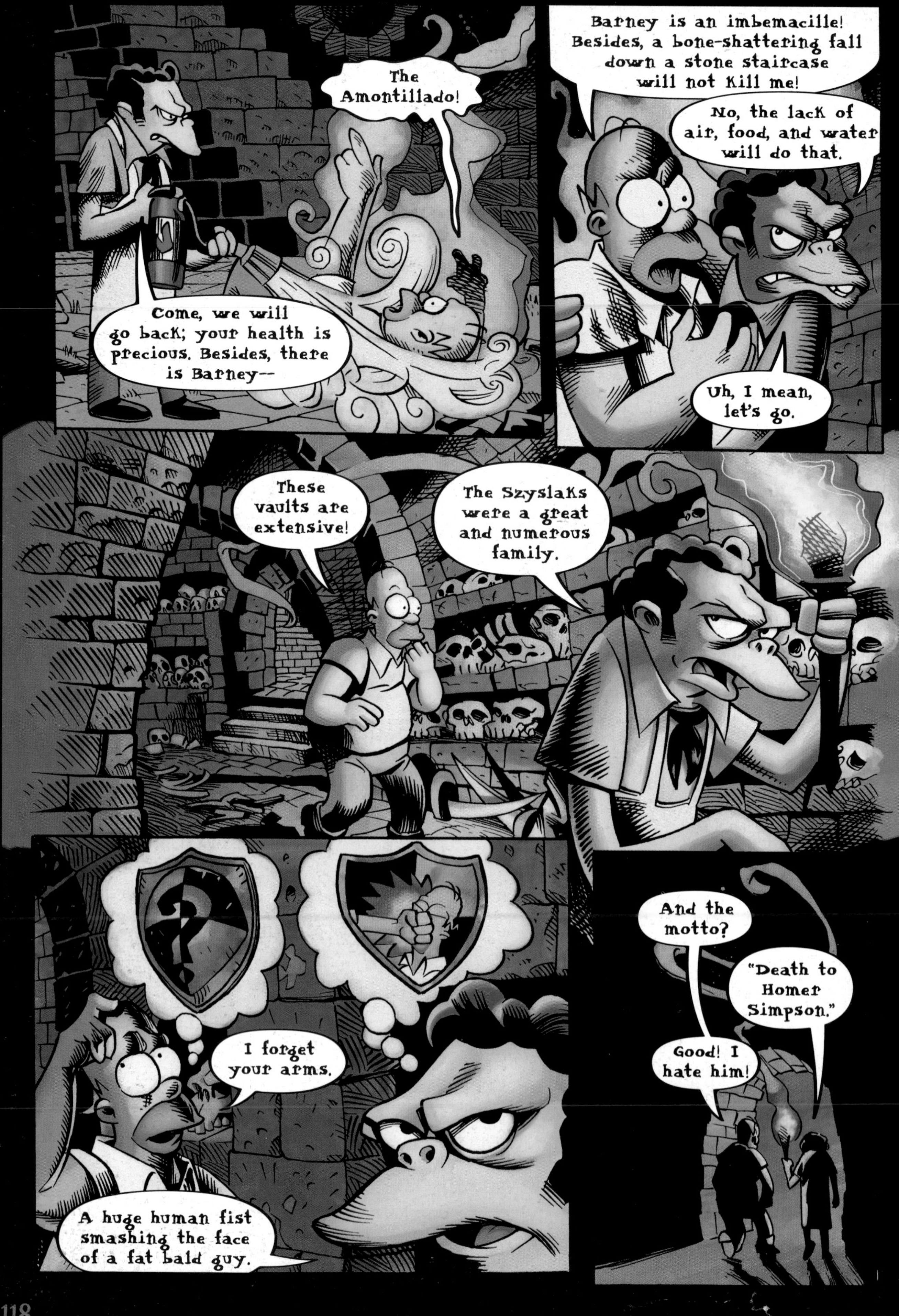
The Amontillado!
Come, we will go back; your health is precious. Besides, there is Barney--
Barney is an imbemacille! Besides, a bone-shattering fall down a stone staircase will not kill me!
No, the lack of air, food, and water will do that.
Uh, I mean, let's go.
These vaults are extensive!
The Szyslaks were a great and numerous family.
I forget your arms.
A huge human fist smashing the face of a fat bald guy.
And the motto?
"Death to Homer Simpson."
Good! I hate him!

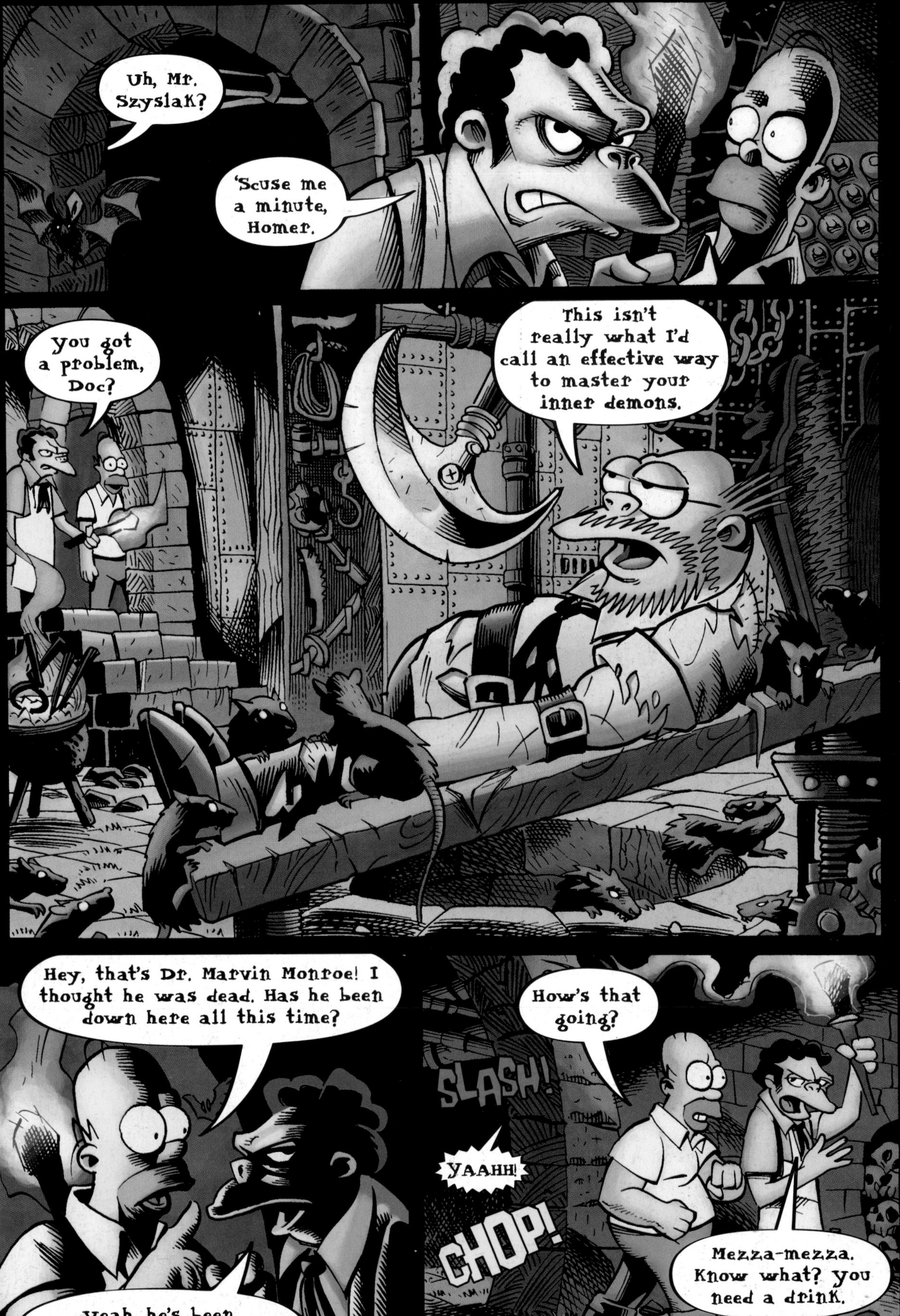
Uh, Mr. Szyslak?
'Scuse me a minute, Homer.
You got a problem, Doc?
This isn't really what I'd call an effective way to master your inner demons.
Hey, that's Dr. Marvin Monroe! I thought he was dead. Has he been down here all this time?
Yeah, he's been helping me work through some anger issues.
How's that going?
SLASH!
YAAHH!
CHOP!
Mezza-mezza. Know what? You need a drink.

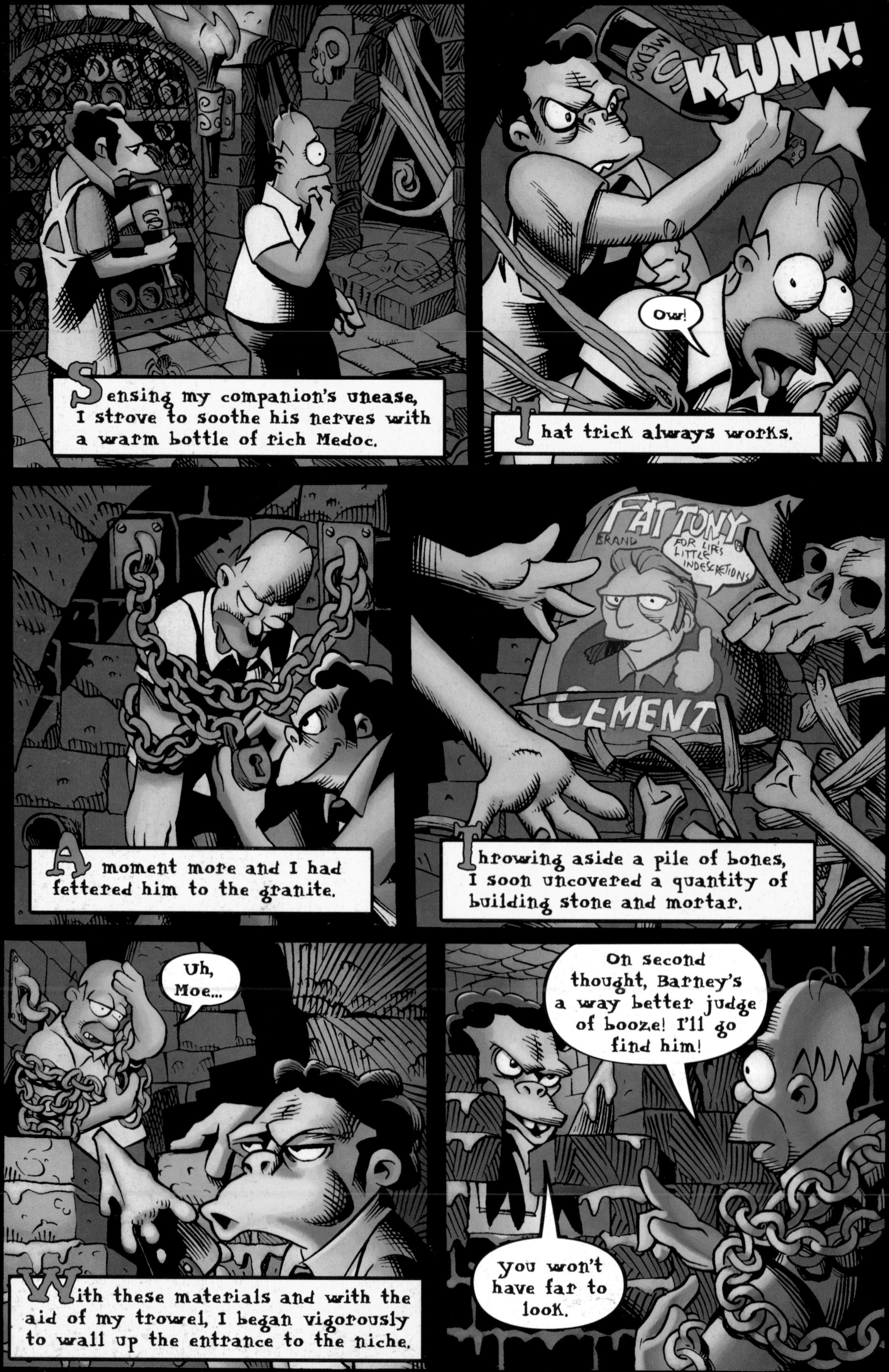
Sensing my companion's unease, I strove to soothe his nerves with a warm bottle of rich Medoc.
MEDOC
KLUNK!
Ow!
That trick always works.
A moment more and I had fettered him to the granite.
FAT TONY BRAND
FOR LIFE'S LITTLE INDESCRETIONS
CEMENT
Throwing aside a pile of bones, I soon uncovered a quantity of building stone and mortar.
Uh, Moe...
With these materials and with the aid of my trowel, I began vigorously to wall up the entrance to the niche.
On second thought, Barney's a way better judge of booze! I'll go find him!
you won't have far to look.

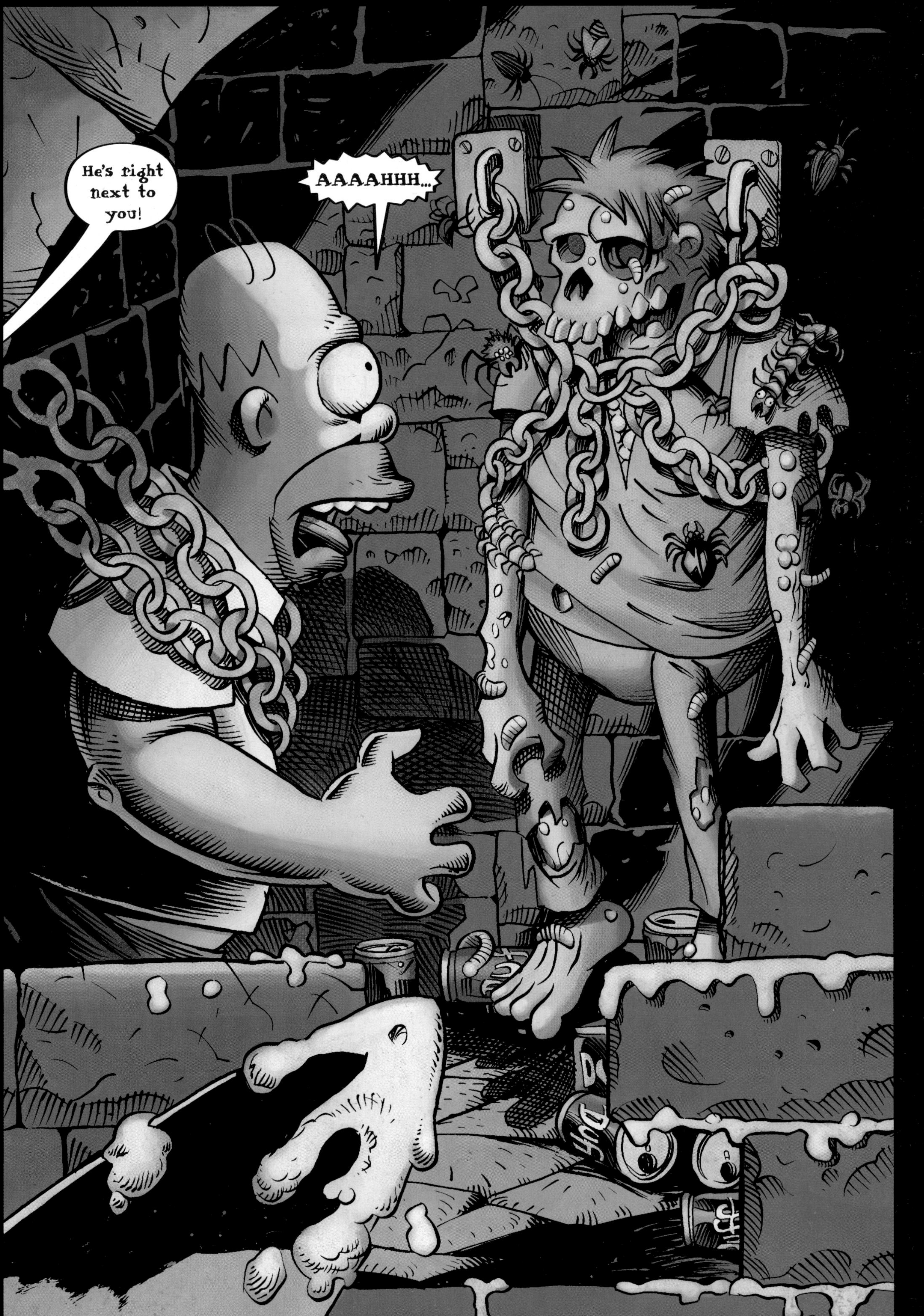
He's right next to you!
AAAAHHH...

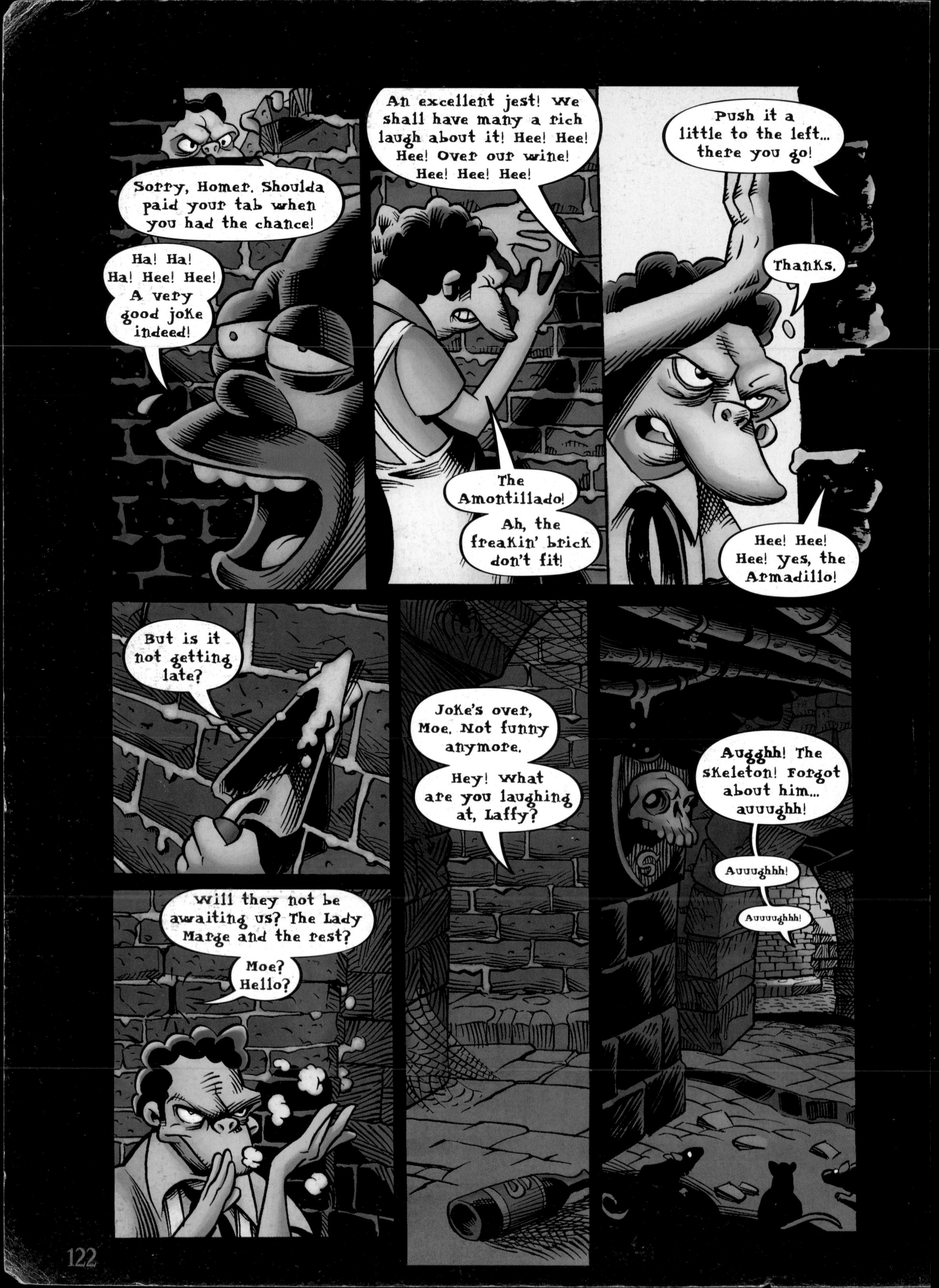
Sorry, Homer. Shoulda paid your tab when you had the chance!
Ha! Ha! Ha! Hee! Hee! A very good joke indeed!
An excellent jest! We shall have many a rich laugh about it! Hee! Hee! Hee! Over our wine! Hee! Hee! Hee!
The Amontillado!
Ah, the freakin' brick don't fit!
Push it a little to the left... there you go!
Thanks.
Hee! Hee! Hee! Yes, the Armadillo!
But is it not getting late?
Will they not be awaiting us? The Lady Marge and the rest?
Moe? Hello?
Joke's over, Moe. Not funny anymore.
Hey! What are you laughing at, Laffy?
Augghh! The skeleton! Forgot about him... auuughh!
Auuughhh!
Auuuughhh!

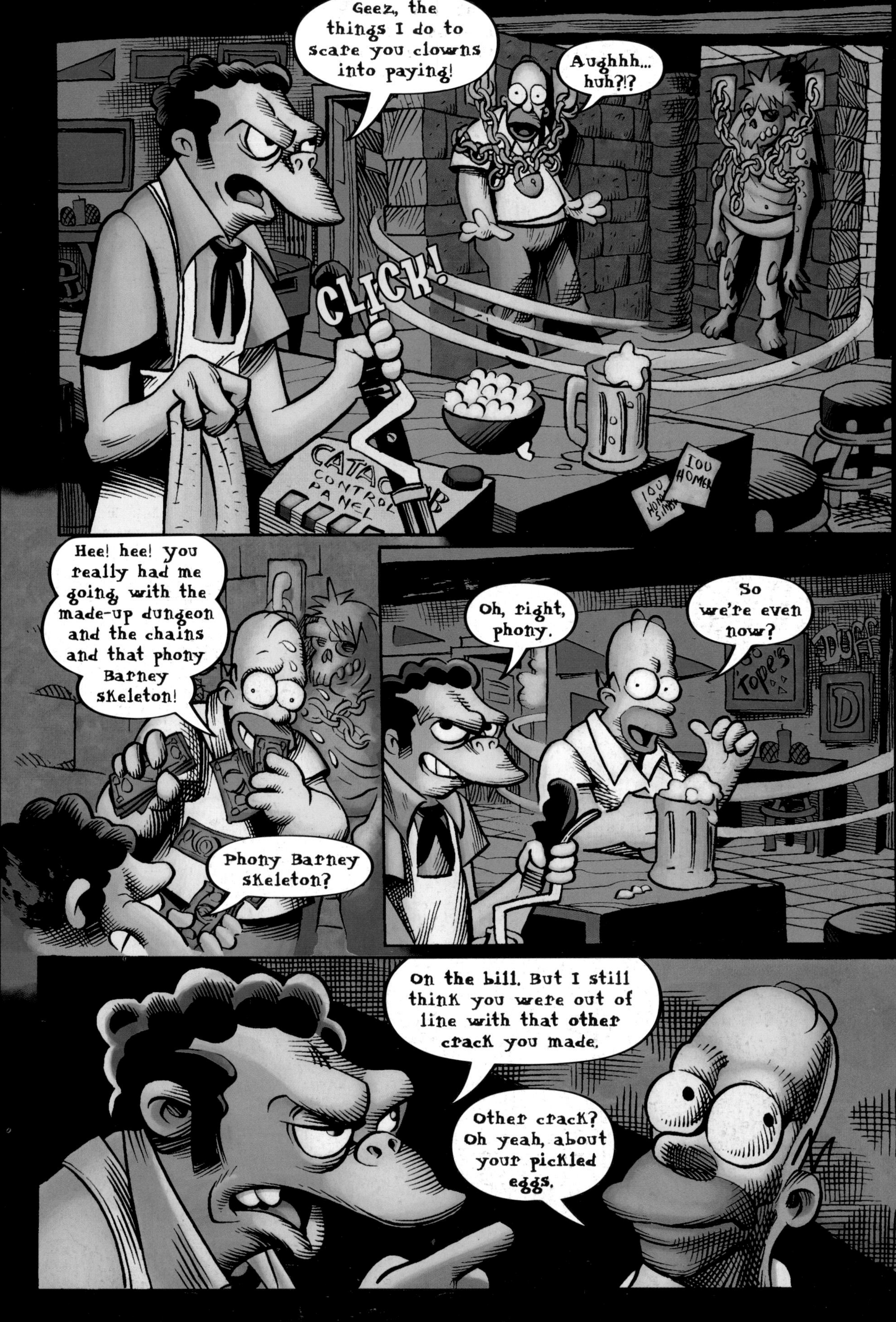
Geez, the things I do to scare you clowns into paying!
Aughhh... huh?!?
CLICK!
CONTROL PANEL
IOU HOMER
Hee! hee! you really had me going, with the made-up dungeon and the chains and that phony Barney skeleton!
Phony Barney skeleton?
Oh, right, phony.
So we're even now?
DUFF
On the bill. But I still think you were out of line with that other crack you made.
Other crack? Oh yeah, about your pickled eggs.

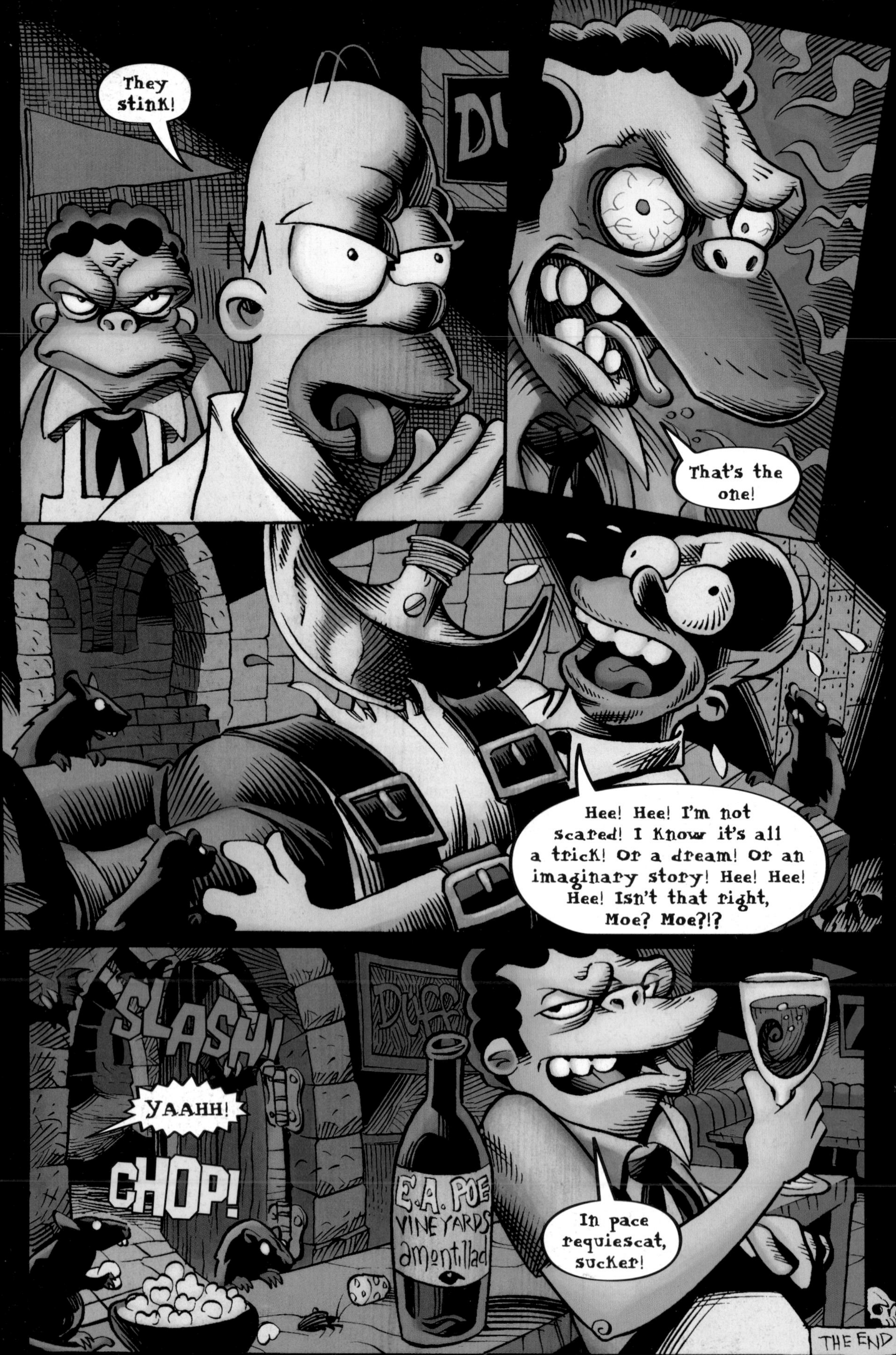
They stink!
DU
That's the one!
Hee! Hee! I'm not scared! I know it's all a trick! Or a dream! Or an imaginary story! Hee! Hee! Hee! Isn't that right, Moe? Moe?!?
SLASH!
YAAHH!
CHOP!
DUFF
E.A. POE VINEYARDS amontillad
In pace requiescat, sucker!
THE END

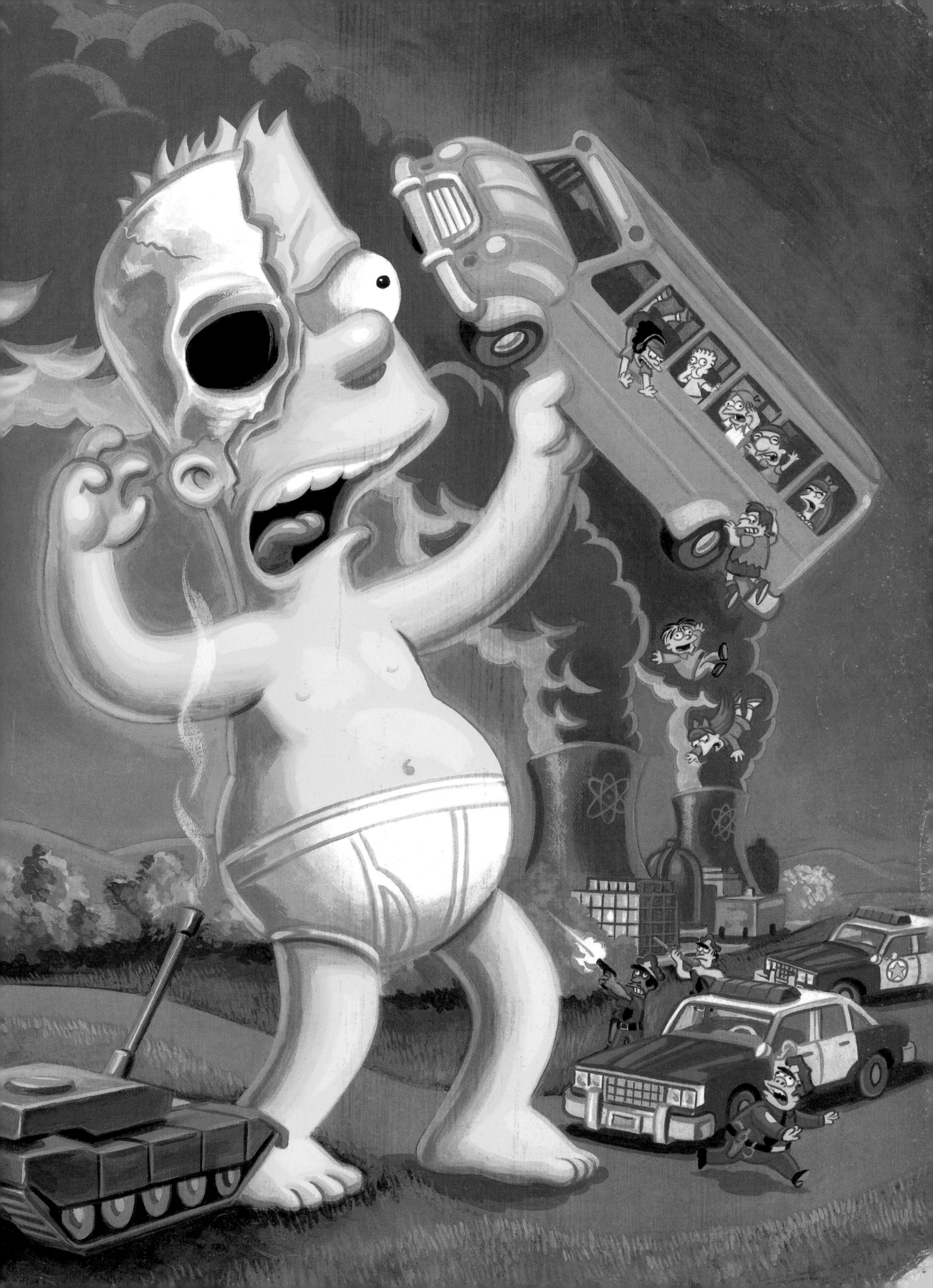

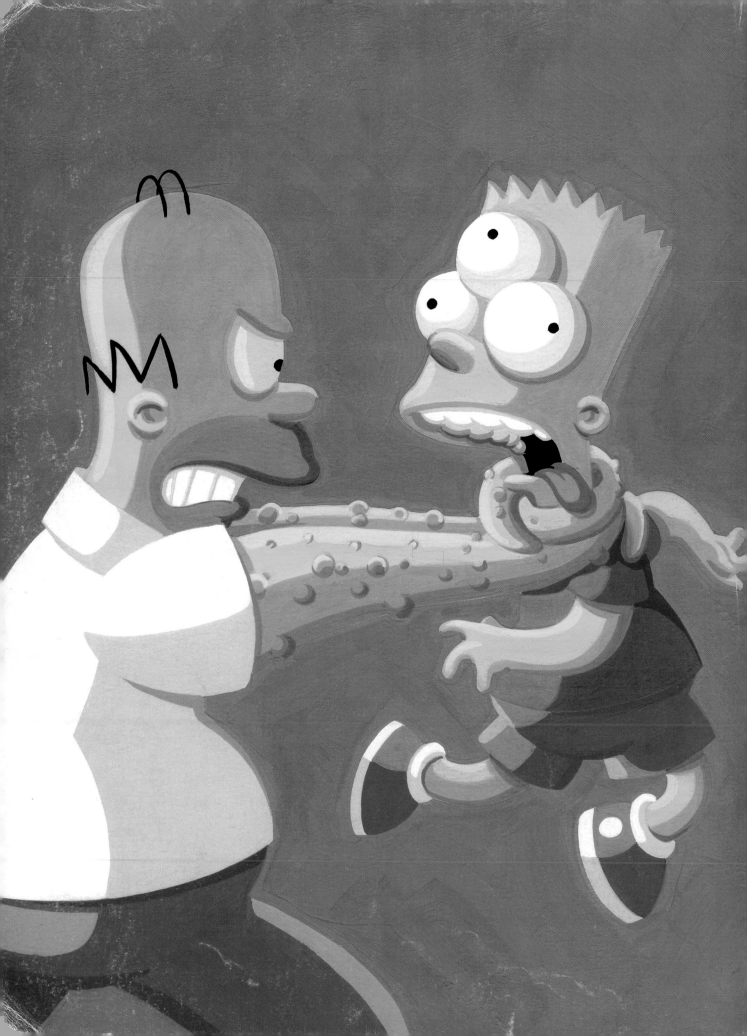

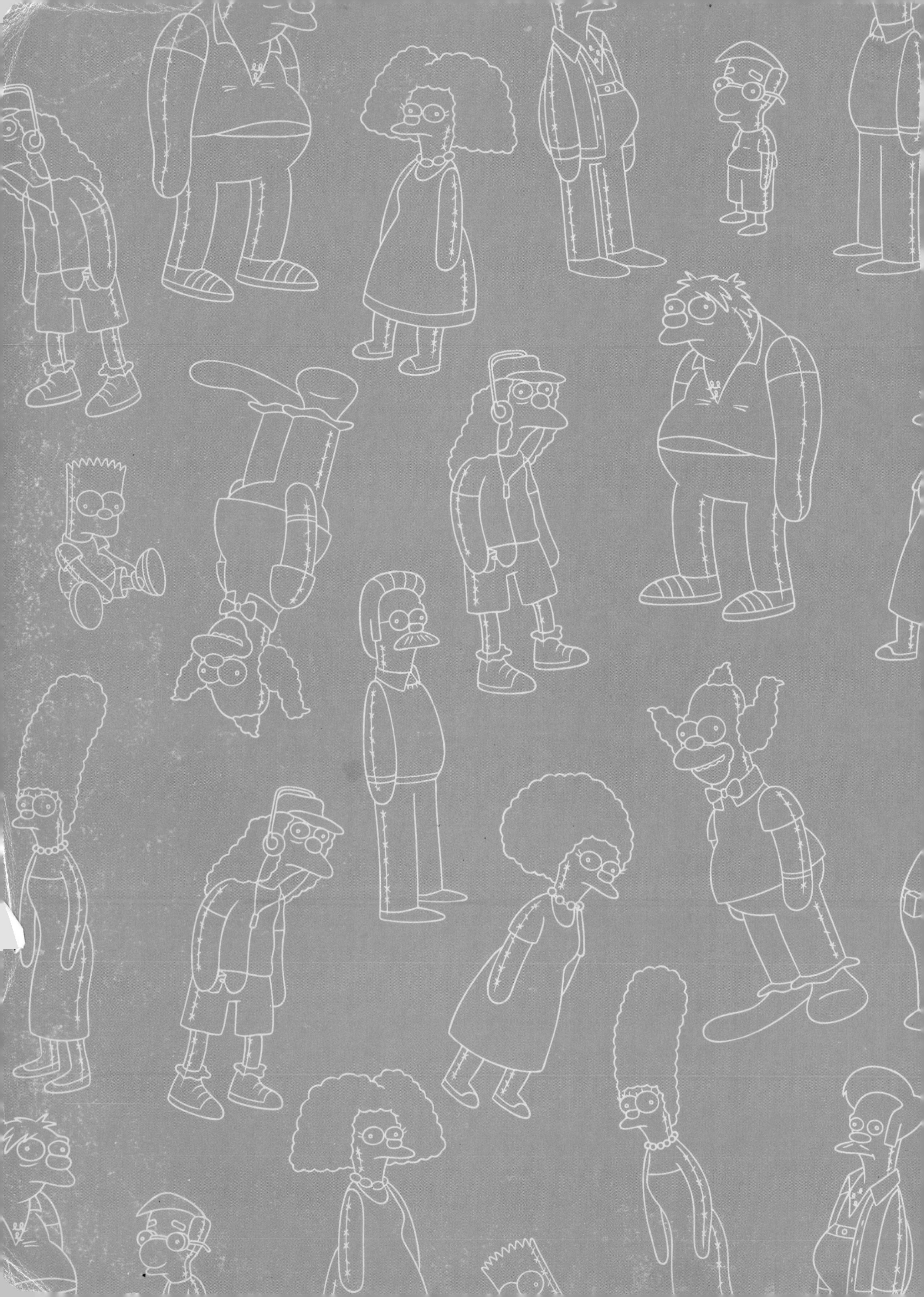